D1594786

Henry Grady's New South

Henry Grady's New South

Atlanta, A Brave and Beautiful City

HAROLD E. DAVIS

The University of Alabama Press   *Tuscaloosa and London*

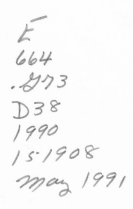

Copyright © 1990 by The University of Alabama Press
Tuscaloosa, Alabama 35487–0380
All rights reserved
Manufactured in the United States of America

The paper on which this book is printed meets the minimum requirements of
American National Standard for Information Science-Permanence of Paper
for Printed Library Materials, ANSI A39.48–1984. ∞

Library of Congress Cataloging-in-Publication Data
Davis, Harold Earl, 1927–
Henry Grady's new South: Atlanta, a brave and beautiful city/Harold E. Davis.
p.   cm.
Bibliography: p.
Includes index.
ISBN 0–8173–0454–1 (alk. paper)
1. Grady, Henry Woodfin, 1850–1889.   2. Politicians—Southern
States—Biography.   3. Journalists—Georgia—Biography.   4. Georgia—
Politics and government—1865–1950.   5. Atlanta (Ga.)—Politics and—
government.   6. Agriculture—Georgia—History—19th century.
I. Title.
E664.G73D38   1990
975'.041—dc19   89–30565 CIP
British Library Cataloguing-in-Publication Data available

The illustration on the frontispiece shows the Commercial Center of Atlanta,
1887. This scene, drawn for *Harper's Weekly* by Horace Bradley, was published
by that magazine on February 12, 1887. At the left is the Kimball House, scene
of much political activity in the 1880s. The fan-shaped building at the center is
Union Station. (Courtesy of the Atlanta Historical Society)

[W]e have raised a brave and beautiful city . . . we have caught

the sunshine in the bricks and mortar of our homes,

and have builded therin not one ignoble prejudice or memory.

—Henry Woodfin Grady on Atlanta, 1886

Contents

Preface

Several years ago, with the encouragement of Malcolm M. Mac-Donald, director of The University of Alabama Press, I began research on Henry W. Grady, managing editor of the Atlanta *Constitution,* often described as the most prominent spokesman for the New South Movement. My efforts took me to Grady's papers at Emory University in Atlanta and to the Georgia State University Library, which had on microfilm an unbroken run of the Atlanta *Constitution* for the time he was associated with it. I also worked in The University of Georgia Library in Athens, which had other newspapers and document collections bearing upon Grady and his associates, as well as the collections of the Georgia Department of Archives and History in Atlanta and the Atlanta Historical Society.

Beginning the research, I had no preconceived notions of Grady beyond those shaped by Raymond B. Nixon's book, *Henry W. Grady: Spokesman of the New South,* published in 1943. That work, a model for accuracy and scholarly care, showed Grady as a relatively selfless man and certainly a courageous one, seeking to rejuvenate the South following the Civil War by creating a new regional economy.

About a year into my studies, I began to perceive a different pattern in the evidence. My Grady would not be the Grady that Nixon described. There would still be much about him to admire, especially his quick intelligence, energy, and oratory, but he was not the selfless developer of the South. He was anything but that. My own thesis, and the point of view of this book, is stated near the end of Chapter 1.

As the work progressed, it developed not into a standard biography but focused instead upon the New South Movement and what it meant to Grady and his principal associates. Chapter 2 contains information about Grady, but for biography, one may consult Nixon with confidence.

Besides MacDonald, many people have made this book possible. William M. Suttles, Clyde W. Faulkner, and Noah N. Langdale, Jr., all administrators of Georgia State University, created a research professorship that gave me time to do this work, and each gave personal encouragement. Several friends and scholars read and criticized the entire work: James C. Cobb of The University of Tennessee, E. Culpepper Clark of The University of Alabama, and William F. Holmes of The University of Georgia. Thomas G. Dyer of The University of Georgia also offered help. Dyer was formerly editor of the *Georgia Historical Quarterly*, and Chapters 3 and 4 were published earlier in different form in the *Quarterly*, benefitting from his own criticism and from that of his referees.

Portions of this work were read by Franklin Garrett of the Atlanta Historical Society. Garrett helped me to check or verify a number of obscure points. Judson C. Ward, now retired from Emory University, read and made important suggestions concerning Chapter 3. Two colleagues at Georgia State University, Kenneth M. England and Harry C. Malone, read parts of the manuscript and made useful comments. Edward J. Cashin of Augusta College read portions concerning Augusta.

Allen W. Jones, professor of history and archivist at Auburn University, directed me to newspapers of the 1880s edited and published by black Americans. Auburn has a considerable collection of these newspapers, and Jones made them available through interlibrary loan.

I am indebted to Edward Weldon, director of the Georgia Department of Archives and History, for reasons explained in footnote seven of the Appendix.

My wife, Priscilla Arnold Davis, who earlier was a professional editor, did much to improve the manuscript. She suggested *A Brave and Beautiful City* as part of the title, and this book is dedicated to her. She and our children—Laurie, Jane, Martha, and Margaret—encouraged me throughout this lengthy effort.

The late E. Merton Coulter, historian and former chairman of the Department of History at The University of Georgia, showed me as a young man how exciting working with history can be, and James Z. Rabun, J. Harvey Young, and the late Bell I. Wiley of Emory University set standards for me that I appreciate and respect.

In the 1930s Raymond B. Nixon gathered up most of the surviving papers of Grady and they have found their way into the special collections of the Robert W. Woodruff Library at Emory. I am most grateful to the staff of that library, and to the libraries of the University of Georgia, the Georgia Department of Archives and History, the Atlanta Historical Society, and the William Russell Pullen Library of Georgia State University for assistance beyond the ordinary. Jane G. Hobson and the interlibrary loan staff of Georgia State University borrowed vast amounts of materials for me.

I intentionally have not troubled the descendants of Henry W. Grady now living in Atlanta. Raymond Nixon worked with Henry Grady's son, now deceased, and from him and other friends and members of the family, got the papers they had, papers now in the Emory Library. Once, however, I was making a speech about Grady at the Atlanta Historical Society and discovered to my discomfort that Grady descendants were in the audience. I need not have been concerned. They did not seem nervous that someone was researching their ancestor, and their behavior to me that evening was of a quality that the original Henry Grady would have recognized and approved.

Harold E. Davis
Research Professor Emeritus
Georgia State University
Atlanta, Georgia

Henry Grady's New South

1
Introduction

To those who barely knew him, the fall of 1889 seemed a glorious time for Henry W. Grady, the popular managing editor of the Atlanta *Constitution*. A cheerful, energetic man of thirty-nine, he beamed goodwill wherever he went. His name was a household word in the homes of most educated Americans. A celebrated orator, he was perceived to be a man of warm heart and generous spirit. His pleasant word and hearty clap on the back made everyone, from millionaire to bootblack, glad to see him coming.

Grady, for whom much was going right, had many things going wrong. He was short of cash. His stock in the *Constitution*, worth about $118,000, was not liquid. Mrs. Grady had had a miscarriage and was not well. On the positive side, the early problems in managing a newspaper were behind him. His partners at the *Constitution* were solid businessmen, and Grady had shown remarkable skill in building the *Weekly Constitution*, a side effort of the daily newspaper, into what some thought was the preeminent weekly in America. With good reason, Grady expected it to enhance his fortune and recover his losses from bad investments.[1]

Grady spent as much time winning political influence as he did performing his newspaper duties. He became the indispensable member of a successful political organization called the Atlanta Ring. In 1889 the political structure, to which the Ring had been central and to which Grady and the *Constitution* had committed far more than was perceived publicly, was threatened. Farmers, doing poorly financially, were sure to register their unhappiness in the statewide election of 1890.

For that reason, Grady embarked upon an urgent campaign to show that he and the *Constitution* were friends of the farmer; he took his celebrated oratory onto the rutted roads of rural Georgia. In place after place, he made a lengthy address entitled "The Farmer and the Cities."[2] Largely ignored by present-day scholars, it was probably the most effective speech that Grady ever made. But the physical and emotional effort involved, along with other worries, wore him out. By December 1889 he was a weakened, almost ill, man.

Grady's political influence was challenged by more than farmers at home. In Washington, Congressman Henry Cabot Lodge of Massachusetts propounded a measure in the House of Representatives that, under certain conditions, would send federal supervisors to the polling places in southern states, assuring that southern Negroes could vote if they wished. Negroes had voted in large numbers earlier, but by 1889 their participation was off, reputedly because of threats and coercion. The Republican party after March 1889 controlled both the White House and Congress and was committed to Negro suffrage upon the practical proposition that blacks would likely vote Republican. Grady and his partners at the newspaper saw in that prospect a diminution of their influence. Thus, when he was invited to speak to the Boston Merchants' Association, figuratively in Congressman Lodge's backyard, he had the opportunity to say to an important northern audience that the South could manage its racial affairs without help.

Grady was in no condition to go. A short time before, talking on the telephone at his home on Peachtree Street in Atlanta, he had fallen to the floor without warning and had spent several days in bed. His physician called it vertigo. Nonetheless, Grady was set on going to Boston. Over the protests of Mrs. Grady and his doctor, Dr. F. H. Orme, he shut himself in his wife's room and began work on the speech that history knows as "The Race Problem in the South." Dr. Orme prescribed medicines for him to take on the journey and gave him the names of physicians in New York and Boston to call if needed. Orme made Grady swear to a plan of minimum exertion: no unnecessary talking and no needless activity. Grady had a slight cold when he and a party of friends left Atlanta in a private railroad car.

Grady reneged on his promise. He talked vociferously in his coach, and during a stopover in Washington, he left the train for two hours to get information for his speech from the Washington correspondent for the Boston *Journal.* Away from the train, he visited newspaper friends and politicians and got into a warm discussion with one of the latter, who insulted him. By then, his cold was worse.

The next morning, feeling better, he sat in the Washington railroad station awaiting the train that would take his car to New York, and he jotted a quick note to his Atlanta friend, Walter A. Taylor. "I've had an easier time today; the growing excitement of my speech nerves the cold and trouble. In every way I am better now."[3] Grady was showing a pattern much remarked upon later. One moment, he would be ill; a short time later, he would seem almost well.

By the time he reached New York, he was sick, and he sent for Dr. E. Guernsey, one of the men recommended by Orme. Grady's chest showed an irritation, and he had a weak and rapid pulse but no fever. Dr. Guernsey was more alarmed at his patient's physical and nervous prostration. Grady appeared to have almost no physical or emotional resources left. The doctor asked that he cancel the trip. Grady acknowledged that the physician was probably correct but said that his appearance had been advertised and he did not like to fail in his engagements. "[P]lease be exceedingly careful in Boston about over-exertion and taking cold," Dr. Guernsey said, as Grady made plans to continue the journey.[4]

In Boston, the Merchants' Association held its great banquet in the principal dining room of the Hotel Vendome, and Grady and his party checked into that hotel. It was soon clear that his momentary recoveries were unrealistic. He sent off a note to Mrs. Grady in Atlanta. "I haven't left my room since I reached Boston, and I don't think I can. . . . I can hardly talk at all."[5]

Grady never showed a sign of canceling any important engagement made by the arrangements committee, even though the schedule before and after the speech would have exhausted anyone. At 5 P.M. on December 12, the night of the banquet, Grady went to a reception in the parlors of the hotel. He was one of three special guests; the others were former President Grover Cleveland and Governor W. L. Putnam of Maine. They spent an hour greeting the four hundred or so persons there for dinner. At six, the party went into the dining hall. At the principal tables were the president of the Merchants' Association, Jonathan Lane, the special guests, and a great number of distinguished persons including Governor Oliver Ames of Massachusetts, Andrew Carnegie, Leverett Saltonstall, many congressmen and federal and state officials, as well as men of affairs from New England and New York. Grady's party from Georgia, itself a distinguished delegation, was prominently placed.

Two and a quarter hours passed before the speaking began, and the first orator was Grover Cleveland, who talked at length in praise of business. When Grady finally got to his feet, he spoke an hour and ten minutes. He declared that justice was at hand for black Americans in the South and that the majority of them was satisfied.[6] Twenty-nine times applause interrupted the speech. Afterwards Grady received the congratulations of those who could reach him. The reactions of some who read the address later were more restrained. The text, taken down by a stenographer, was soon available. Staunchly Republican newspapers were unconvinced by what Grady had said, and the black press was hostile. Comment from Democratic newspapers was friendlier, and southern editorial comment elevated the speech to the pantheon of great public address in America. Andrew Carnegie spoke after Grady, and the exhausted Georgian got to bed after 2 A.M.

The schedule of the next day was worse, and Grady, with gimlet-eyed fanaticism, kept every detail except the last one.[7] The weather was now an enemy, for that morning, a wintry blast struck. The day began with breakfast with members of the Merchants' Association, and at 10 A.M., an unperceptive friend came with an open carriage to drive Grady around Boston. Grady's Georgia companions tried to keep him at the hotel, but he put on an overcoat, turned the collar over his neck and ears and rode for an hour in the freezing wind. He and his party then left by train for Plymouth Rock. There, standing on the Rock with his head uncovered, he made a short speech. Returning to Boston, the Georgians attended a reception given by Governor and Mrs. Ames. They then visited the Bay State Club, a Democratic organization, where Grady spoke again, by this time so hoarse that he worried about being heard.[8] Edward Atkinson invited the party to an early dinner. Atkinson was the Boston economist sometimes credited with suggesting the Atlanta Cotton Exposition of 1881. That evening, the Georgians were to attend a play at the Hollis Street Theater in Boston, but Grady probably did not go.

The next morning the party left for New York, and at the Boston depot, a crowd gathered to say farewell. Grady stood in the car shed as cold wind from the east whipped through it. His friends asked him to get inside the railroad car; finally, a member of the party laid a hand on Grady's shoulder and felt something like a spasm. There was no choice then. His friends pushed him into the car.

In New York some hours later, the party checked in at the Fifth Avenue Hotel. Snow covered the ground and Grady canceled some of his schedule, but not all. He got out of bed, closed himself into a carriage, and went to a private luncheon with Grover Cleveland, able to stay only thirty minutes. Back at the hotel, he gave a difficult interview to a reporter from the New York *World* and saw a representative of the New York *Herald*.

That evening, Grady stayed at the hotel while his friends dined at Delmonico's, the triumphant scene three years earlier of his "New South" speech, his first nationally celebrated address. Grady wrote a note to his Atlanta friend, Taylor. "I am a prisoner, my eyes running with cold till I can't see. . . . It is a terrible snow outside, piled up deep, and I sit like Cinderella in the ashes. . . . I am coming home if I die." A doctor who lived in the hotel was called and found Grady in a chill.[9]

Grady wanted to leave New York but he worried about traveling.

His car finally left at midnight on Sunday, December 15, for the long trip home. During a stop in Washington, one member of the party was so alarmed that he thought of sending for Mrs. Grady, but a few minutes later Grady seemed so bright that there appeared to be no danger.

The train was to arrive at the Atlanta depot at 11 A.M. on Tuesday, December 17, completing a journey of thirty-five hours. From a copy of the *Constitution* bought as the train passed Toccoa, Georgia, Grady learned that a reception for him was prepared in Atlanta, and he knew that he was too sick to go. He asked a traveling companion, Evan P. Howell, editor in chief of the *Constitution*, to represent him. As the train passed the village of Lula a few miles down the road, Grady telegraphed Dr. Orme to meet him at the Atlanta depot.

The train was three and one-half hours late. At 11 A.M., the posted time of arrival, Atlantans assembled at the station, unaware of conditions up the track. At the Chamber of Commerce, a gala celebration awaited. Told that the train was late, the crowd broke up for the time being.

About 1 P.M., it assembled again, and Dr. Orme then got his telegram. The train arrived at 2:30, and people pressed forward as Orme bolted to the door of Grady's car, followed by Donald Bain, a friend. With these men supporting him, Grady stepped from the train to great cheering. An open carriage drawn by four horses waited to take him to the Chamber of Commerce, but instead, Grady was half carried to Dr. Orme's carriage, the crowd instinctively making an opening so he could get through. A victor's wreath was cast across Grady's shoulders, and he bore the flowers away. Soon, word spread that he was seriously ill, and Orme issued a statement: Grady was feverish with bronchitis. He was prohibited from seeing anyone and could not attend to business. Some time would pass before he could handle his affairs again.[10]

Grady finally felt the comfort of his own bed at midafternoon of Tuesday, December 17. He was not expected to die. Bronchitis was not considered serious, and Grady was a vital man. Not until the following Saturday did large numbers of people realize that matters had taken a serious turn. By church time on Sunday, his friends knew that death was coming. Bronchitis was now pneumonia, and Dr. Orme said later that Grady was as good as dead when he got off the train.

Orme and a team of consulting physicians did all they could do, but Grady died at 3:40 the next morning, Monday, December 23, 1889. Close friends who had left the house shortly before were recalled to be present at the end. The *Constitution* held its presses, and a death notice appeared on the editorial page, with column rules reversed to print bands of mourning.

The funeral was held on Christmas afternoon, with services at the First Methodist Church, a few blocks from Grady's home. Floral and verbal tributes came in from Atlanta, from Georgia, and from the nation. Grady's death drew the attention of every major newspaper in the country. Merchants on Peachtree Street decorated their shop windows with tributes.

The body lay in state at the Grady home and finally in the church, where 7,000 to 9,000 persons passed by to see it. Mrs. Grady wanted no music and no uniforms in the funeral procession, but the line of march was lengthy, with delegations from the stewards of the First Methodist Church, the Gate City Lodge of the Masonic order, the Chamber of Commerce, the Young Men's Democratic League, the Piedmont Exposition, the Fulton County Veterans' Association, the Traveling Protective Association, and Grady's beloved Chi Phi fraternity. Delegations represented the government. Governor John B. Gordon, out of town when Grady died, rode all night to be present.

From the church, twenty-three carriages and many marching mourners went with the coffin to Oakland Cemetery, where a crowd of several hundred awaited the cortege. The Grady family had no plot there, so the body went temporarily into the tomb of a friend to await removal to a new cemetery, Westview, where it lies today.[11]

Grady's friends rallied around his family and his memory. A few of the wealthier ones, realizing there was little liquidity in the estate, started a fund to pay off the mortgage on the Grady home. Led by

W. A. Hemphill, business manager and owner of a substantial block of *Constitution* stock, these men subscribed $5,600 and retired the mortgage without fanfare.[12]

The colleague thus honored was ordinary in appearance but in little else. Grady was about five feet eight inches tall; his head and face were round, and his hair seemed to be black but had an underlay of brown. Although many of Grady's young and middle-aged friends wore moustaches, he was clean-shaven. His skin was olive and his eyes were brown. He bore himself as a man who loved sports and exercise. As a young man, he briefly owned a skating rink and zipped around it in high spirits. As a mature man, he had his own gymnasium. He once gently reproved a young friend for not caring enough about baseball and other sports. "Don't make the mistake of standing aloof from these things and trying to get old too soon."[13]

Mirth and laughter marked his personality. He doubled over at his own jokes. He once counseled a young person to live in the sunshine, for men who sat in the shade mildewed. He liked to be agreeable and preferred compromise to argument. In an early newspaper piece, written when he was nineteen, he said that if anyone offended him, or if he offended anyone, all injured parties should meet quietly in his backyard where differences would be peacefully adjusted.[14] Where disagreements were on the surface, he took that course; where they were substantive, he was a formidable opponent.

A friend said that if the art of conversation were dead when Grady was born, he reinvented it. Some men with reputations as talkers waited for a subject to arise upon which they could be brilliant, then seized the moment. Grady did no such thing. He took any commonplace subject that came up and suffused it with wit and imagination. He explained his readiness with words in a way that would offend modern readers. His father was an Irishman, he said, and his mother was a woman.[15]

With his high energy and sharp mind he could do two or more things at once. Visitors told of him seated on a couch in his office, dictating to his secretary and at the same time entertaining callers.

Early in his career, an unwelcome woman trapped him at his desk. As she talked on and on, Grady found time to write off a note to a friend: "That damn'd woman is in the office now, smiling like a she fiend! What *have* I done to deserve all this? She came in the office humming 'Come Birdie, Come.' "[16]

It was said he could do the work of three people. A sometime partner said he was a composite character, energetic, warm, poised, and tactful, yet also extremely conservative. Passion never governed him in things that mattered, and in difficult circumstances, he behaved with control and judgment.[17]

His personal conservatism was old-fashioned. He usually dressed formally in a blue suit with a white handkerchief protruding from the breast pocket. Sometimes he had a flower in his lapel.

When Clark Howell, son of Grady's editor in chief, was twenty-one years old, Grady had no money to buy him a large present. His main gift was a letter of advice, which was all the more impressive because it was advice that Grady followed. It had three parts.

Young Howell was never to gamble. It was a poor investment, poor business, and poor fun. "A man who plays poker is unfit for every other business on earth."

He was never to drink. Grady admitted that he loved liquor and the fellowship involved in drinking. But, he said, "It is much easier not to drink at all than to drink a little. If I had to attribute what I have done in life to any one thing, I should attribute it to the fact that I am a teetotaler."

Howell was to marry early, for early marriage had a steadying effect. "By marrying young your children grow up when they are a pleasure to you. You feel the responsibility of life, the sweetness of life, and you avoid bad habits."[18]

Grady's own homelife was ideal. He was married to his childhood sweetheart and they had a son and daughter. He spoke lovingly of the son in his speeches. And once when unable to walk to kindergarten with his daughter, as he usually did, he worried about her disappointment and by the time he reached his office, he was sending her a bag of candy by messenger, along with a note: "Papa loves his baby with all his whole heart and it makes him happy to walk with her, but he has so much work that he has to hurry all the time." He told her to share the candy with her friends.[19]

Grady was at home on most evenings. He and Mrs. Grady entertained a stream of guests, many of them people who could help him accomplish some purpose or other: well-connected Georgians visiting Atlanta; visitors from out of state; members of the General Assembly, for whom he once had a fiddling contest in his home. Four legislators fiddled away at the top of their form, and the prize went to Thomas E. Watson, then a first-term representative from McDuffie County, who was destined to make a mark of his own. Watson later became one of Grady's harshest critics but held back a time before assigning mean motives to him.

There was audacity, or at least risk, in holding the fiddling contest, for one egotistical legislator triumphed while three others suffered by comparison; but Joel Chandler Harris said that even as a little boy, Grady had "moral audacity," his willingness to try the unexpected making him a leader among his childhood friends.[20] When as an adult, mature judgment, personal charm, connections, and directed energy were added to audacity, Grady seldom failed to accomplish his objectives. Those objectives were usually limited, and therefore winnable: triumphing in an election for some candidate he had chosen, sponsoring a Chautauqua, making a successful speech, bringing about a civic improvement for Atlanta.

Having no malice, he disarmed those who opposed him, and few rancid personal comments about opponents ever came from him. When things did not go to suit him, he usually shrugged them off. Once, watching his candidate get trounced in a debate, Grady listened carefully, then muttered, "My God! he has killed him too dead to skin!" That was all.[21]

Of the great orators America has produced, Grady may have bloomed the latest. When he died after a life spanning thirty-nine years, few remembered that he had been a celebrated speaker only for his last three. Before he was thirty-six, he spoke little, and never on weighty subjects. All at once in New York, in the New South speech, he became a man everyone wished to hear. Even then, he spoke seldom for so celebrated an orator.

His voice was high-pitched, but ringing, and he appeared to speak without preparation, using no text. He sometimes spoke with his right hand in the pocket of his trousers, rocking gently. He seized quickly upon occurrences of the moment, such as an event in the audience or a remark by his introducer, and incorporated them into his speech. Such interpolations gave his addresses a sense of being products of the moment. Actually, they were carefully prepared in his mind and had been written out, although the preparation underwent changes once he was on his feet. Often, when he had written something for the *Constitution* with which he was pleased, the better lines from that piece found their way into his speech.

When Grady spoke outside Georgia, he traveled by special rail car. He always invited a party of distinguished Georgians to accompany him, persons as carefully selected for present and future usefulness as any honors list in the nation.

In the oratorical style of the day, references to God and Providence appeared in his addresses, but little suggests that Grady was religious in more than a nominal sense. He was a baptized member of the Methodist Episcopal Church, South, and was a member of the First Methodist Church in Atlanta, where he occasionally attended services. Before he made his New South speech in New York in 1886, he appeared at the front of the congregation one Sunday morning to make a profession of religious faith. Thereafter, he was for three years a member of the official board of the church, but if records are correct, he attended only one meeting.[22]

Grady set forth his religious concerns in 1881 in an article he wrote for the *Constitution*. He perceived a tide of atheism in America, and he warned against it. He feared that social control would slip if religious practice eroded, and it was social control that concerned him. Conventional writers in the 1880s saw religion as snatching guilty souls from the burning, but not Grady. Jesus is barely present in his piece. The "lowly Nazarene" gets one mention, but the name of Jesus appears only in the last sentence in a quotation from someone else.[23]

Grady had some of the impulses associated with religious people. He was generous to the poor, although sometimes condescendingly. He believed that rich people who lost their money by accident suffered more than people who always had been poor. In the organized charities sponsored by the *Constitution*, he chose the persons to be helped, excluding those he thought unworthy of assistance. He felt that many people deserved to be poor; helping them encouraged vagrancy.[24]

Grady's cheerfulness, openness, and, toward the end, his large local and national reputation attracted hordes of people to him. Following his death, his younger admirers wanted a permanent memorial for him and were ready to pay for it. More than one hundred of them crowded the editorial rooms of the *Constitution* to discuss a monument, which when completed was a statue of Grady in an oratorical pose, standing upon a granite base and rising twenty-five feet into the air. Dedicated in October 1891, this work in bronze still stands, with its spectacular green patina, on an island in the middle of Marietta Street in downtown Atlanta. As the monument committee finished its business, another group worked to build a great hospital in Atlanta named for Grady. Henry Grady Memorial Hospital was dedicated on May 25, 1892. Greatly expanded, it exists to the present time, providing health care with a special mission to the poor.[25]

These honors and Grady's death at an early age were enough to validate a local legend, a story handed down to subsequent eras which perhaps is not verifiable in all of its aspects. His legend grew as companies of military cadets were named in his honor and as innumerable boy babies received the orator's name. In 1905 and 1906, Georgia created and organized a county named for him, situated on the Florida line with Cairo as its county seat. A high school in Atlanta bears his name, as does the School of Journalism and Mass Communication at the University of Georgia.

The legend, however, became more than a local thing, receiving all-important help to do so. The New South Movement was a phenomenon of its own, and the Grady story fitted neatly into it. Around the Movement and the times immediately preceding it, an intellectual consensus formed purporting to say in heroic cadences what both the times and the Movement meant. The meaning of Grady's life and career were thus viewed within a particular framework. The consensus ran as follows:

Carpetbaggers, scalawags, and radicals took charge in the southern states following the Civil War, fixing upon white southerners bad governments shot through with graft, corruption, and ignorance. Black men, unprepared for leadership, held conspicuous public offices. Under such regimes, white southerners were misgoverned, humiliated, and justifiably embittered. These governments were replaced by others led by southern white men, often called Redeemers because they "redeemed" the South from alien rule. Many of these Redeemers had been Confederate officials or military officers. Their governments were honest, frugal, and prudent.

The New South Movement then took wing. Fermenting earlier, by 1880 it promised southerners a way out of economic trouble and a grip on self-respect. Its promises were almost universal. It would industrialize the South, making new jobs in factories for those who wanted them. It would put southern agriculture on a better footing, bringing prosperity, or at least improved conditions, to the farms. It would give justice to black southerners, plus all the opportunity they could manage. The South would forgive the North for defeating it and would extend its hand in friendship.

The Movement had critics in the South, but the region needed it. Huge numbers of people were poor, with scant hope, and they were ready for an optimistic program, one in which scarcely a tincture of cynicism showed. Brave and disinterested leaders might bring such a program to fruition.

Grady began the decade of the 1880s as such a leader, but after the New South speech in 1886, he was the preeminent leader, or was perceived as such. He seemed to embody the Movement, for he was widely accepted as an extraordinarily able and selfless man. He was even as heroic as Confederate soldiers on the front line, although the dangers he faced were different and his courage was of another kind. In 1886 he stood solitary in New York before an untested audience of putative adversaries making the first speech of his life on a substantive subject; and there he charmed the nation and convinced many important leaders that the South really did accept the outcome of the Civil War and wished to be friends. In 1889 he stood alone before an even more dangerous assembly in Boston. Then he died still youthful in a matter of days.

Seen in that light, Grady's life was a struggle for his region and his people, in whose behalf he finally laid down his life. Upon those terms, his legend would grow.

Grady's friends helped it by publishing a memorial volume within a few months of his death. The body was unburied when people at the *Constitution* talked of collecting his speeches and some of the tributes that followed his death and prefacing them all with a biographical essay by Joel Chandler Harris, Grady's friend and colleague. The immediate idea was not to promote a legend but to make money for the Grady family. The copyright would belong to Mrs. Henry W. Grady.

Harris and his associates undertook their project with haste and alarm. Within seven weeks of Grady's death, they warned against an Atlanta publishing house which was assembling another volume. That product would drain off money.[26]

Harris had his book in the hands of reviewers by early April 1890, about three months after Grady's death.[27] It was titled *Life of Henry W. Grady, Including His Writings and Speeches*. Scholars and serious readers thereafter had a well-produced volume of 630 pages, containing acceptable texts of seven of the ten significant speeches that Grady gave in his lifetime. The volume contained several other pieces and essays written by Grady, as well as some 350 pages of editorials, speeches, memorials, letters, telegrams, and poems of praise and memory. Harris's preface comprises sixty pages of biography. There are errors in the essay and in the rest of the book, but as memorial volumes go, the one on Grady holds up well.

The book represents Grady as his grieving friends wished him to be remembered. They chose the line of argument, the themes, and the vocabulary through which he was offered to the public, and Grady himself could scarcely have improved upon their efforts.

The rival volume, produced by H. C. Hudgins and Company of Atlanta, also appeared in 1890. Titled *Life and Labors of Henry W. Grady: His Speeches, Writings, Etc.*, it was also published in other cities under differing imprints. The work generally is inferior, its strength lying in personal statements and recollections of Grady's friends. The volume presents one speech not in the Harris volume. Despite its flaws, the book added to the public record of Grady's life.

Another work of less scope also appeared in 1890. In the final weeks of his life, Grady wrote six articles for the weekly New York *Ledger*. These pieces were published as *The New South* (New York, 1890), and the work included a character sketch of Grady by Oliver Dyer, a friend from the New York *Sun*.

Within fifteen years, the New South Movement itself began to interest serious writers, and the raw materials of Grady's life and work were available for consultation, or at least the portion that his friends had elected to present.

Thereafter for about a half century, scholars and writers cast the legend of the New South Movement and its leaders mostly in terms of the historical consensus referred to. In 1905 Philip Alexander Bruce, for a time corresponding secretary of the Virginia Historical Society, advanced the story in a much-acclaimed volume titled *The Rise of the New South*. The book was Volume XVII in *The History of North America* series, edited by Guy Carleton Lee of Johns Hopkins University. Lee, in a foreword, said that the years between 1865 and 1905 were so triumphant that he required self-control to avoid overstatement. In the volume that followed, Bruce exalted improvements in the South in almost every field.[28]

Bruce was not a professional historian, but Holland Thompson, born in North Carolina and for forty years a distinguished faculty member at the City College of New York, was. In 1919 he produced a work through the Yale University Press that, with minor qualifications, swung the weight of a university scholar behind the New South consensus. Thompson called his book *The New South: A*

Chronicle of Social and Industrial Evolution, and it was the standard book on the Movement for thirty years. Holland argued that the New South was an extension of the Old, noting within it a political consolidation of the white population united in self-defense, an interpretation often heard from Grady's lips. Acknowledging that white farmers were unhappy, Holland said their affairs might be getting better. As for blacks, the condition of many of them had improved. Industrialization had arrived in an important way, Holland said, especially in the South Atlantic states.[29]

A rather unusual champion followed Holland. Broadus Mitchell, born in Kentucky and brought up in Virginia and in South Carolina, claimed to be a Marxist and an exponent of the New South all at once. Mitchell, in *The Rise of Cotton Mills in the South,* chronicled the surge of industrial growth, finding in it romance, creative tension, and triumph enough to invest the Movement with the halo of dogged heroism, a characterization that would have astonished Marx but which pleased Mitchell's readers, who found conviction in the work.[30]

There were minor protests,[31] but they were swamped by a contribution from Harvard. Paul H. Buck put his reputation behind the proposition that reconciliation between North and South occurred under New South auspices, a contention of Grady's. Buck's work, *The Road to Reunion, 1865–1900,* won the Pulitzer Prize. Although Buck believed that Grady had few original ideas, he said the Atlanta newspaperman was the "recognized apostle of the new faith." His faith and optimism were "living fire peculiar to the New South he served."[32]

Perhaps the finest hour for the Movement came in 1941 when W. J. Cash, an editorial writer for the Charlotte *News,* published *The Mind of the South.*[33] This book, popular in its time and since, depicted a heroic and romantic South recovering from its past, building up the region while holding to what it perceived as the best of its values.

As the reputation of Cash burgeoned, Raymond B. Nixon, then a professor at Emory University, published a full-length biography titled *Henry W. Grady: Spokesman of the New South.* Nixon cemented the Grady legend of glamor and heroism, showing the newspaperman and orator as the attractive figure depicted by his friends and taking him at his word about the values he enunciated.[34]

However, nothing goes on forever. The framework in which Grady's reputation stood was about to be ravaged. C. Vann Woodward earlier had written a youthful work on Tom Watson, the Georgia populist who had won Grady's fiddling contest. In 1951 Woodward published *Origins of the New South,* a frontal assault on the New South Movement. In a memorable phrase coined much later, Woodward said he turned the Movement upside down and celebrated Black Mass atop it. In place of honest governments run by Redeemers, he found absconding state treasurers, dishonest deals, and favoritism defensible under no decent standard. He discovered exploitation by business leaders, repression of blacks, and poverty on farms.[35] As the reputation of the New South Movement declined, Grady's reputation sank with it, although he himself escaped sustained attack.

Since the publication of Woodward's work, and in part because of it, the Movement has been opened to searching examination. Along with others, Paul M. Gaston, Jonathan M. Wiener, Dwight B. Billings, Jr., David L. Carlton, Carl N. Degler, Gavin Wright, Michael Wayne, Barbara J. Fields, and James C. Cobb have examined a number of questions about it: whether the New South was an exercise in mythmaking; whether there was conflict between industrialists and agrarians and what was its nature and result; what was the nature of continuity between the Old South and the New; what was the nature of change; could continuity and change be measured and evaluated? Quite logically, an occasional scholar wondered whether the argument was moving along the most creative lines.[36]

The present work has both limitations and a point of view. It is limited to the study of one decade, the decade of the 1880s when Grady was most active and influential. It is largely about Georgia.[37] It is almost entirely a work about Grady, his immediate confederates, and what they did under the aegis of the New South Movement.

A part of the title, *A Brave and Beautiful City,* suggests something of the point of view. In 1886 in New York, Grady talked of his beloved Atlanta before an audience that included General William T. Sherman. "I want to say to General Sherman, who is considered an able man in our parts, though some people think he is a kind of careless man about fire, that from the ashes he left us in 1864 we have raised a brave and beautiful city; that somehow or other we have caught the sunshine in the bricks and mortar of our homes, and have builded therein not one ignoble prejudice or memory."[38] From that sentence, another apt though clumsy title could have come: *Somehow Or Other,* a phrase suggesting that Grady used everything at hand to accomplish his ends, including things that perhaps were inappropriate.

Grady said all the right things to show that he wished to industrialize the South, that he longed for reconciliation with the North, that he was committed to improving agriculture, and that he wanted something approaching justice for black people. On the surface, he espoused those things and pulled the shining threads of the Movement together and wove them into a fabric presenting just such a picture. Its front, like the face of a tapestry, showed an irreproachable pattern of advancement for the South and became the image that men acclaimed; but like a tapestry, it had a backside where the threads bunched and knotted. The backside forms a picture of its own, one seldom seen, a truer one, a more human vision. In the rear, one sees not a perfect picture but a creditable work.

Except in a general and sentimental sense, Grady's heart belonged not to the whole South, but to Atlanta, proclaimed at the height of his powers as his "first and only love."[39] It was for Atlanta that he used most of his instincts, intelligence, energy, and time. This book will explain that, somehow or other, he strove to make a difference for Atlanta, leaving the rest of the South to enjoy what the city could not garner for itself. In that vein, this book seeks to define what the New South Movement really was to Grady, a definition based in part upon his words, which always were eloquent, but more upon his works, which always were interesting. It is the backside of the tapestry that we shall examine.

Aside from theses, dissertations, and an occasional article, Georgia in the 1880s has, in modern times, had serious study comparatively recently. An excellent monograph by Numan V. Bartley is a necessary starting place in the field, as is Charles E. Wynes's section of a contemporary general history of Georgia. Bartley sees contention between farmers and urban communities as an important theme of the decade. Pertinent parts of the present work fit comfortably into that concept. Other scholars have also dealt with this theme in different ways and with differing emphases upon Georgia: Steven Hahn, Robert C. McMath, Jr., Stephen J. DeCanio, Lewis Nicholas Wynne, and Charles L. Flynn, Jr. Other works by Roger L. Ransom, Richard Sutch, Joel Williamson, and J. Morgan Kousser, although not concerned exclusively with Georgia, have vast implications for the state and have influenced the present work. Excellent studies of Atlanta and of Augusta by James Michael Russell and Edward J. Cashin shed light upon themes found here.[40]

In a justly famous monograph, Richard C. Wade studied the rise of cities in the American West and concluded that they often behaved like imperial states. "Like imperial states, cities carved out extensive dependencies, extended their influence over the economic and political life of the hinterland, and fought with contending places over strategic trade routes. . . . Like most imperialisms, the struggle . . . left a record of damage and achievement. It trampled new villages, smothered promising towns, and even brought down established metropolises."[41] The New South Movement in Georgia as led by Grady was in this pattern of urban imperialism. Atlanta moved to become the preeminent city in Georgia, a preeminence indicated but not yet established in 1880. Grady and his allies did not quite trample new villages, smother promising towns, or demolish established metropolises, but the New South leaders of Macon and Augusta believed they were seeking to do so. The leadership of Columbus and Savannah watched with nervous eyes.

Students of southern history are accustomed to sagas of struggle, and readers of the present study will recognize that theme here. Struggle and contention are central to the works of Woodward. More recently, David L. Carlton has described some of the consequences of the rise of the textile industry in South Carolina, a rise that left a trail of contention in its wake. The work of Jonathan Wiener gives a noteworthy account of the founding and development of Birmingham, Alabama, laying bare the clashes of interest that went into that undertaking.[42]

Before looking at Grady's efforts in behalf of Atlanta, it is necessary to examine the man himself and the newspaper upon which he founded a reputation, and which, with his oratory and his political dexterity, was an instrument of his power.

2
Grady and the Atlanta *Constitution*

During the 1880s the Atlanta *Constitution* was one of two southern newspapers read and admired in the North. Only in Louisville, Kentucky, where Henry Watterson edited the Louisville *Courier-Journal,* was there a publication to rival it. The *Constitution* had a point of view; it had leadership, and it was financially stable.

Stability was lacking in many publications of the era, and the births and deaths of newspapers were unremarkable occurrences. Little suggested that the *Constitution* was launched for the long haul, for it was created to serve an end.

When the first edition appeared on June 16, 1868, Georgia was under Reconstruction rule and some Georgia Democrats thought a publication was required to attack the government every time the presses rolled. The leading newspaper in Atlanta, the *Intelligencer,* was not vigorous enough to please them. Carey W. Styles, a colorful character who in a long lifetime was associated with at least twenty-one newspapers, was the motivating founder of the *Constitution,* but he needed more money than he had. He got it by taking on two business partners: William A. Hemphill and Hemphill's father-in-law, James Anderson. They raised funds to buy a small and undistinguished newspaper called Atlanta *Daily Opinion,* which they renamed the Atlanta *Constitution. Daily Opinion* had supported Radical Republicans in Georgia; its finances were insecure and when bought, it was owned by a group of printers. The *Constitution* was as Democratic as *Daily Opinion* had been Republican, and the renamed publication pledged a fight for southern rights.[1]

Hemphill, not Styles, was the key to survival for the *Constitution*. Styles, following a pattern he showed during much of his life, left the newspaper quickly, before the end of 1868, and Hemphill's father-in-law knew nothing about newspaper management. Neither did Hemphill, but he learned fast. When the three men started the *Constitution,* Hemphill had been a soldier, a schoolteacher, then administrator of a small academy. He was twenty-six years old, but a mature twenty-six. Like many young southerners he had spent the years of his majority mostly in the Confederate army. Born in Athens, Georgia, on May 5, 1842, he was graduated from the University of Georgia in 1861. Hemphill enlisted in the Troup Artillery attached to the forces of Robert E. Lee in Virginia, and he spent the war in service. He was wounded at Gettysburg. After the war, he moved to Atlanta and founded the Male School.

As business manager of the new publication, he was a major stockholder. A man of few words, he was a fanatic on promptness and on keeping his word. He once told a group of young men almost scoldingly that if they expected to amount to anything, they must always be punctual, whether in appearing at the exact moment promised, in paying a note, or in keeping an engagement in court. "Success comes to the prompt man," he said. Business associates of the *Constitution* could deal with such a person.[2]

During its early years, the newspaper had several editors. Styles attracted attention by attacking the government, and when he left he sold his stock to Hemphill. He was followed by James R. Barrick, Isaac W. Avery, and Edward Y. Clarke. Of these, Avery was the most important and served the longest tenure, from May 1869 until April 1874. Avery subsequently was executive secretary to three governors of Georgia, a political fixture in his own right.[3] He wrote a biased but useful history of his times.

Not until 1876, when the newspaper was eight years old, did a second great leader arrive to join Hemphill. Evan P. Howell was born in Warsaw, Georgia, but from the time he was nine, he lived near or in Atlanta, and he had a lifetime association with the city. At twenty-two, he joined the Confederate army, fought under Stonewall Jackson and Joseph E. Johnston, and rose from noncommissioned officer to captain. He was "Captain Howell" for the rest of his life. Although a lawyer by training, he had been city editor of the Atlanta *Intelligencer.* His business interests achieved focus in October 1876, when he bought a substantial block of stock in the *Constitution* and became editor in chief.[4]

Grady became a reporter on the *Constitution* in 1876 and managing editor four years later, and the corporate leadership to carry the newspaper through the decade was then in place. The directors and principal owners of the Constitution Publishing Company were Hemphill, Howell, Grady, and N. P. T. Finch. Finch, the associate editor, joined the newspaper in 1872 as a minority owner and was one of its best editorial writers until he retired in December 1885. There were other small stockholders, including Robert A. Hemphill, brother of William A. Hemphill. Robert Hemphill was important in the business department, supervising subscriptions and advertising.

The *Constitution* earned about $31,500 a year on its $100,000 capital, but the principal owners took only $1,800 a year each at first, wisely putting the rest back into the newspaper. The directors met the fifth day of each month to review the business. Howell was president of both the company and the board of directors, and until 1886 Finch was secretary.[5]

During the 1880s, the Constitution Publishing Company held to its policy of reinvesting profits. Improvements in all categories were made as fast as the books would permit. When Grady became managing editor, the directors had just made a blunder, buying a press that was too small and slow to allow much expansion. One of Grady's first decisions was to increase the size of the paper and the space available for news, which also meant more room for advertising. He pushed the inadequate equipment to its limit.

The *Constitution* usually ran four pages of eight columns on weekdays and more on Sundays. Grady doubled the pages, cut the columns to six, and changed the type so that the newspaper was less gray. On Sundays the press ran for eleven hours, until 9 A.M., an inconvenient hour for the circulation department. The management was not proud to admit it, but subscribers living below Macon got an inferior product. The paper for that market, the "midnight edition," had a copy close at 10:30 P.M., before many important items were ready. Patrons in central and south Georgia complained, but a later edition would have been twenty-four hours out of date.[6]

The first copies of Grady's "new" newspaper appeared on September 6, 1881. By then, the daily *Constitution* had a circulation of perhaps 6,000 and the weekly claimed 11,000. Whether the enterprise would grow depended upon the wisdom and energy of the management. Except for Finch, each of the principal stockholders was the ideal man to lead the *Constitution*. Hemphill was the perfect business manager; Howell had political judgment as well as business sense; and Grady was a man of personal, professional, and organizational gifts.[7]

In 1882 or 1883 the partners made expensive decisions that freed the *Constitution* to expand.[8] The Constitution Publishing Company bought a corner lot at Alabama and Forsyth streets, knocked down two new brick stores, and built a six-story building that was a model for its time. A double steam engine supplied power. If one side failed, the other switched on. The boilers were under the sidewalk, encased in masonry. Steam heated the building, and electricity, generated on the premises, lighted it. No gas lamps, fireplaces, or gas fixtures were allowed, and the structure was said to be fireproof.

A new press, a Hoe Perfecting model, was in the basement, which was the first floor. It cost as much as three railroad locomotives, and after the press fitted into its routine, it printed 10,000 newspapers an hour and was capable of more. The old presses were in the basement for job printing. The circulation department and mail room took up the rest of the space.

Visitors entered on the floor above, which accommodated the offices of two of the owners and directors. The handsome office of William A. Hemphill connected by folding doors with that of Howell, and their offices were made into one room by opening the doors. Near their suite, clerks stood behind windows to receive subscribers and advertisers. Two elevators, one for people, one for freight, tied the six floors together and went from the top to the bottom of the building in six seconds. The front elevator for visitors was of mahogany and mirrors and was said to be the finest south of Washington. The company leased the rest of the floor, a part of it to Western Union. It also leased the two floors above.

Grady's domain was the fifth floor. As visitors got off the elevator, they entered an anteroom, where the office boy received them, then went through glass doors into the library. The library and an adjoining room were offices for three important colleagues and editorial writers: Finch (until 1885), Wallace P. Reed, and Joel Chandler Harris. Grady's private office and his consultation room opened off the library. From their windows, the colleagues saw Stone Mountain and Kennesaw Mountain.

The news staff, directed by Grady, was on the top floor. When Grady was absent, the man in charge was Clark Howell, night editor and the young son of Evan P. Howell.[9] Clark Howell oversaw most of the details of production, editing, and makeup. He was assisted by P. J. Moran, the news and telegraph editor, who wrote occasional copy for the editorial page, and by the city editor, Josiah Carter (after 1887, J. K. Ohl).[10] Reporters and copy editors had desks near Howell and Carter. Back of this suite was the composing room, where men stood before banks of type, setting it by hand.

The schedule of the newspaper as well as the design of the building assured that the people most responsible for the company had access to one another. Unless one or more of them were out of town or sick, no day passed when they did not consult.

At about 9 each morning, Evan P. Howell, Hemphill, and Grady met in Howell's office. Other editorial writers occasionally attended this most important conference of the day. Policy was fixed on current issues, and editorials were suggested or assigned. Grady sometimes wrote editorials, but his responsibility was the direction of the news staff. When the conference ended, he went to his office to start the news day, going through the mail. Sometimes if he were zestful, he finished the task, went into the room where Harris, Reed, and others were working, sat on Harris's desk and regaled them with jokes and a running satire on events.[11] Then he put on a serious face, went into his office with his stenographer, slammed the door, and worked furiously.

He studied a schedule of occurrences in the state that day. His eye noted conventions, elections, and hangings, and if they were out of town, he wrote a telegram to a correspondent telling him to cover it. Grady sent as many as fifty of these dispatches a day. He went through the exchange newspapers, marked for him by Reed.

At noon, the city editor appeared. He and Grady reviewed a roster of events in the city and made assignments, each written out and laid on reporters' desks. Each reporter also had a beat: the police reporter went to the station house and to the courts; the department reporter went to the post office, State Capitol, and related offices; the market reporter went to the exchanges; the railroad reporter went to the depot and the offices of the rail companies, and the personal reporter went to the hotels to see who was in town and why. On days when there were many stories, editorial writers and some executives took assignments. At the *Constitution,* nobody was too good for any task. When regular personnel could not handle everything, the city editor called in men who worked on space rates.

By 2 P.M., early copy was finished. Howell had done his brief editorials on practical subjects. Finch's editorials were ready on foreign affairs and on statistical matters; Reed had done his essays, and Harris, who wrote on anything, had put the final touches on his work. Moran, if he were writing anything that day, had turned in a collection of shorts called "Georgia Gossip."

As telegraph editor, his busiest work was before him, for items were by then arriving from the Associated Press, as well as copy from special correspondents in Augusta, Athens, Savannah, Macon, Columbus, Rome, Montgomery, Birmingham, Chattanooga, and Columbia, South Carolina. Each correspondent checked in daily whether he filed or not. The *Constitution* had exchange agreements with the *News and Courier* in Charleston and with the *Times-Union* in Jacksonville, and some of that copy arrived by 2 P.M. Other material came by mail.

By 6 P.M., Clark Howell was at work. Up to then, Grady and his subeditors had run the news department, but in the early evening,

Grady went home for dinner and remained there to be with his family and to read. He had one of the first telephones in Atlanta and stayed in touch with the editorial offices and with Howell. If he wrote anything, a copy boy went to his house and picked it up. Grady trusted his night editor absolutely, even though Howell was only twenty when the *Constitution* moved into its new building in 1884.

All through the evening, Howell fed copy to the composing room. The much-criticized "midnight edition" was abolished, and the press start was at 2:30 A.M. rather than 10:30 P.M. Newspapers were fast arriving in the mail room a bit before 3 A.M.

Speedy work was required. Trains that took the *Constitution* to subscribers and to customers left the depot beginning about 4. Workers sacked the papers by destination, threw them onto carts, and hurried them to the station. The *Constitution* took advantage of all augmented train service. In the fall of 1884, three months after the newspaper got its new building, the East Tennessee, Virginia, and Georgia line put on a fast mail train that left Atlanta at 4:45 A.M. Before 8 A.M., the *Constitution* was in every town between Atlanta and Macon. At 8, the train left Macon for Brunswick on the Georgia coast, dropping the paper along the line. In the early evening, people in Jacksonville, Florida, could read it. By 1889 readers in Valdosta near the Florida line could have their copies by 4:23 P.M. on the day of publication.[12]

Before 1884 the *Constitution* was called a daily paper by courtesy only; there was no Monday edition. With the new press, that changed. On November 3, 1884, the *Constitution* published for the first time on a Monday, giving the edition to readers without additional charge. The press start for the weekly edition was now noon Monday, and work on it continued until 11 P.M., with its run falling between daily editions. By 1886 the weekly was up in circulation, and the press could not print the whole run on Mondays. The remainder was produced between daily editions on Tuesdays, with the Tuesday product reserved for out-of-state subscribers.[13]

During the 1880s, the daily *Constitution* held subscription rates steady while increasing charges for advertisements. Circulation for the daily was near 20,000. By 1888 copy and advertising pressure on Sunday was such that the Saturday paper swelled from eight to twelve pages to relieve it. The Sunday paper had thirty-two pages, and for the first time readers could subscribe to it alone.[14] In the 1880s, and indeed until 1914, no institution existed to audit circulation figures reliably, so all newspaper claims were suspect. The *Constitution* threw open its press register, mailing lists, cashbooks, postage accounts, and paper bills for public inspection to try to prove it spoke the truth about its circulation.

The *Constitution* sold guns, sewing machines, watches, and books at reduced prices to subscribers; but mainly it printed the news, always letting the public know that it spent large sums to do so. In 1883, at much expense, the *Constitution* began printing lengthy news items sent by telegraph from other Georgia cities. Delivery of such stories by mail was the earlier standard and had been considered acceptable, even though publication was delayed for a day or two. When, in the spring of 1886, Georgia had a flood, the *Constitution* in one edition printed almost 12,000 words received by telegraph from special correspondents, plus its Associated Press budget of 8,000 words. In one month, correspondents wired in nearly 150,000 words, after which the newspaper told its readers that its special telegraphic charges equaled the combined charges of every daily paper in six nearby states. Grady's spending once dismayed Evan Howell, who had just seen the telegraph bill for one week, but neither he nor Hemphill restrained their colleague, or tried to do so.[15]

Employees of the *Constitution* sometimes did their duties in ways that money could not buy. In the flood just mentioned, the correspondent in Rome stood on a Western Union table with an operator, and he wrote and the operator filed until the instruments were submerged. In West Point, a doctor who wrote for the paper filed for hours until water broke the wires.[16]

Such events were the stuff of which legends were made, and the editors happily publicized them, but such occurrences would never have made the *Constitution* a distinguished newspaper. Its growing reputation owed much to the organizational skills of Henry Grady, skills no less remarkable for having been undemonstrated before he became managing editor.

Grady's background lay in the commercial middle class in the university town of Athens, some sixty miles from Atlanta.[17] His parents christened him Henry Woodfin Grady. His father, William Sammons Grady, was a dour but idealistic merchant who struggled in the 1850s to improve the lot of his growing family. Besides half-interest in a store, he owned half of a plant which made gas from pine wood, and he invested in a sawmill. As the Civil War approached, William Sammons Grady and family were doing well. His wife, Ann Gartrell Grady, was the lively member of the household. Like her husband, she was a member of the Methodist Episcopal Church, South, and abjured liquor and cardplaying, but her spirit was happy. She liked games, such as checkers and backgammon, which she played ferociously. Into this household, Henry Grady was born on May 24, 1850. The following year, William Sammons Grady, Jr., arrived, followed in 1855 by Martha Nicholson (Mattie) Grady. Five Negro slaves were members and servants of the household.

Grady's boyhood was filled with frolic and good humor, but he also loved books. He read everything in the Grady home plus what he could borrow. He mastered much of what he read and showed a gift for recalling detail.

He probably did not grasp the meaning of the issues unfolding in America during his childhood in the 1850s. His father understood them all too well and became convinced that troubles harmful to his business would follow the election of Abraham Lincoln in 1860. William Sammons Grady sold his part of the store three weeks after the election, although he kept half interest in the building, the sawmill, and the gasworks. The money went into real estate, a wise move.

The father had wished to preserve the federal union, but after gunfire at Fort Sumter, he cast his lot with the Confederate States of America. He organized a military company and was soon a captain in the Twenty-fifth North Carolina Regiment and on his way to Virginia. Other children had arrived in the household—Annie King and Julia Kennon—and just after Captain Grady left for Virginia a sixth child, Elizabeth, was born and died. Shortly thereafter, scarlet fever killed Annie and Julia. The father, now a major, hurried home on a short leave. Another son, Minor Graham Grady, was born in January 1863 but lived little more than a year and a half.

On leave again in the summer of 1863, Major Grady bought the Taylor mansion on Prince Avenue in Athens, the first grand house that the family owned, and with the house came a 338-acre farm. Major Grady never lived in the house. In July 1864 he was wounded at the head of his command at Petersburg. There was hope that he would live, and Mrs. Grady went to a military hospital at Danville, Virginia, and took him to his brother's home in Greenville, South Carolina; he died there in October. Mrs. Grady and the surviving children moved into their new house in the summer of 1865. The farm that came with it and the other real estate were the salvation of the family, for the property was sold bit by bit to produce money needed to live on.

Henry Grady was fifteen as the war ended, and his education needed attention. The University of Georgia had closed during the war. In the fall of 1865 a preparatory academy started in Athens, which Grady attended briefly; then he entered the reopening university, where the student body was mixed. Boys like Grady mingled with veterans of the Confederate army, some bearing battle wounds. Social life was sparse, but two debating and literary societies, Phi Kappa and Demosthenian, were active, and university rules required that all students be members of one or the other. Grady joined Phi Kappa and took part in a debate a month later. He was a conspicuous debater and a more than competent one, but legends dating from a later time ascribe to him the same oratorical powers as a youth that he had as a man. Contemporary records do not show how developed his talents were. In 1868, representing Phi Kappa as commencement orator, he made a fanciful address entitled "Castles in the Air," a future vision of the South different from the troubled realities of that commencement year. He left the university with a degree, an excellent record in history, literature, and rhetoric, and a poorer one in science and in mathematics.

From Athens, Grady went to Charlottesville to attend the University of Virginia. He registered as a postgraduate student in modern languages, history, and literature, but his real interest was debate. The leading societies were the Jefferson and the Washington, and Grady affiliated with the latter. The honor he coveted was that of "Final Orator" at graduation representing the Washington society, and almost every letter he wrote during the period deals with his plans to win it. He was all but certain that he would, but the winner was selected by election and Grady failed. He wrote a despairing letter to his mother, asking to stay in Charlottesville for another year to try again.[18] He did not stay, but slipped off to Richmond with a few friends. For the only recorded time in his life, he got drunk briefly and even that failed to help. Twenty years later, the loss of the honor still hurt. Invited to speak at the University of Virginia, he praised the charity of that institution for sealing "in sorrow rather than in anger" his stormy career there, and for its kindness in asking a "scapegrace son" to return, language that suggests more happened in Charlottesville in 1869 than was recorded. He left the University of Virginia without taking a degree.[19] Although he had spent much of his time in college learning to speak in public, he abandoned the platform except for minor talks at country schools and a brief address to a group of firemen.[20]

William A. Hemphill accidentally steered Grady into journalism. He, like Grady, grew up in Athens and the two knew each other when Hemphill was superintendent of the Methodist Sunday school. When in 1869 Grady needed encouragement, Hemphill gave it. After the disappointment in Charlottesville, Grady wrote a snappy newsletter which he sent to Hemphill; Hemphill liked the style and turned it over to the editor, Avery, who printed it under the pseudonym "King Hans." A second letter was also published.[21] Hemphill encouraged Grady, and the *Constitution* gave him reporting assignments once he was back in Georgia. One assignment sent him on a press excursion to northwest Georgia. Rufus Bullock, the Republican governor, was also a guest on the trip, and the *Constitution* did not wish to consort with him more than necessary, so it used Grady rather than a regular editor or reporter. Grady's work brimmed with humor and style, he was noticed by other newspapermen, and he soon had a full-time job in Rome, Georgia, near the Alabama border. In September 1869 he became associate editor of the Rome *Courier.*

The new journalist, then nineteen, thus embarked on a career marked by failures for seven years and by mixed successes during the four years after that. Even so, the years were not wasted, for Grady learned his craft and perfected those personal traits which for the rest of his life made him welcome in almost any group he chose to enter.

His reporting and editorial efforts were respected, but the financial rewards were disappointing. After ten months on the *Courier,* he took most of the money he had left from his father's estate and, in a sudden move, bought the Rome *Commercial,* later acquiring the Rome *Daily* and its weekly edition to combine with it. The *Commercial* became a daily newspaper, criticizing Governor Bullock and his friends with glee.

Although the Ku Klux Klan was allegedly disbanded in 1869, elements of it remained active. Governor Bullock, seeking to bolster his unpopular government, convinced the federal government that the Klan was terrorizing blacks and Republicans and that only help from Washington could keep order, meaning that he needed assistance to stay in power.

An incident then occurred that has convinced some persons that Grady was affiliated with the Ku Klux Klan. Perhaps he was, but the evidence is inconclusive. Grady had had a pleasant disagreement with B. F. Sawyer, associate editor of the *Courier* after Grady left. The two men exchanged jibes in their newspapers, and Sawyer told of seeing a giggling little fellow in a spotted shirt riding a mule at the end of a Klan procession. He suspected that "the tail end of the ku klux was no one else than our facetious young friend, Henry W. Grady." Grady put Sawyer's clipping in his own scrapbook with a note beside it saying that because of a jest, Sawyer "thus came down on me." A select committee of the United States Congress investigated Klan activities in Georgia and Grady's name was mentioned in the testimony, but he was not asked to testify. Sawyer testified but had no new details concerning Grady. It is probable that both Grady and Sawyer had been present at some Klan activity either as members or observers. In an editorial a short time later, Grady said that Klan activity sometimes produced undesirable side effects, adding that if there were an "inexorable necessity" for Klan action, the least action possible should be taken.[22]

The Rome *Daily Commercial* was a financial failure. Grady had money to spend and he let the paper run on a long string. At times he labored mightily on its behalf, then abandoned his duties to his foreman.[23] Rumors said that Grady was plagued by creditors.

During this time, Grady married Julia King of Athens, his childhood sweetheart. Her father was a physician and later mayor of Athens. When Grady was fourteen and she was twelve, he proposed marriage. As he liked to tell it, Julia agreed to signal her answer to him at a picnic the following day. If it were "yes," she would wear a yellow dress and wave her handkerchief. Grady described the desperation with which she waved in what became a family joke.[24] The wedding took place on October 5, 1871, in the Methodist church in Athens.

About a year later, in the fall of 1872, Grady and a friend sought the aid of Robert Toombs to buy half interest in the Atlanta *Constitution*. Toombs, a hot-tempered man, had been a United States senator before the Civil War, then Confederate secretary of state and a general in the Confederate army. He never sought pardon for his past and could not vote or hold major office, but he was influential nonetheless. The attempted purchase failed, but Grady signaled his willingness to leave Rome and shortly thereafter an opportunity appeared. Stopping one evening at the Kimball House in Atlanta, he fell into conversation with Robert A. Alston who suggested that Grady buy one-third of the Atlanta *Herald,* a morning newspaper in competition with the *Constitution.* Within an hour, Grady agreed, making Alston wonder whether there was insanity in Grady's family. Only a lunatic would move so rapidly. Grady hurried back to Rome, sold the *Commercial,* and on November 11, 1872, he and Julia moved to Atlanta.

Three partners owned the *Herald*—Grady, Alston, and Alexander St. Clair Abrams, who had founded the newspaper. Now it was

Grady's turn to wonder at the sanity of his associates. Abrams was a volcanic Creole. Alston had little self-restraint. Eventually he was murdered, but that was after his association with Grady was over. Abrams became editor of the *Herald* and, in a move that passes understanding, Grady, who had failed at business in Rome, became business manager. Abrams had learned his craft at the hands of a master, James Gordon Bennett of the New York *Herald,* whose specialty was sensationalized news. The Atlanta *Herald* published a full measure of crime and scandal and, when criticized for doing so, said that it showed the world as it was, good and bad. The newspaper was full of interesting reading, but its finances were chaotic.[25]

The editors plunged into the presidential politics of the 1872 election. President Ulysses S. Grant was opposed by Horace Greeley, running on the Democratic ticket with the endorsement of some Liberal Republicans who could not abide Grant. The *Constitution* supported Greeley; the Atlanta *Sun,* of which Alexander H. Stephens was editor, opposed him; the *Herald* professed to find a position between the two, but its stand was more confused than convincing. The *Herald* also criticized former Governor Joseph E. Brown, president of the state-owned Western and Atlantic Railroad.

The newspaper endorsed several Georgia politicians with eyes more on the future than the past, men such as Alfred H. Colquitt, John B. Gordon, and Benjamin H. Hill. On March 14, 1874, Grady published an editorial which he called "The New South," in which he set forth principles that later years would link to his name. He called for the erection of a regional economy with industrialization as a principal component.

By the time Grady wrote that editorial, the *Herald* was in trouble. It had readers but money went out faster than it came in. Bad decisions complicated the situation. The schedule of the mail train that took copies to Opelika, Alabama, and to points in between was changed, and the newspaper hired an engine and a mail car to deliver the papers. When a night train to Macon was taken off, the *Herald* hired another engine and car. The two trains cost $150 a day, more than the income generated by the service.

The Panic of 1873 and its aftermath added other strains, for loans were keeping the newspaper afloat. If the notes were called, the paper would die. One loan from Toombs caused a nasty break with that strong-willed man; but the Citizens Bank in Atlanta, controlled by Brown, whom the *Herald* had been afflicting, held the dangerous one. Unwisely, the newspaper also had promised to give $7,000 in prizes to its subscribers. There was a series of lawsuits over unpaid bills. Grady's mother finally sold her home in Athens and the half interest in the store building to help prop up the failing newspaper. Abrams suddenly left, citing differences over management, and following his departure, Alston took over business affairs, and Grady became editor. Matters seemed to improve when Avery left the *Constitution* to join the *Herald* as partner and colleague. Bad health retired him within a year, with Alston buying Avery's one-third interest. The management was reorganized again, and Alston became president and Grady managing editor. Alston's behavior was a humiliation. He prepared to fight a duel with the new editor of the *Constitution,* Edward Y. Clarke. Dueling was against the law in Georgia, so the men expected to fight in Alabama but were stopped by officials of that state.

The *Herald,* by now headed for ruin, alleged that Brown was setting up a monopoly to raise rail charges. The bank that Brown controlled foreclosed its mortgage immediately and the *Herald* was doomed. On February 6, 1876, it was advertised for a sheriff's sale.[26] The *Constitution* bought the subscription lists and some of the assets, and the *Herald* ceased to exist.

Somehow Grady and Alston raised money to start another daily, the Atlanta *Courier,* but it lasted little more than a month. Grady then began a weekly, the *Sunday Telegram.* It published five issues. Three newspaper ventures connected with Grady died within five months, and he cannot be absolved of substantial blame. In all of his career, he had had no qualms about neglecting all or part of his duties.

Such a harsh estimation overlooks what Grady had learned, however. Not restrained by traditional ways of doing things, he insisted upon aggressive reporting and stylish writing, fast becoming hallmarks of successful newspapers in America. He did not draw back from flippant headlines. If sometimes he approached a mild sensationalism, he was not troubled so long as coverage was solid. He personally demonstrated the power of a relatively new form, the interview. At the *Herald,* Grady had a spectacular success interviewing L. Q. C. Lamar, the congressman from Mississippi who was an early advocate of reconciliation between the North and the South, a theme that Grady expanded. He used interviews with success throughout the rest of his career. Even his flawed ideas had a soundness about them. Harris believed that running expensive trains up and down the tracks was not a mistake in concept. It was ahead of its time.[27]

Nevertheless, Grady failed. By now he and Julia had a son to support. Henry King Grady, who later changed his name to Henry Woodfin Grady, was born on June 6, 1873, and by the time his sister, Augusta King Grady, arrived on August 16, 1875, the fortunes of the family were low. The final collapse of the *Herald* and the deaths of the two ventures thereafter coincided with the end of any money from the estate of William Sammons Grady, Sr.

Henry Grady, then a few weeks short of twenty-six, earned a little money as a writer for the Augusta *Constitutionalist,* but financial pressures required a new start. He turned down an editorship in North Carolina, borrowed fifty dollars, and hurried to New York, where he appeared in the offices of the New York *Herald.* Grady knew no one there but presented himself to the managing editor who invited him to write a story about Georgia politics. Grady sat down, turned out the piece, and left it for inspection. The next morning, the *Herald* printed it, and Grady became Georgia correspondent for the newspaper. His pay was figured on space rates and remuneration was poor, for only a little news from Georgia interested *Herald* readers. From July to October 1876 the family lived with little income. Finally, on October 18, Grady packed a suitcase and started to the Atlanta depot to take a train to Augusta, where he had been offered the editorship of the *Constitutionalist.* At that moment, fortune smiled.

On the street he met Evan Howell, who the day before had

bought a substantial interest in the *Constitution* from Clarke, and who was now editor in chief. Howell engaged Grady as a reporter on the spot, and before the train to Augusta left the station, Grady was on his way to the *Constitution*.[28] Howell took Grady's suggestion that he also hire Joel Chandler Harris, then in Atlanta with his family after fleeing a yellow fever epidemic in Savannah.

Grady needed big assignments to hold his interest, and one appeared immediately, the biggest in the nation. Rutherford B. Hayes was the Republican candidate for president of the United States in 1876, and Samuel J. Tilden was the Democratic nominee. On election evening, most newspapers believed that Tilden would be president, but results in Florida, Louisiana, and South Carolina were open to question. If Hayes carried the three states, he would be elected. Reconstruction governments were still in place there, and President Grant sent federal troops to oversee the vote recount. In Florida, results could most easily be manipulated.

Upon urgent instructions from the *Herald* in New York, and on behalf of the *Constitution*, Grady took a train to Tallahassee, traveling with federal soldiers on the way to their duties. Both Republicans and Democrats sent representatives to guard their interests. One of the Republicans was General Lew Wallace, later the author of *Ben Hur,* and one of the Democratic observers was former Governor Brown of Georgia, the man who controlled the bank that killed the Atlanta *Herald.* Grady avoided the bars where many who had congregated in Tallahassee reveled. He needed no liquor to make him happy. He used his time to meet almost everyone connected with the recount. His cheerful demeanor opened doors for him, and he came to know General Wallace well. He came to know Brown and to respect and like him enormously, a surprising development with auspices.

Predictably, the Canvassing Board of Florida said that Hayes had won the state. The board had three members, two Republicans and a Democrat. The results were announced on a day when the telegraph wires were down, a fact that Grady learned earlier than other newspapermen. He was prepared. As soon as the count was handed out, Grady leapt into a horse-drawn buggy and left at high speed for the nearest town with a functioning office. He and General Wallace arrived almost together, and Grady deferred to the Republican to send brief notices to Hayes and to the Republican hierarchy; then he began filing both to the *Herald* and the *Constitution.* Those newspapers led the nation in reporting that Florida was for Hayes. Other newspapermen arrived in the office and Grady tied up the line, transmitting pages from a spelling book to keep his competitors from using it.

The Florida decision, with those from the other two contested states, gave Hayes the presidency by a count of 185 electoral votes to 184. The election was probably stolen, and for a time, a confrontation seemed possible. Grady stayed with the story to its end, working in Florida and later going to Washington. In the spring of 1878, about eighteen months later, he was still dealing with its ramifications. Hayes was nevertheless secure in the presidency, for much of the Democratic leadership had acquiesced in his election in exchange for an agreement to remove federal troops from the South. The coverage of the disputed election of 1876 did much for Grady's self-confidence, for he had triumphed against the best competition that his field could offer. He knew some of the most prominent newspapermen in America, and he signed up as a correspondent for the Philadelphia *Times* and the Cincinnati *Enquirer,* while continuing to write for the New York *Herald.* This arrangement did not interfere with his job at the *Constitution,* and his financial situation became easier.

He interviewed famous people. Mrs. Thomas "Stonewall" Jackson, former President Jefferson Davis of the Confederate States of America, Generals James Longstreet, Gordon, Toombs, and William Tecumseh Sherman all spoke through Grady's pen. The Chicago *Inter-Ocean,* Louisville *Courier-Journal,* and Detroit *Free Press* took him on as a correspondent, giving him an income from six northern newspapers. He stopped going to the *Constitution* daily, working for it on space rates rather than as a reporter waiting for assignment.

During this period, he used bad judgment more than once about news values. Grady was moved by the plight of a fourteen-year-old white female convict working in a camp alongside male prisoners. Her name was Sallie, and she said that she was homeless, being punished for vagrancy. Grady undertook a crusade in her behalf, helped her get a pardon from the governor, attended a dinner in her honor given by Howell, found her a room in a charity home, and got her a job. The judge who sentenced her said that she was sixteen rather than fourteen, and that she was a prostitute, not a vagrant. Sallie shortly proved the judge right, leaving Grady the butt of jibes.

Like so many things in his career, this embarrassment had good results, for Sallie helped to get Grady back on the speaker's platform. A comical mix-up led him unintentionally to misrepresent the topic of an address that a visiting lecturer would give in Atlanta, so Grady himself agreed to prepare a lecture on the advertised subject, "Just Human." Grady's talk was about Sallie and the need to withhold harsh judgments.[29] He gave it on June 12, 1877, and repeated it in Augusta and in Macon.

His second such venture came a few months later. While at the *Herald,* Grady wrote a piece about an Atlanta well-digger who lived in a patched-up shack. The man's name was Lewis Powell, but Grady called him Mortimer Pitts. To Grady's romantic eye, the Pitts shanty symbolized the longing of every person for a home. He ascribed bliss to it and took it as the subject of his next talk, the "Patchwork Palace." No text for it was written out fully, but notes show that it was an evocation of the hearthside virtues that Grady loved.[30] He repeated the lecture in Augusta, Gainesville, and Athens to great acclaim, which made the embarrassment that followed all the worse. As the praises of the "Patchwork Palace" were sung, Powell, or Pitts, beat up Mrs. Powell, was put out of the house, and taken to the police station.

Despite the imperfect behavior of his real-life subjects, Grady could now take gossamer topics and make them entertaining. On July 17, 1878, he gave a talk at Emory College in Oxford, Georgia, now Emory University, entitled "The Philosophy of Happiness." That appearance was his severest test to date, for Emory students of that day were rude to speakers. They were so even to their own president, the much-respected Atticus G. Haygood. Often they stalked out of the hall, creating a disturbance. One of these students, W. T. Turnbull, later described the day that Grady spoke:

> I shall never forget his appearance, boyish in face and feature, but not disappointing in the least. . . . He wore a business cutaway, and defied the austerity of his surroundings by a single rose dangling in his button hole. Upon being presented to the audience he advanced promptly, but with the utmost composure, and with an impatient gesture simultaneously flung his handkerchief upon the speakers table and launched the current of his utterance, which with the steadiness born of the exhaustless sea from which it flowed, never ceased for one moment during the two hours he held the audience. . . . We were willing to be enslaved and followed him blindly and gladly.[31]

Turnbull's account, written after Grady was famous, was certainly colored by that fact, but by 1877 or 1878, Grady could create an effect as a speaker anytime he wished. It is remarkable, and in a way mystifying, that he did not choose to do so again for eight and a half years.

He was making money from his writings, and perhaps he could not spare the time for speechmaking, even though there were profits there, too. He and Harris were involved in a weekly publication called the *Sunday Gazette,* of which little is known because no file survives. Increasingly, he was fascinated by railroad matters and wrote about them, a natural turn of events since his friend Howell and the *Constitution* were interested in the subject and the prosperity of Atlanta depended in great part upon railroad development. Even so, Grady was not happy. In a document written for him alone, he said that his life lacked system. It was "brilliant but rudderless."[32]

Interest in railroads led Grady indirectly to the assignment that finally was big enough for him, the managing editorship of the Atlanta *Constitution.* In 1879 E. W. Cole, president of the Nashville, Chattanooga, and St. Louis Railroad, visited Atlanta, and Grady covered that story, soon writing news of railroad agreements and combinations that helped the city by extending its network of lines. Both Grady and the *Constitution* believed that more such news was coming. Drawing an advance from the business office, Grady set out on a journey that took him to more than a dozen states and threw him into the company of H. Victor Newcomb, shortly to become president of the Louisville and Nashville Railroad.[33]

Grady and Newcomb were taken with each other, and Newcomb sought vainly to employ Grady as his secretary. They traveled together, and when they reached New York, Grady visited the Stock Exchange and spent time with Newcomb in the investment offices of Cyrus W. Field, the financier who had promoted the Atlantic cable.

Field liked Grady although he scarcely knew him, and when Grady produced a telegram from Howell saying that one-fourth of the *Constitution* could be bought for $20,000, Field lent him the money. The promissory note specified only financial conditions, including repayment within a year at 6 percent interest, but allegations were made that the *Constitution* was giving unusual attention to Stephen J. Field, associate justice of the United States Supreme Court who wished to be president of the United States.[34] Stephen Field was Cyrus Field's brother. Howell was a Field delegate to the Democratic convention of 1880, supporting him until his hopes collapsed. Grady heaped lavish commentary upon the candidate. An agreement to help Stephen Field may have been made, but it cannot be proved. Rumors abounded that Cyrus Field gave or loaned one of Grady's associates $20,000 to fix the Georgia delegation for his brother, but Field denied the allegations, saying that persons who never had 20,000 cents should not bandy around such sums as 20,000 dollars.[35]

W. A. Hemphill brought business ability to the *Constitution;* Howell brought judgment and resolute character, and Grady brought energy and a sense of joy that gave his staff an *esprit de corps* that would have credited any organization in the world. Men felt that it was an honor to work for him.

Grady soon embodied the spirit of the newspaper. He took plea-

sure in a saucy little symbol that the *Constitution* adopted—a minia-
ture homemade cannon that discharged upon occasion. Like the
Constitution, it had its peculiarities, such as those described in 1888
when it was fired at a Chautauqua sponsored by Grady. "The fuse
was no sooner touched off, than the little gun turned a back somer-
sault, belching its fiery salute in mid-air and lighting on its wheels
with a tranquility that would be difficult to describe." The cannon
could be heard in seven counties, the newspaper claimed. The *Constitution* intended to be heard in the 137 counties of Georgia and beyond, an effective advocate for the things it espoused. It gloried in
its victories. As the decade progressed, the *Constitution* said that it
spread a gospel of "cheerfulness, liberality, frankness and hope."[36]

The newspaper, like Grady, worked hard at hospitality. The public was urged to come to the press room to watch the printing, and
the staff cheerfully received out-of-town reporters, editors, businessmen, and just about anybody else. The newspaper made a good
showing at being a happy family. When city editor J. K. Ohl married
the society editor on a happy Monday evening, and three other
weddings of employees followed within a week, the newspaper
claimed credit, attributing the joyous events to an editorial written
by Clark Howell entitled "Woman's Love."[37]

In 1885 the newspaper hired the facilities of the Kimball House
and gave a banquet for 400 of its "family," from proprietors to elevator boys, regretting that it could find no place big enough to entertain the 3,000 persons who circulated the paper. Even so, at
Grady's instigation, the local carriers were honored, the boys who
jammed the crowded basement of the *Constitution* to pick up their
papers. They resembled nothing so much as a cargo of monkeys, it
was said, fighting "just as fiercely for precedence in that long room
as older men fight in politics or business." Their lives were hard.
"The weaker boys are driven to the wall, and the stronger come to
the front." Grady's dinner for them was at first intended as a *Constitution* affair alone, but word got out and various persons wished to
contribute. They did, and the feast was magnificent, the tables presided over by prominent women from Atlanta society.[38]

But even a newspaper preaching optimism and good humor had

enemies. The *Constitution* intentionally chose a few, preferring distant foes without local friends, such as Republican politicians who sought to participate uninvited in southern affairs, or trusts headquartered in far-removed locales. The *Constitution* admitted having one local enemy. It hated the Macon *Telegraph*, a dislike heartily reciprocated. Language approaching the violent poured upon the Macon competitor even as the *Constitution* blandly and unconvincingly insisted that it loved the people of Macon.

Other than the continuing attack upon the *Telegraph*, the *Constitution* used scathing words selectively. It was careful about what it said, for Atlanta was regarded by many as a bad neighbor and the *Constitution* was seen as the spokesman for the city. Rather than denouncing rivals outright, the newspaper usually used other techniques. In 1885, for example, Atlanta and the *Constitution* had just had a harsh exchange with Augusta and the Augusta *Chronicle*, when the editor of the *Chronicle*, Patrick Walsh, appeared in Atlanta on one of his frequent visits. The *Constitution* profusely welcomed Walsh to the city without acknowledging that any problem existed. He would never be so welcome as the day when he arrived to occupy the governor's mansion, a prospect sure to give Grady, Howell, and Hemphill apoplexy had it ever had the slightest chance of occurring.[39] Walsh, for his part, was never silly enough to believe that anyone at the corner of Forsyth and Alabama streets in Atlanta wished to see him governor.

The preposterous salute to Walsh was pure raillery, a device used regularly to discountenance rivals short of making ill-tempered attacks. The Mobile, Alabama, *Register* once criticized the *Constitution* for its endless promotion of Atlanta, promotion seen in Mobile as unjustified puffery. The *Constitution* urged the *Register* to drop its paste-pot and to get to puffing on behalf of its own city. All good wishes were extended to Mobile, which, it was hoped, would grow, thrive, and export ice to New Orleans.[40]

The *Constitution* believed that Savannah was a sleepy, indolent town, a throw-back to another age, and the Atlanta newspaper regarded the people of Savannah as nonworkers who rejoiced mostly in their ancestors. When John Schwartz, a Bavarian immigrant who had arrived in Savannah as a pastry cook, was elected mayor, the management of the *Constitution* almost exploded with amusement. According to them, Schwartz had gone around town during the campaign peddling bread and clanging his cart bell as usual. His election, they said, had set off a flutter in a metropolis made up almost entirely of first families, but Schwartz would make a splendid mayor because he knew the needs of the poor at firsthand. From time to time, spokesmen for Savannah suggested that Atlanta was usually ahead of the truth.[41]

Concerning truly serious matters, the raillery could be awesome. Grady and the *Constitution* had a disagreement in 1886 and 1887 with Francis W. Dawson, editor of the Charleston *News and Courier,* that at bottom had to do with who the preeminent New South leader was. By then, Grady believed that he was, and in late 1886, Grady had a triumph that suggested that indeed he was. Dawson was silent as acclaim poured in upon Grady from many directions. Dawson, who was jealous, was supposed to have asked, "Who is Grady, anyhow?"

The *Constitution* suddenly discovered that Dawson, a proper man of English birth and upbringing, was better addressed as Francisco rather than Francis. It allegedly found that he wore socks costing an outrageous $1.75 a pair, when thirty to forty cents was the standard price. Dawson was proclaimed a man of incredible good looks, and the *Constitution* wished to know through the Associated Press whenever the handsome editor changed his high-priced socks. Pressed to say whether the man was really as beautiful as reputed, the *Constitution* concluded that he was. He could not quite be called voluptuous, for that carried a suggestion of weakness, but certainly he was sumptuous. "His enemies have charged that he is knock-kneed. We admit there is something more of bunchiness about the inside of his lower thighs than the strict line of grace permits, but like the lisp of a pretty woman, it is a defect that provokes praise rather than censure." Atlanta never would inquire, "Who is Dawson, anyhow?" It knew him well as the "Star-Eyed Beauty of the Coastal Plain." Dawson, said the *Constitution,* was one of the most beautiful persons in existence, regardless of sex.[42]

The treatment of the South Carolinian illustrates another technique of the *Constitution*. When Dawson was murdered in 1889, the Atlanta newspaper praised him extravagantly, forgetting earlier disagreements. Conciliation, or reconciliation, was a striking element of the public face of the *Constitution*. Dawson, no longer acclaimed as beautiful except in spirit, was an undisputed leader. "To his infinite and lasting honor it can be said that this leadership has never been abused, its opportunities never wasted, its power never prostituted, its suggestions never misdirected." A month before his death, Dawson had written the editors of the *Constitution* a warm letter expressing appreciation for a small courtesy, and the *Constitution* had replied in a sentiment that it hoped abided with him to his much-lamented death.[43]

The *Constitution* regularly sought to conciliate local political opponents once it defeated them. After drubbing a dangerous rival in 1883, the newspaper lavished generous praise upon him. He was a gallant gentleman, a blossoming statesman, and it was vaguely suggested, although without much conviction, that the editors wished to be friendly. A few of the politician's associates had been intemperate and had caused any bad feeling that existed. The newspaper predicted that Georgia would in time crown the man with honors, something that occurred, but not so long as Henry Grady could prevent it.[44]

To achieve its ends, the *Constitution* spoke with one voice on issues of the day. With one exception, there was no dissent within the leadership of the newspaper itself. That exception, however, involved the most embroiling local issue to afflict Atlanta during the 1880s, and enemies far and near watched the furious turmoil with amusement and joy.

The issue was prohibition. In 1885 a local option law passed in Georgia, and any county could vote on whether liquor could be sold if one-tenth of the voters petitioned for an election. Fulton County, in which Atlanta lay, was the first to petition. Amid vast excitement, an election was held on November 25, 1885, and the county went dry by 228 votes. Liquor was supposed to go out for a two-year trial period, but in fact it was not that long. Saloon keepers had seven months to close. The county went dry on July 1, 1886. On the day before liquor was outlawed, society women converged on the spirits shops with the dainty suggestion that a little brandy would season many a dish. Men came into town with empty jugs to be filled, then put them on a horse-drawn street car. For a nickel, the conductor dropped the jug off at the home of the patron. All through the day reports came that liquor dealers were abusing the circumstances to sell their worst stock, the "meanest, vilest truck that was ever stilled."[45] The *Constitution* had covered the election and subsequent events thoroughly, but Grady hung back from committing himself.

The matter was sure to come up again and it did so in a second election, held on November 26, 1887, at the end of the trial period. Except for his Richmond adventure, Grady was not a drinker, although he served alcohol in his home for important visitors. Howell was a convinced wet. At length and after listening to delegations from both camps that beseiged his office, Grady and Hemphill came down as drys, although there were those who believed that Hemphill did not really care. Samuel M. Inman, a wealthy Atlanta cotton merchant who owned a block of nonvoting stock in the *Constitution,* also was dry. In the campaign that followed, Howell led the wets. Grady shared the leadership of the drys with Judge George Hillyer, who had just finished a term as mayor of Atlanta and was a noted layman in the Baptist church. With the partners of the *Constitution* divided, the newspaper kept editorial silence on the question but gave it much attention. Anyone could get an opinion published by paying for it, and such opinions were labeled "Communicated," a term generally understood in that day.

Cynics believed that the leadership of the newspaper positioned its executives on both sides of the issue while the *Constitution* kept silent and made money from the advertising. The Macon *Telegraph* saw Hemphill's role that way. "Grady is dry and Howell is wet, but all's fish that comes to Hemphill's net."[46]

Both Grady and Howell gave everything they had to the campaign, coming into oratorical competition on the evening of November 17, 1887, but not face to face. Grady addressed an enormous throng in a cotton warehouse, and Howell enthralled another audience in DeGive's Opera House, wondering why prohibitionists needed a law to stay sober. He claimed that business was better when liquor was legal and said that it should return. A portion of Grady's peroration became a Bible for prohibitionists for several decades. He urged that Atlanta continue to shut liquor out. "Don't trust it. . . . Tonight it enters an humble home to strike the roses from a woman's cheek, and tomorrow it challenges this republic in the halls of congress. Today it strikes a crust from the lips of a starving child, and tomorrow levies tribute from the government itself. There is no cottage in this city humble enough to escape it—no palace strong enough to shut it out. . . . It is flexible to cajole, but merciless in victory. . . . It can profit no man by its return."[47]

The campaign was a vicious one with supporters on each side attacking the leadership of the other. Judge Hillyer was quoted as saying that to the best of his recollection, he had drunk no liquor as a beverage since prohibition started. A wet wondered why he said "to the best of my recollection." "Afraid of the next witness, say? 'As a beverage.' Good! How many times did you take it 'as a medicine?' "[48] Of the leaders, only Grady and Howell escaped disparagement. No future lay in criticizing men who owned a printing press.

Voters turned out massively on election day, terribly disappointing the drys. The wets carried the county by 1,122 votes out of 9,244 cast.[49] Analyzing the outcome, Raymond B. Nixon explains why Grady, who almost never lost politically, was counted out on this one. For the first time in his life, he was on the opposite side from the big money.[50]

If the outcome was no surprise, neither was the reaction of the *Constitution,* which launched a campaign of conciliation. No issue in 1887 caused deeper divisions than alcohol, for huge numbers of persons equated drinking with religious damnation, while those who thought otherwise believed their liberty was invaded when men told them what they could not do. Such an issue made men mad. It also caused factionalism which, if not controlled, could wreck grand political structures and divert a city from its destiny. The partners at the *Constitution* feared exactly that. Drys talked of protesting the election and of running men for office sworn to reverse the hated results. It was then that the policy of reconciliation had its severest local test, and no better person could soothe the distressed than that crusading dry, Grady. "Is the hatchet too hot to be buried?" asked the newspaper. "We trust not."[51]

Grady called the leaders of the drys to the *Constitution,* where he said that he knew there had been voting irregularities, but that he opposed both protesting the election and running prohibitionist candidates in the forthcoming city election. Then, in a note delightful to the militants, he suggested wrapping the liquor regulations around the necks of the wets and making them enforce all of their provisions, some of which were troublesomely detailed. Inman agreed with what Grady had said.[52]

Numerous clergymen swung into line and, without changing their views about alcohol, preached unity for Atlanta. The purpose of the partners was to confine all disagreements over alcohol to special elections, and at regular times to pick fusion slates of candidates to run the city. On such slates, each faction would have equal representation; but in a disturbing move, the wets at the last moment offered a slate that swept into office on December 7, 1887. So displeased was the *Constitution* that it barely acknowledged their victory.[53]

These unwelcomed results meant a year of tension before the next municipal election, scheduled the following year on December 5. Accord was badly tattered. Grady appeared before a crowd of distraught prohibitionists urging that a fusion ticket be supported and that differences be put aside for the welfare of Atlanta. If ever the issue of alcohol came up again in a special election, he pledged himself to the drys; but for now, an "Atlanta" slate must be elected. Monumental exertions carried the fusion ticket in with John T. Glenn as mayor. The win was comfortable but there was a vast dissenting vote. In the mayor's race, Walter Brown polled almost 2,000 votes of some 4,650 cast. Quickly, the mantle of conciliation was thrown around Brown. His vote was greatly to his credit and his campaign was gallant, said the *Constitution.* "[A]ny man who, by his own influence, can poll two thousand votes in so one-sided a campaign, certainly owes deep allegiance to the city in which his constituents live."[54]

This determination to overlook differences and to build upon common interests took surprising turns. In 1880 or 1881 Alexander K. McClure of the Philadelphia *Times* visited Grady's home and was astonished to see who the dinner guests were. Governor Colquitt was guest of honor, which was not surprising; but also at the table were former Governor Bullock and Hannibal I. Kimball. Both Bullock and Kimball had in earlier times been denounced as obnoxious by the *Constitution* and by Grady, and both were Republicans, a genus that never ceased to be odious. Yet there they were, in Grady's house, discussing politics without reserve, agreeing on state policy with Colquitt and Grady and other Democrats. Although no partner at the *Constitution* could say a kind word for the politics of these gentlemen, Bullock and Kimball merited an ever-ready personal acceptance, for they were building up Atlanta.[55]

Even so, no amount of conciliation, cheerfulness, optimism, joyousness, or good management by themselves could make the *Constitution* a successful newspaper. Readers subscribed to it and advertisers put it into their budgets because it printed the news, and news was the business of Grady. Harris once said that Grady borrowed from no one in his techniques.[56] He may have been correct, but Grady's experiences with the New York *Herald* cannot be discounted. Although Grady never met James Gordon Bennett, Sr., he may have learned indirectly from that journalistic pioneer that successful newspapers spend money to get news; not only do they spend it, but expenditures are minutely planned and watched for results.

Grady's genius went into directing the news staff, and anything he had left over went into an occasional editorial that underlined or backed up what his people had done. Almost everyone who spoke of Grady during this period commented upon his enormous grasp of detail. Alexander McClure was startled by it.[57]

Thomas W. Reed, a seventeen-year-old graduate of the University of Georgia, employed in 1888 as the newest member of Grady's writing team, appeared for duty while the managing editor was out of town. Reed was assigned to do a story on Atlanta clergymen spending their vacations in Europe. He had never been to Europe, but he let his imagination fly and produced a two-column story with which he was pleased. He then did a second assignment on how local clergymen spent their vacations in Atlanta. Grady returned to the office, summoned Reed, went line by line over the stories with a blue pencil, then handed the four printed columns back to him. About four inches of copy were left. What remained was so stripped that it should have gone to jail for public indecency, Reed said. Grady patted him on the shoulder and sent him back to his duties wiser and not in the least depressed. "He possessed real genius in organizing his forces for active and effective work," Reed said.[58]

On the evening of August 31, 1886, Grady was working in the living room of his house on Peachtree Street when the chandeliers began to swing, the house began to shake, and a nearby chimney crashed through a roof. Grady hurried on foot to the *Constitution* and discovered through telegraph reports that the Eastern Seaboard was hit by an earthquake. The damage in Atlanta was slight, although the fright was considerable. One telegraph office on the Atlantic coast, Charleston, South Carolina, was silent. Grady was sure that the city was hard hit, a suspicion confirmed a few hours later when telegraph service resumed. Accompanied by Howell and a small group, Grady took a train to Augusta which was about halfway to Charleston. There he found a terrified populace and some damage. He also discovered that his path to Charleston was blocked, for the earthquake had ruptured a dam and washed out the rail line.

Grady telegraphed the superintendent of the South Carolina railroad and called for an engine to meet him on the Charleston side of the washout. Then he chartered a livery carriage which took him to the lake caused by the break. He got a boat over to the engine. As the train backed its way to Charleston, devastation lay on both sides of the track. In Charleston, Grady worked like a man possessed, interviewing survivors, talking to those conducting relief operations, and even tracking down Dawson, not yet acclaimed as the Star-Eyed

Beauty of the Coastal Plain. Grady filed thousands of words to the *Constitution*, to the New York *World*—by then under the direction of Joseph Pulitzer, who knew a good story when he saw one—and to other northern newspapers. Grady called for a relief effort to help Charleston. His work was printed in the North under his full name and was acclaimed as brilliant. The earthquake moved Grady close to national prominence.[59]

Grady managed such personal feats magnificently, but his supervisory accomplishments were equally stunning, and ultimately more important. Early in his managing editorship, he wanted next-day election results from the Seventh Congressional District of Georgia, a mountainous area with tortuous roads. In the past, two weeks passed before an accurate count from that district was published. There was broad interest in the election, as an Independent candidate threatened the Democratic establishment. Grady set up a courier system with relays of horses, and neither money nor horses were spared getting the results to the telegraph offices. Grady sent his reporters and editorial associates to key spots to supervise and to help as needed. He personally selected one courier, who rode forty miles over the mountains along bad roads and through rushing creeks. That man, like the others, reached the telegraph station at the appointed time. The next morning, the *Constitution* had complete results.[60]

Grady expanded this kind of service to all of Georgia by 1888. In the October election of that year, there were 1,508 voting precincts in 137 counties, more than 1,000 of them not on railroads. About 20 counties had no railroads at all, and an even larger number had county seats with no telegraph service. Almost everywhere, rural precincts were six to fifteen miles from the county seat.

Grady hired almost a thousand horses and arranged for telegraph operators to stay on duty until the "specials" galloped up. There was one failure. A correspondent did not cover his full assignment, possibly because a letter of instruction miscarried. In October 1888 the *Constitution* presented the best next-day coverage ever seen in Georgia. Every state senator was named and every state representative was identified except one, the result of the oversight.

Long before then, the *Constitution* turned election nights into parties for anyone who came to downtown Atlanta. The newspaper projected the latest figures by stereoptican camera upon a small screen inside its building, where visitors had seats, and upon a huge screen outside where thousands stood.[61]

The triumphs of the news staff and the hard-working manager became legendary, but nothing more distinguished Grady than his success with the weekly edition of the *Constitution*. In 1880 when he assumed his office, about 7,000 copies a week were published. The weekly was not thought to have a future. Grady's partners believed that if it ever got 10,000 subscribers, the market would be saturated. By the end of the decade, however, circulation was almost 200,000, and it was perhaps the largest weekly in the nation.

Most successful weeklies in the country depended upon some specialty. The Detroit *Free Press* had the sketches of M. Quad, and the Toledo *Blade* featured the letters of Petroleum V. Nasby. Grady would not allow his weekly to emphasize a specialty, although it had the letters of Bill Arp, Sarge Wier, and Betsey Hamilton, all humorists. He also got M. Quad from the *Free Press*. He ran sermons of famous preachers, such as T. DeWitt Talmage and Sam Jones; farm advice from Dr. W. L. Jones of the University of Georgia, and a panoply of other features. He paid about $10,000 a year to special writers and to artists to draw sketches and illustrations. After each daily paper was printed, the best type was saved and much of it found its way into the next weekly. Some of these issues are collector's items, such as the one with the account of the death and burial of Toombs, which appeared on December 21, 1885.

Grady watched the circulation with enormous care and whenever the new subscriber list slowed down, he shut himself up with the appropriate subordinates, made changes, and within about two weeks, subscriptions started coming in again. He often rejected the suggestions of colleagues who thought they had a perfect item for the paper. Grady once said that if the weekly ever got 2,000 new subscribers in a day, he was ready to die. Ironically, on the train that bore him home from Boston, he was handed a message from Robert

A. Hemphill reporting that the previous day, 2,000 new subscriptions came in.[62]

The weekly claimed patrons in every state. By 1886 advertisements for it ran in 1,492 newspapers. The message was a simple one: "Send for a sample copy of the Atlanta *Constitution,* the great southern weekly," plus details on how to do so. Agents gave out circulars, cards, and pictures, and the newspaper offered premiums. On the sensible thesis that persons who read the weekly would read other things, Grady offered books by Scott, Dickens, DeFoe, Cooper, Verne, Bunyan, and Bulwer for sixty cents a volume plus postage.

The weekly usually had twelve pages and sold for $1 a year for most of the decade, finally going to $1.25. Most of the revenue came from advertising. Of seventy columns of space, from twelve to twenty went to advertising. By 1888 Robert Hemphill needed two assistants to go through the mail with him each morning; they took money orders, postal notes, checks, and cash from envelopes and tossed all into a basket in the center of the sorting table. The growth was phenomenal. From 7,000 subscribers in 1880, a colorable claim was laid to 37,000 by August 1885; 70,000 by April 1886; 81,000 by November 1886; 118,000 by August 1887; almost 200,000 by December 1889.[63]

Grady's ability to organize people and resources appeared universal and included almost anything that helped Atlanta. Scarcely a civic enterprise occurred in which he was not involved, usually as instigator. Three international expositions bore the stamp of Grady's mind and work and attested to the power of the *Constitution* to bring events to fruition. The Young Men's Christian Association got a new building because of Grady and the newspaper. The Young Men's Library, in deplorable condition early in the decade, was reorganized and financed along workable lines. Funds were raised for a Confederate Veterans Home; lectures and cultural events were arranged; a Chautauqua was created and spectacles of a grand nature were organized to memorialize great events and to draw visitors to the city.

Baseball, played by amateurs before 1884, was organized on a professional basis. Grady became president of the Southern Baseball League, made up of teams from cities with more than 25,000 people. He was often at the games, dictating accounts of the play to his secretary. He organized walking contests, one of the crazes of the era, with reporters from the *Constitution* as participants in intercity meets.

The feats of the *Constitution* dealt setbacks to competing newspapers. Atlanta had always been a graveyard for newspapers, and during the 1880s the *Constitution* pretty much occupied the morning field by itself. In 1883 the Atlanta *Evening Star* made a brief appearance before going the way of most underfinanced ventures, and the Atlanta *Evening Capitol* met the same fate. Only the Atlanta *Evening Journal*, later the Atlanta *Journal*, offered anything approaching competition in the daily field, and it was an afternoon newspaper. The *Journal*, founded in 1883, started without an established telegraphic service and throughout the decade it ran incomplete reports from places outside Atlanta. Although it boasted of correspondents in some Georgia cities, the *Journal* was a local newspaper, concentrating upon local coverage. It was no match for the well-financed engine supervised by Grady. Its daily paper usually ran to four pages, with larger editions on weekends. In 1887 Hoke Smith, an energetic Atlanta lawyer, got controlling interest in the *Journal*. Although the newspaper later became a rival of the *Constitution*, that development awaited another decade.[64] The principal competitors of the *Constitution* in the 1880s were the Augusta *Chronicle* and the Macon *Telegraph*, and, to a lesser degree, the Columbus *Enquirer-Sun*, the Savannah *Morning News*, plus vigorous daily and weekly newspapers in smaller localities in Georgia.

Grady, Howell, and Hemphill in the 1880s were in a position to exercise vast influence, and they did so to the discomfort of many who otherwise admired their purely journalistic performance, or were jealous of it. Their instruments were the *Constitution* itself and the loosely knit political aggregation called the Atlanta Ring.

3
Politics and the Atlanta Ring:
1880–1886

The unpopularity of Atlanta in the rest of Georgia was due in part to jealousy but also to what some saw as a disagreement over values. In its early decades, the city had a reputation for bawdiness, which spread as farmers drove wagonloads of produce to market and remained long enough to experience the sinful delights of the new town. Everyone knew that Atlantans had no regard for proper ancestry. In 1870 more than one-third of the largest property owners came from outside the South. The road to status lay through an open door through which any white man of capability could pass if lucky, shrewd, and ambitious.[1] Henry Grady said that if a man had ability, Atlantans did not care if he were hatched in a stump.[2] Atlantans hurried. They pushed and shoved. To the successful among them, business was king.

Some Georgians remembered that the hated Republicans favored Atlanta when they controlled the state. The capital had been satisfactorily located in Milledgeville since 1807, but when Republicans took charge, they called a constitutional convention, wrote a new constitution, and as a result of all this, the capital moved to Atlanta. Major General John Pope, commander of the Third Military District and in fact head of the federal army of occupation, actually entered the hall where the new constitution was being written. An unsympathetic historian computes that of one hundred sixty-nine delegates who wrote the document, only twelve were southern white men of conservative views. The remainder were Negroes, northern carpetbaggers, and southern scalawags.[3]

The constitution of 1868 was a despised document to many Georgians, mainly because of its sponsorship. The dislike, however, was not universal. Some people of New South views saw merit in it because it expanded the power of the state government to help businesses and railroads. In a word, it was probusiness. Much of the leadership of Atlanta held that view, as did a representative New South man such as Isaac W. Avery, former editor of the Atlanta *Constitution*, staunch Democrat, and executive secretary to three governors.[4]

Help given to railroads angered many Georgians, however. By the 1870s, railroads owned one-fifth of the property in Georgia, but before 1874, only their income was taxed, not their property. Public outrage caused the General Assembly to correct the matter, but resentment against railroads ran high as the state bonding provisions under which some of them built lines were abused. Rates of the roads also appeared to be unfair. Some manufacturing and mining companies also got much-resented benefits.

In 1873 a state representative from Baldwin County (Milledgeville) suggested that Georgia needed a new constitution. His bill to call a convention died a quick death, but thereafter, the subject did not die. Some persons wished to repudiate the railroad bonds the state issued under the constitution of 1868. Many people thought the state government was wasteful. Salaries of officials were perceived as excessive. One governor spent $98,300 in three years advertising his proclamations in newspapers. The General Assembly of 1869 and 1870 sat for 328 days and cost almost a million dollars. More Georgians were moving to town, but taxes remained in the countryside. The location of the capital in Atlanta was always an emotionally wrought issue. Finally and after much discussion, Georgians voted to call a constitutional convention.[5]

The Atlanta *Constitution*, an organ of probusiness and New South views, was the only daily newspaper in Georgia to oppose it. Ellen Barrier Garrison examined the strategy of the newspaper as it sought to forestall the convention and called it "insidious." "[T]he paper regularly allocated front-page space to letters, speeches, and editorials by obscure convention supporters endorsing a convention as the way to eliminate the homestead, dismantle the public school system, establish literacy and/or property qualifications for voting, and revive the whipping post and debtors' prison." No convention supporter of standing was for any of these ideas.[6]

The Augusta *Chronicle and Constitutionalist* maliciously divided the opponents into three camps, "Capital, Office, and Bonds." Atlanta was in all three. It had the capital and wanted to keep it. It was home to state employees who valued their jobs. It was also home to people who owned some of the railroad bonds authorized by the old constitution.[7]

The convention met in Atlanta on July 11, 1877. No one knew what it would do, but it would likely do something the Atlanta *Constitution* would not like. It would not be probusiness. One hundred delegates out of 194 called themselves either planters or farmers. The figures should not be taken at face value, however, for many men called themselves planters or farmers who were also in business or professions. The numbers, nevertheless, were significant to the outcome.[8]

The convention voted at once to dispense with the constitution of 1868 as a model and proceeded to demonstrate a high and arrogant sense of itself. Grady said with tongue in cheek that the delegates were the most independent collection of men in the universe. The first day, they declared themselves independent of the United States government. The second, they voted themselves independent of the governor by refusing to invite him to speak. The third day, they declared independence from God Almighty by refusing to pay a chaplain.[9]

Robert Toombs was the dominant member of the convention. A hater of what he saw as railroad abuses and suspicious of all corporations, he represented the interests of the planter class. He turned his oratorical skills, honed to an art in the practice of law, in the United States Senate, and in the Confederate government, upon the business interests. Under his persuasion and that of like-minded delegates, the state government was reduced to strict economy, and the hated railroad bonds were repudiated.[10]

The term of the governor was cut from four years to two, with the right to succeed himself. Members of the Assembly got two-year terms. Senators formerly had served four. The Assembly was shorn of power to elect several important state officials, that power passing to the people. A minor adjustment was made in the apportionment of the House of Representatives but urban citizens remained underrepresented.

Financial help to railroads and to corporations became illegal. The General Assembly got authority to regulate freight and passenger rates, a stunning development. Rebates were forbidden, and buying up stock in other railroads or corporations which would lessen competition was unlawful. Any railroad or corporation not liking the strictures violated the law if it lobbied to change them.[11]

For persons to whom business was supreme, these provisions were bad tidings; but for advocates of Atlanta, there was a more dangerous development. The convention went home without settling two issues, one of them the permanent location of the capital. Voters would decide in a referendum whether to leave it in Atlanta or move it back to Milledgeville.[12] The new constitution would be voted on in the same referendum.

The decision to elect where the capital would be was a brilliant ploy by the convention managers. Opponents of the new constitution in Atlanta were held hostage, for if they attacked the document, they stood to irritate its supporters, who might then vote to send the capital back to Milledgeville. There is no doubt about the views of Atlantans concerning the convention itself. When the vote was taken on whether to call it, only 8 percent of Fulton Countians (Atlanta) voted for it. The count was 94 for and 1,176 against.[13]

Scholars agree that the constitution of 1877 is out of line with the probusiness ideals of the New South. Judson C. Ward says that the document "fastened upon the state a government so weak that it could no longer help business directly." Ellen Barrier Garrison says that by striking a set of alliances within the convention, rural interests shaped the document. Charles E. Wynes is convinced that the convention was effectively in the hands of agricultural interests, and that the result increased the power of rural counties at the expense of more heavily populated ones. Lewis Nicholas Wynne believes that the results were more spectacular. He computes that changes in the reapportionment of the House of Representatives assured that the planter class, which had enjoyed great power before the Civil War, now had 86 House votes out of 175 upon which it could rely absolutely. It was within two votes of a majority, and two votes could be produced on almost any issue. The constitution of 1877 forbade creation of new counties, so the system could not be disarranged.[14] Planters, however, had no wish to conduct a running battle with the urban areas of Georgia and the two groups coexisted happily enough, their differences seldom coming into sharp focus.

With the capital to lose if matters went awry, the Atlanta *Constitution* endorsed the constitution of 1877. Saying that "nearly every intelligent voter with a turn for criticism" could discover something to object to, the newspaper nevertheless found it "worthier of commendation than of condemnation." At the same time, the *Constitution* launched a campaign on behalf of Atlanta as the capital, keeping it as good humored as possible.

The opposition from the Milledgeville *Union and Recorder*, the Macon *Telegraph*, the Augusta *Chronicle*, and a host of other leaders and newspapers was vigorous. They represented economic interests in central Georgia that had been damaged when the capital, with its payroll, moved to Atlanta. Departing central Georgia with the payroll were state deposits in banks, which eased credit wherever placed. Merchants in Augusta, and doubtless in Macon as well, were pinched economically. When Georgia legislators attended sessions, they placed large orders of goods for themselves and for their friends with businessmen in the capital area. As long as the Assembly sat in Milledgeville, Macon and Augusta got a part of that trade, being connected by rail with Milledgeville. Now, the money went to Atlanta.[15]

Another consideration was important in Macon and in much of central Georgia. The capital was the locus of political power in the state, and Macon had for many years wished to be the capital. It was satisfied as long as the seat of government was in Milledgeville, and in 1877 supported its relocation there. However, there was a difference between being satisfied and being pleased. Macon wanted it for itself. The city fathers early reserved four square blocks of prime downtown real estate as Tattnall Square Park, an area to which the capital and the governor's mansion would be relocated once matters could be arranged. The issue was alive after 1877 although, in effect, it was moot for a time. Nevertheless, Macon attempted to secure capital removal as late as 1925.

Avery watched the capital referendum of 1877 with amusement, and he said that the campaign bordered on the outrageous. Out-of-control Atlanta advocates said that Milledgeville was stagnant and fit for fossils. Milledgeville supporters said Atlanta was responsible for every horror of Reconstruction. Avery, an Atlantan, said that his city "fought the struggle with characteristic liberality and enterprise," having her committees flood Georgia with documents. Evan P. Howell managed the Atlanta campaign, helped by two men who were principally advisers. "[H]e left nothing undone," said a contemporary.[16]

The *Constitution* sensed that the efforts were going well, for even before the votes were cast, it threw a mantle of conciliation around Milledgeville by congratulating its newspaper. "That paper, although laboring under the disadvantage of being only a weekly, has really led the Milledgeville campaign. Its tactics, if not always judicious, have been vigorous and effective." Had they been more effective, the *Constitution* might have thought otherwise. However, the voters went to the polls on December 5, 1877, approved the constitution by a count of 110,442 to 40,947, and confirmed Atlanta as the capital 99,147 to 55,201.[17]

The issue left a deposit of bad will even as the state put up a handsome new capitol on the old city hall property in Atlanta. The government of Georgia itself was without power to do many of the things desired by New South leaders; and this fact meant that the most vigorous of them would try to use personal and political influence to fill the void. That is what Grady, the Atlanta *Constitution,* and their allies tried to do for Atlanta in the 1880s.

During the 1870s, Atlanta Democrats had influence within the party, and persons who objected often referred to the political organization called the Atlanta Ring, which they said was the instrument of power for the city. The Ring in fact controlled the Atlanta city government for a time and used such influence as it could in the legislature, the Democratic party, and the state. Ring leaders cultivated poorer white voters and tried to keep blacks from the polls. Policemen, chosen by the council, were an essential source of patronage. In 1872 a Ring representative in the legislature sought to give all Atlanta police officers and marshals then holding office life tenure. The leader of the organization, Samuel B. Spencer, was a sometime mayor of the city. Some Atlanta businessmen opposed the Ring and, through means open to criticism, got a new city charter, which diminished the power of the organization. The Ring was nearly impotent after 1877 when Spencer departed Atlanta.[18] Its name survived, however, and politicians in the state continued to denounce it, apparently unaware that it was all but defunct.

Grady, Howell, the *Constitution,* and an unbelievable set of circumstances gave birth to a new Ring after May 1880. None of the structure carried over from the old to the new. Only the name remained, supplied by enemies. Grady would have preferred to call it nothing, and he and the *Constitution* sometimes denied it existed.[19] After 1880, however, the new Atlanta Ring is easily defined, usually by what it did, and more particularly, by what Grady did.

Neither the Ring nor Democrats as a whole were much concerned with great matters of principle. During the 1880s, Georgia Democrats saw alike on broad issues. Planters, industrialists, and businessmen agreed that government should operate in an economical and minimal way, although some came to that conclusion with difficulty. They agreed that the supremacy of the white race and the inferiority of the black race were settled facts, and that nothing should disturb the social quiet. They believed that Republicans were obnoxious as a party, but some Democrats, especially in Atlanta, accepted individual Republicans as friends and business associates. Because planters and industrialists required differing things from the labor market, a potential source of disagreement existed there but, in fact, never was an important issue during the 1880s. Only on the tariff, a national issue, was there a major difference on principle.

If there was an agreement on major matters, why was there an Atlanta Ring? Why was there also a group dedicated to the advancement of Macon, and why did Augusta, Savannah, Columbus, and even Athens, Dalton, Albany, and little Milledgeville have such tenacious advocates?

The answer is that each community was out for itself. Atlanta was seen as abusing the state in its quest for dominance, although the *Constitution* put it more delicately. "[T]his city has a sort of habit of coming along before it gets too dark to travel." Milledgeville, fretting over the capital, feared travel by night less than robbery by day. It alleged that Atlanta gloried only in itself while feeding on the rest of the state, valuing only a "blind, unscrupulous adherence to the material interests of the city." In the little town of Eastman in Dodge County, the Atlanta Ring was seen as wishing to control state politics absolutely; and the Macon *Telegraph* said that the people of its city and the rest of Georgia refused "to be dominated and disgraced by the Atlanta ring." With such sentiments commonly held, the *Constitution* professed love for everybody but occasionally ran editorials titled "Atlanta and Her Enemies."[20]

Between 1880 and 1886, the period of greatest cohesion within the newly constituted Ring, there were five principal members, of whom three held political office. They were Joseph E. Brown, Alfred H. Colquitt, and John B. Gordon. The two who held no office were as important as the three who did. They were Evan P. Howell and Grady.

The new Ring had no officers, and nothing except circumstance and ability selected Grady to be its most important leader; yet he was indispensable to it. Enemies attributed more power to the Ring than it had, and more than it ever sought. "A button, when pushed in Atlanta moved another smaller wheel in nearly every court house in

Georgia," said one.[21] That characterization made the operation sound lockstep, something it never was. Grady was sometimes rebuffed when he tried to use Ring influence. In 1884 a political leader in Meriwether County reproved him, as Grady reported to a fellow member of the Ring: "He says he has been working for the 'Atlanta ring' all his life and has never had anything for it but abuse."[22]

The men running the state, mainly allies of the Ring after 1880, were sometimes accused of corruption, and there was some. Graft was rampant nationally as well as in Georgia. Dishonest or ambiguous activities were charged to two Ring members, Brown and Gordon, but voters were never disturbed enough to defeat them at the polls or to eject either from office. Corruption was alleged and proved during the governorship of Colquitt, but he was not implicated.

Grady and Howell were spared such charges. Grady never held political office of any sort. Howell from time to time occupied posts in the Democratic party, but he never was in public office higher than president *pro tempore* of the state senate and, later, mayor of Atlanta.

Colquitt was originally from Walton County, had lived in Columbus and Macon, and after his wife acquired a plantation in Baker County in south Georgia in 1848, he moved there, practicing law and politics. The plantation was of great use to him in politics. He lived in the satellite community of Edgewood just outside Atlanta and was identified with the New South after Reconstruction ended, but his ancient ties to the planter class led planters to claim him as their own. He had been a general in the Confederate army, also an advantage. In the period of Grady's earliest interest in him, he was a candidate for governor.

Brown was a native of South Carolina but early became a Georgia mountaineer. He told of plowing with a yoke of oxen as a boy, but he never was the kind of farmer planters liked. By 1855 he was judge of the Blue Ridge circuit in north Georgia, but soon he swept down from the mountains to serve four two-year terms as governor when Milledgeville was the capital. During Reconstruction he became a Republican but was forgiven by many Georgians when he reentered the Democratic party. He established his home in Atlanta and was president of the state-owned Western and Atlantic Railroad, of which he was a lessee.[23] His principles in the 1880s were those of a tough and articulate New South advocate.

John B. Gordon may have been the most interesting of the three office-holding members of the Ring. When the Civil War began, he came down from the hills of northwest Georgia as captain of a company called the "Raccoon Roughs." Although he lacked military training, he had the stuff of heroes. Within two years he was a brigadier general, and by the end of the war he was a major general. He should have been a lieutenant general, but the papers did not go through in the closing days of the Confederacy. At the Battle of Sharpsburg, he was wounded twice and refused to leave the field, remaining to be wounded three times more before losing consciousness. He fought almost everywhere: Manassas, Seven Pines, Malvern Hill, Chancellorsville, Fredericksburg, Gettysburg, Spotsylvania Court House, Second Winchester, Monocacy, Cedar Creek, Fort Stedman, Petersburg, and Appomattox, where his troops made the last charge of Lee's army. His handsome face bore a scar probably made by a northern Minié ball but which his friends said was from a Yankee saber. The scar was an asset. The irascible Toombs, who put men in their places, said that if Gordon's scar had been on any other part of his anatomy, he would have failed as a politician.[24]

Gordon was considered an Atlantan after Reconstruction, although he, like Colquitt, lived in a satellite community. His home in Kirkwood actually lay just over the line in the next county, DeKalb, a fact that Gordon occasionally cited to prove he could not be a member of the Atlanta Ring. He had a plantation in Taylor County in middle Georgia, but contemporary accounts and even legends current in the county to the present day say that he was a terrible farmer. Nevertheless, he had support in the planter class because of his Confederate record and his style.

In 1868 Gordon had run for governor of Georgia and was probably elected, only to be counted out by partisan election officials. In

1873 he was elected to the United States Senate and everyone assumed that he was serious about politics.

Historians often call the three office-holding leaders of the Ring the Bourbon Triumvirate, or simply the Triumvirate. The name "Bourbon," applied to them and to other leaders, never fit but enjoyed broad currency.[25] As for the Triumvirate, it had limited significance of its own, and it was never anything other than the leaders of the Atlanta Ring who held high office.

Two members of the Triumvirate, Brown and Gordon, despised each other even while working together. Derrell C. Roberts, who has studied Brown closely, says the dislike grew from a disagreement over the settlement of the Hayes-Tilden election dispute in 1876. Roberts found disparaging remarks about Gordon written in the margins of the Brown scrapbooks, presumably by Mrs. Brown.[26] The dislike was intense throughout the eighties, especially after Gordon questioned the treatment of state convicts whom Brown leased and used in one of his enterprises. In view of this tension, the role of Grady, Howell, and the *Constitution* in reformulating the Ring and holding the Triumvirate together in any sort of harmony becomes a story in itself.

There would have been no Ring in the 1880s had not each member wanted something that the relationship supplied. All members shared ideas about how the South could be developed, but these ideas constituted an agreement in principle about which it was unnecessary to do much as a group. What Brown, Colquitt, and Gordon wanted was something specific and personal: to be appointed, elected, or reelected to office. Between 1880 and 1886 each of these men hit a point at least once where his political future was in doubt. Each time, Grady, with the help of Howell and the *Constitution*, helped and probably rescued the man in danger with other Ring members assisting at crucial points. Grady and Howell made this effort for three reasons:

First, the threatened politicians were all Atlantans, and their elections spoke to a broad, differentiated audience of the power of the city. Grady and Howell were convinced that appearances were as important as actualities and that to be strong, Atlanta must seem strong. Strength attracted capital and ambitious men. Also, the Atlanta officeholders could do favors for their city, if only small ones. The state government was weak and the federal government had not established a large role for itself. There was still another side to the proposition. When Atlantans held high office, they shut out other men who wished the city ill or who represented competing cities or localities.

Second, Grady and Howell threw themselves into the effort because Atlanta was home. The fortunes of both men were related to the well-being of the city. Especially was this true for Grady; his liquid wealth was small and his family was expensive. During one of his last Christmases, he could buy only inexpensive presents for his loved ones.

Third, Grady and Howell had their pride to lose if Ring politics failed. They embarked initially upon serious political manipulation unable to see the road ahead. As the pathway became clearer, they could not get off it. With pride to forfeit if beaten, they contended with all their might.

Grady became a force to be reckoned with suddenly in 1880 at the same time he became a member of the *Constitution* management. While he was in New York negotiating the Cyrus Field loan, a political crisis arose which could have changed the political landscape to the disadvantage of Atlanta. Gordon became no longer interested in politics. He turned to his closest friends and, pleading poverty, said he would resign from the United States Senate and take a job that paid more money. Colquitt was in the governor's chair and would name a replacement, then stand for reelection himself shortly thereafter. Colquitt was in grave danger, and Atlanta stood to lose both the governor and a senator if matters were not dealt with correctly. The new Ring coalesced in this threatening situation.

Grady made the first move. There is no sign that anyone asked him to do so. He simply took charge, becoming the intermediary and negotiator for the controversial events that followed.

Grady wanted Brown to have the Senate seat, thus saving it for Atlanta. To disguise what he was doing, Grady made up a secret code so that he could telegraph messages confidentially. He wrote the code out on his own letterhead and had it delivered to Brown in a railroad envelope.[27] The code involved word substitutions; wherever *Smith* appeared, for example, it meant *Brown,* and so on. When a word was not in the code, it stood for itself.

On May 15, 1880, Grady wired Brown: "William will pass play certain,"[28] which, when translated, meant: "Gordon will send in resignation certain." Other coded telegrams followed in which Grady helped to arrange a job for Gordon with the Louisville and Nashville Railroad. This arrangement was open to sinister interpretations, because Brown, who was to get the Senate seat, was to have his own railroad pay a portion of Gordon's salary. It was widely said that a Senate seat had been bought and sold. Unusual and probably irregular accommodations were certainly made, but their details are now lost.

On May 17 Brown got a telegram from Grady saying that everything was arranged. "Williams play pass to Jim and Jones shoots that Smith shall hold wood and wash but says in adjusting Williams salary four slow should come from Smith's road";[29] which meant that everybody involved agreed that Brown should hold the presidency of the Western and Atlantic Railroad and the Senate seat simultaneously, but that Brown's railroad should pay Gordon four thousand dollars a year.

The situation was potentially destructive to the governor. Contemporary reports say that he asked Gordon to delay his resignation for a little time; but on May 19 he moved ahead and telegraphed Brown, then in Nashville attending a dinner for Confederate General Joseph E. Johnston, that Gordon had resigned. "[I]f you can accept appointment to vacancy please notify me and return immediately."[30] Brown accepted and returned.

One Georgian, not meaning it as a compliment, said it seemed that Georgia had swapped senators between dark and daylight.[31] An enormous outcry occurred from people who sensed irregularity. Public meetings in Muscogee and Pike counties denounced Colquitt, Brown, and Gordon. Anger and a vicious campaign of vituperation were directed at the governor, then ten weeks away from a Democratic convention called to accept or reject him for another term. Delegate selection was about to begin.

During the 1870s a substantial and well-led body of Independents had showed remarkable political strength in Georgia. In 1878 Independents took two congressional seats which the Democrats regarded as their own, nearly took a third, and Democrats held onto a fourth only after a dangerous battle. The leader of the Independents, Dr. William H. Felton, was congressman from the Seventh District, and he laid ferocious attacks upon the Bourbons governing Georgia.[32]

As Colquitt faced the convention, no one could measure the dissatisfaction within the electorate. His administration had been embarrassed by the impeachment and conviction of its state comptroller, and by investigations of the treasurer, the agriculture commissioner, the state school commissioner, the public printer, the office of secretary of state, and the penitentiary system.

Even good fortune damaged the governor. Payments from unanticipated sources came into the state treasury, and the rancid jealousies created by the presence of the money were pure poison. Patronage problems beset the embattled governor. Beginning in 1877 an army of men wanting appointments beseiged him. "There will never, in the history of Georgia, be such another universal rush for office," wrote Colquitt's executive secretary. Severe need pushed hundreds of people to apply for positions without saying which one they wanted; anything would do. Others declared with terrible specificity what they wanted. More than one hundred men wished to be principal keeper of the penitentiary. An equal number wanted to be state librarian. Thirteen well-qualified lawyers envisioned themselves as solicitor of the South Western circuit. Eleven saw themselves as judge. Bestowing each appointment, the governor kept one friend and made a swarm of enemies. Thousands of men contended for about thirty places,[33] and by the time Colquitt faced the nominating convention, many of them nursed angers that had smoldered for three years. In Georgia the struggle for the

Democratic nomination was usually the real election. In 1880 matters were different.

Nomination was done by delegates selected in the counties. A majority of delegates often chose the nominee, but sometimes the Democratic party required a two-thirds vote. Colquitt supporters correctly foresaw trouble in getting two-thirds but believed they would go to the electorate stronger if they nominated that way. Colquitt had a majority but not two-thirds, and after a tumultuous convention lasting six days in which the anti-Colquitt minority yielded hardly an inch, the convention "recommended" Colquitt for governor rather than endorsing him. A group within the minority approached Dr. Felton to run as its candidate against Colquitt, but Felton declined and maliciously made their overture public.

At length, those dissatisfied with Colquitt settled their candidacy upon Thomas Norwood of Savannah, a former United States senator and a poor choice. He was a pedestrian speaker and a cold man who related badly to black Georgians, who voted in considerable numbers then; but even against such a man, the reelection of Colquitt was uncertain.

It was then that Grady became the master manipulator of Georgia politics for the election at hand and for others stretching into the future. The new Ring was forming, and Grady became its master when a group of young businessmen from Atlanta, seeing their friend and neighbor Colquitt in trouble, put together a campaign committee to help him. The obvious person to lead that combination was Howell. He was the senior editorial person on the *Constitution* and could bring the newspaper to bear in behalf of the effort. He had successfully run the statewide campaign to ratify Atlanta as the state capital three years earlier. In the past session of the legislature, he had been president *pro tempore* of the state senate and he knew almost every legislator in both houses as well as other officials and had working relationships with many of them.

Grady, on the other hand, had presided over several failed newspaper ventures and had never managed a political campaign. He had been managing editor of the *Constitution* less than three months. His skill in getting Brown appointed senator was done in private and was not known.

Grady became campaign manager by taking charge, vastly helped by the fact that the campaign to save Colquitt was not universally seen in 1880 as an effort to promote Atlanta. Many persons saw it as a crusade to save the Democratic party. That fact was a crucial one. In that campaign, Grady had the help of newspapers and of people who a short time later would become bitter enemies as they perceived this brand of Bourbon politics to be helpful to Atlanta more than anybody else. Patrick Walsh of the Augusta *Chronicle* and J. H. Estill of the Savannah *Morning News* helped Colquitt in 1880 and paid a price for it in their communities, where their positions were not appreciated by some of their friends. The Macon *Telegraph* also assisted, marking the last time that Grady joined that contumacious organ in an enterprise of importance. The other two Ring members, Gordon and Brown, worked indefatigably for the Colquitt candidacy.

In short order, Grady was running the campaign. In its Atlanta offices, he unleashed energy and cunning that took people by surprise. He polled the sheriffs and ordinaries in the counties to see how the campaign was going. The result was that he had a correct view of the relative strengths of Colquitt and Norwood. When Colquitt's record was criticized, unfairly so in the opinion of the campaign manager, Grady learned and perfected an ingenious device that he used for the rest of his life. He found a way to print a letter so that each copy looked like an original. A letter from Colquitt, thus prepared, went into all the counties and into the hands of voters, who were flattered to have a personal letter from the governor. The letter helped to turn the campaign.

Colquitt's executive secretary said that Grady's command was "undisputed," his enthusiasm was "irresistible," and his executive capacity was "extraordinary." "He threw himself into the struggle with his whole heart. He watched every point, kept the whole State in his observation, devised means, wrote letters, sent myriads of dispatches, strengthened doubtful localities, and placed help wherever it was needed."[34]

This unexpected ability to manage a campaign was noticed, but Grady said nothing, demonstrating a characteristic he showed thereafter. He commented on his political activities only when he had to, although they were central to his purposes, consumed much of his time, and sometimes worked him to the edge of collapse. The election results confirmed the correctness of the strategy used. The vote was 182,353. Colquitt got 118,349.

The campaign had an interesting detail. When Colquitt spoke in Macon in an appearance that almost turned into a riot, he was introduced by a vigorous lawyer from that city, a member of the state House of Representatives, and Speaker of the House. His name was Augustus O. Bacon. The gubernatorial campaign of 1880 also marked the final time that Grady and Bacon made common cause, for the men were about to become deadly adversaries. Bacon was the catalyst that converted the politics of the decade into pro-Atlanta and anti-Atlanta camps, and the threat that he and his friends posed to Atlanta gave the new Ring a continuing reason to exist. Bacon, in short, became the vehicle by which central Georgia and much of the rest of the state sought to shift political power away from Atlanta.

At age forty, Bacon believed himself prepared to serve as governor at the earliest opportunity. For years, he had done his duty to the Democratic party of Georgia. He held offices great and small: city attorney for Macon, several terms in the House of Representatives both as Speaker *pro tempore* and as Speaker, and he labored mightily within the party structure. He was an efficient presiding officer in the House, scrupulously fair, and he attached himself to members and former members all over the state. They were a ready-made political organization for him.

Yet he was a cold man. Even in the courtroom, he was a judge's lawyer rather than a jury's lawyer. His best strokes came in legal motions. He could not understand why he was considered as icy, for he never intended to be. Often elected, he sometimes ran behind his ticket.[35]

He made terrible blunders. In a race for Congress once, the canvass took him into Twiggs County where he saw an old-fashioned woman sitting at the door of the courthouse trying to sell several pairs of socks she had knitted. Bacon rudely rebuffed her. "No madam, I don't wear that sort of socks at all, and I don't want them." Bacon's opponent, following in his footsteps a few days later, encountered the same woman and bought several pairs, saying they would do nicely for him and his children. Word concerning both episodes got around. Bacon lost Twiggs County and the election.[36]

Abrupt behavior aside, Bacon was a formidable candidate every time he ran for office, which was frequently. In 1882 Colquitt could not offer for reelection, and the situation seemed ready-made for Bacon except for one thing. The Independents were still a force even though their leader, Dr. Felton, had been narrowly defeated for reelection to Congress in 1880. Out of Congress, Felton had time to seek a vigorous Independent candidate for governor while he ran for his congressional seat again. Felton made overtures to an old friend, Alexander H. Stephens, Georgia congressman from the Eighth District. Stephens had been vice-president of the Confederate States of America and his name was known to every Georgian and was revered by many. His celebrated public service had come in an earlier time when agricultural interests called the tune, and he was never at home with Bourbon Democrats, especially not with those who most loudly espoused New South ideals.

In 1882 Stephens was unwell, a stubborn and contentious man in a wheelchair. From time to time, he hinted that he might retire from politics, but in a long career he had never been governor, and election to that post might be a splendid capstone to his public life. Both he and Felton deplored much of what the New South leaders stood for, and if Stephens were enticed onto the Independent ticket, a new arrangement of political power was possible in Georgia, one with priorities that many Atlantans would not care for.

The Democratic party was in peril once more, and measures were needed to preserve it. Confusing messages were passed at conferences and meetings, and at length, and to the astonishment of some, Stephens agreed to run for governor of Georgia, but on the regular Democratic ticket. Dr. Felton felt betrayed, for Stephens had gotten a blessing of sorts from the Independents, who in understandable confusion had recommended him. Meanwhile in Macon, Bacon was ready to make the race on his own and the Macon *Telegraph* held his candidacy aloft as long as it could.[37] When finally his name was withdrawn, Bacon nursed his disappointment privately. He sat out the election, refusing to support Stephens actively. General Lucius J. Gartrell, a cousin of Grady's, ran against Stephens, getting a respectable vote from Independents and Republicans.

In the midst of the campaign, the senior senator from Georgia died. Benjamin H. Hill was not from Atlanta, but he was perfectly acceptable to the Atlanta leadership. He embodied many of the New South ideals, especially reconciliation with the North. With the Senate seat vacant, Grady saw another opportunity for which he fortunately had a few weeks to prepare.

The duty of choosing a new senator fell this time to the legislature, which picked Middleton Pope Barrow of Athens, a respected figure but a man without much of a political base. Hill's term was about to expire. Barrow would be in the Senate briefly unless reelected in November, an unlikely prospect.

Stephens won the election for governor on October 4 with a majority of the votes, but with enough opposition to show that the situation had been dangerous. He was inaugurated on November 4, 1882, as the legislature prepared to elect a United States senator for a six-year term.

Grady's plans again involved the elevation of an Atlantan. Colquitt had just finished his term as governor and was available. J. C. C. Black, a charming lawyer from Augusta who had been a member of the state House of Representatives, also wanted the seat and worked to get it. Black had supported Norwood in the gubernatorial election of 1880 and had done all he could to thwart Grady's efforts in that campaign. Grady would have none of him, determined that the post would go to Colquitt. Atlantans would sit in both Senate seats.

As the hour of election neared, Grady, as Colquitt's campaign manager, worked the halls of the General Assembly and the rooms and parlors of the hotels where the legislators stayed. On election day, only two ballots were needed to sweep Colquitt off to Washington amid cheers. Colquitt's gratitude to Grady took concrete form when he had an expensive gift delivered to him: a pair of reddish-brown horses.[38]

Politics appeared settled for at least two years. Stephens was not Grady's first choice to be governor, but he was needed. Grady intended to influence Stephens, and although Stephens was no man to be used lightly, he was old and sick and could be beguiled, an art at which Grady was supreme.

Beguilement became moot exactly 120 days after Stephens's inauguration, for he died in the executive mansion on Peachtree Street. Grady had had little chance to use Stephens as governor when alive, so now he used him dead. Grady had perfected the technique of arranging grand occasions for the benefit of Atlanta. The death of the sad little man in the wheelchair, respected governor of Georgia, an authentic relic of the Confederacy, touched the hearts of many people. Grady took charge of the funeral. Down Forsyth Street, he marched military companies and bands from all over Georgia as the Dead March reverberated through the city. The hearse taking the tiny body to a temporary resting place in Oakland Cemetery passed through tens of thousands of visitors, packed into the city by train. Some Georgians believed they were seeing the Confederate flag pass in review a final time. Alexander Stephens, unknowing in death, performed his last service for Atlanta. Any city that could put on such a spectacle was a formidable place.

The corpse was scarcely cold before the candidacy of Bacon rose once more. James Boynton of Griffin, president of the state senate, assumed the governorship and signified an understandable willingness to remain in office, but other people had different ideas. Columbus wanted Judge Martin Crawford, Savannah backed Rufus Lester, and other candidates included Philip Cook. The race seemed to be between Bacon and Boynton when Henry D. McDaniel announced that if he received the nomination, he would accept it.[39] The *Constitution* had not yet entered the picture beyond showing lukewarm satisfaction with Boynton and frigidity toward Bacon. A nominating convention was summoned to meet in Atlanta on April 10, to be followed by an election on April 24.

Early ballots in the convention showed that estimations had been wrong. Boynton was not ahead as thought, but Bacon was leading. On five ballots held the first day, Bacon led on all but the fourth. McDaniel had a few votes as did Cook, and the other candidates were out of the running. Alarm struck the offices of the Atlanta *Constitution.* On the second day, the convention recessed after the seventeenth ballot, with Bacon leading. Cook seemed to be withdrawing, and McDaniel was likely to do so. Bacon was on the edge of triumph, and the political locus of Georgia seemed about to shift southward.

Two unfortunate things then happened for Bacon. His campaign manager, Nathaniel E. Harris, left the convention suddenly because of the illness of a son; more important, Henry Grady arrived at the Kimball House hotel, where the political caucuses were in session. Grady's personal situation was awkward, for he and Mrs. Grady had houseguests and he was wanted at home; but at the Kimball House, he saw Bacon about to become governor. He forgot home, explaining to his guests what happened in a letter written later.

Grady discovered in the corridors and caucus rooms that his friends and allies had stopped working. He himself was lied to as he tried to come to grips with the details of the situation. He was "in torture," and he said that if he had left the hotel, Bacon would have been governor.[40]

During the long night of April 11, 1883, Grady guided the convention toward empowering a special committee to recommend a nominee. Grady then worked with the prospective committee members to assure that on the following day, McDaniel would be recommended and Bacon pushed aside. The next morning, one of Grady's friends made the motion to appoint the committee, and the Bacon forces made their final stand against it, losing 203 to 147. The committee met at 1 P.M., and by 6 P.M. came forth with the name of McDaniel,[41] who was nominated, elected, and inaugurated.

McDaniel was from Monroe, but his father had been an Atlanta merchant, and the governor had gone to school in the city as a young man. The leadership of Atlanta regarded him as satisfactory if absolutely unspectacular. Grady could influence him. The governor had a terrible stutter and sometimes could barely speak at all. Woodrow Wilson, then an unhappy lawyer in Atlanta, watched the crowds assemble for the inauguration of McDaniel and wrote down a vicious comment made by a Tennessean. Georgia, the Tennessean said, was exchanging a governor who could not walk for one who could not talk.[42]

Many persons opposed McDaniel's elevation and were never reconciled to him. Three years later, one country editor was still saying that up to the time of McDaniel's nomination, his name had been unknown in the race. When McDaniel retired from the governorship, the Macon *Telegraph* showed that feelings never smoothed insofar as it was concerned. "It may be said that he returns to his position in private life with less reputation than he brought out of it."[43]

Pleasing Macon and the Macon *Telegraph* was no concern of Grady's. He was bent upon perpetuating the political situation. Senator Brown and Governor McDaniel would face election again in a little more than a year, and although the power of incumbency would help both and probably assure reelection, Grady had a special plan. He wanted them reelected without a fight. Fights were costly and used resources better saved for a later day. The way to avoid struggle was to return them to office without opposition.

Grady thus became manager of the technically nonexistent campaigns of Brown and McDaniel. We know much about his activities, for in 1884 Senator Brown was in Washington and Grady could not communicate with him in detail except in writing. Some of his exceedingly candid letters were marked "confidential," and Grady certainly considered that all of them were destined for the fire once read; but perhaps because they were so detailed that they could not be memorized, Brown kept them.

Early in the year, after Grady decided to run his candidates without opposition, he disclosed the plan to Brown after calling upon the governor to explain it to him. "I have just had a *long* talk with

Gov. McDaniel. He is *thoroughly* in line, and will quietly do all he can, which means, *with me at his side* a great deal. I showed him that all incumbents who offer for re-election this year have *common cause* in a *quiet* race, and in keeping down opposition."[44]

Grady and Howell threw themselves into the effort, embarking the *Constitution* on one of the most calculated uses of a newspaper ever documented in Georgia. They stirred up a diversionary issue to distract attention from local politics. The Republican president of the United States, Chester A. Arthur, had problems with his party and it looked like a Democratic year. Many Democrats thought that Samuel J. Tilden had been elected president in 1876 and that victory had been stolen from him. Now, eight years later, Tilden was a sick man of seventy years, a venerated figure in his native New York and an icon in the Democratic party. The mention of his name stirred sentimentality everywhere and fervor in some quarters. If the *Constitution* could excite the electorate of Georgia about a new Tilden candidacy, the voters were less likely to become exercised about candidates who might rise up against McDaniel and Brown.

On March 4, 1884, the *Constitution* launched its campaign to name Tilden the nominee once more. "The renewal of the Tilden agitation comes in such shape that there is no room for doubt." Some weekly newspapers swung into line as the *Constitution* developed its theme: only Tilden's refusal to run, or death, could keep him from becoming president. Whether Tilden would cooperate was the question. Georgians were assured that he would make any sacrifice for the party. The paper pursued its campaign through April, reporting favorable signs of activity and averring that wherever people could speak, they spoke for Tilden: in West Virginia, Iowa, Pennsylvania, Oregon.

"We repeat what we said more than a month ago. There are but two things that can prevent Mr. Tilden's nomination and election to the presidency of the United States in 1884. One of these is his absolute refusal to accept the nomination. . . . The other is—death." The campaign moved into June. On June 10, Tilden said he would not run. The *Constitution* printed this news on June 12. As vigorously as the newspaper had supported Tilden, it switched to Grover Cleveland, who was nominated.[45]

In Washington, Senator Brown, who otherwise might have been confused at the presidential support given to a sick man, had been told at the outset what was going on. "The Tilden boom we have started is doing immense good in tying things together. It reawakens hope, turns attention to national politics and discourages the idea of factional differences here at home."[46]

There was a chance that the strategy would not work. In Macon, Judge T. J. Simmons, a vigorous and respected man of forty-six who was less noxious than Bacon but who still lived in the wrong place, wanted to run. He had been president of the state senate and was regarded as an expert on finance. With naïveté, Simmons let McDaniel know that he was thinking of making the race but would not do so unless Grady would help him. By 1884 there were telephones in Atlanta, and McDaniel lost no time in calling Grady, warning him that his support was about to be solicited. Grady laid a plan to see Simmons that evening and to "switch him off the track."[47] And thus Simmons, who divined gubernatorial qualities in himself in more than one election year, was put off the track and switched back to Macon.

By then, Grady was working as though his candidates had life-and-death opposition. Senator Brown would have to be reelected by the legislature, and thus legislative races were important. Grady half-threatened Frank L. Haralson, the state librarian, if he did not help to bring in a shoal of pro-Brown people from the mountains of north Georgia. Howell made plans to bribe the editor of a weekly newspaper, who also was a candidate for the state senate. Grady used every connection he had to follow legislative contests all over Georgia. At night at home, he wrote reports to Senator Brown by gaslight. In five such dispatches, he reported on races in 27 of the 137 counties, and he asked Brown for information about three.[48]

In the end, the plan worked. McDaniel went back into office unopposed, and Brown returned to Washington, only a little miffed that the legislators had not chosen him unanimously. If ever two noncampaigns had a masterful manager, Henry Grady was that manager in the uncontested elections of 1884.

Grady could not afford to be pleased for long, for electoral politics would not stand still. The leadership in Macon and in much of central and south Georgia now believed that the Atlanta Ring had gone too far. It was thus that 1886 was seen as the year of Augustus O. Bacon.

Technically, McDaniel could have run for governor again, because he had not served two full terms; but Bacon was regarded as having a powerful machine with the votes to elect him all but counted. If McDaniel ran again, he probably faced defeat. The governor announced on March 13, 1886, that he would retire at the end of his term.

Grady had nobody with whom to face the confident Bacon. Any lukewarm person would fail, for Bacon had been running since 1882 and some said since 1865, adding acidly that the statute of limitations should have expired on him.[49] Perhaps Grady's mind turned back to 1882 when the Confederate flag ran in the person of Stephens. It would take the flag again to unhorse Bacon.

The machinery of the Democratic party was on Bacon's side. A convention called by the Georgia Democratic Executive Committee would select the nominee, and delegates to it would be picked in the counties, usually by caucus. Caucuses were easy to manipulate. The people calling them, usually the courthouse ring, could set them at hours when their supporters could be present. Other people could come only when their work would allow. If the courthouse crowd wished to confuse matters, it could call two or more caucuses on different days, one to nominate a candidate for Congress, one to nominate candidates for other positions, and one to nominate gubernatorial delegates. The courthouse rings belonged mostly to Bacon.

Twelve years earlier a few places in Georgia had begun to use primary elections to choose delegates. Fulton County (Atlanta) in 1874 held what probably was the first one, and the practice spread a bit, including to Bacon's home county of Bibb.[50] The Democratic executive committee in each county decided whether to hold a caucus or a primary, and in 1886 most chose caucuses.

Only two things could save the governorship for the Atlanta Ring. Grady must find a good campaigner who could appeal to Confederates, and he must either invade the county caucuses or persuade the counties to switch to primaries. The assignment was nearly impossible, but there is no sign that Grady hesitated for an instant.

Nineteen days after McDaniel withdrew, the Macon *Telegraph* notified the world that the Ring was about to produce Gordon.[51] Gordon had been a splendid general but not much of a business success since leaving the Senate. He failed at innumerable ventures. In 1886 he was an erect fifty-four, his splendid face dominated by the scar. Events over which Grady initially had no control helped enormously.

Alabama was ready to lay the cornerstone for the Confederate Monument on its Capitol Hill. Mayor Warren Reese, of Montgomery, and others persuaded the ailing former president of the Confederate States of America, Jefferson Davis, to leave his home in Mississippi and to come to Montgomery as honor guest. Alabama veterans who had served under Gordon asked him to be principal speaker. Davis was too ill to make a long address.

The Montgomery exercises were set for late April. In Atlanta, Grady hit upon a plan for another great occasion for his city, one that would help to propel Gordon into the governorship. He arranged for Davis to come on to Atlanta from Montgomery to appear at the dedication of a statue of the late Senator Hill. Gordon would be with Davis, conspicuous in his presence, rekindling the fires of the Confederacy in tens of thousands of Georgia hearts and forming the basis for a resplendent campaign, founded upon General Gordon, Confederate veterans, their families, and the Lost Cause.

During the Civil War, there was grumbling by many Georgians about Davis and the war. Not until the 1880s did these same people, especially the military veterans living lives of tedium in a generally unprosperous decade, realize that the war had given them the most exciting days of their lives. They were absolutely ready for a hero and a dose of nostalgia, and they were about to get both.

On April 29 a train banked with flowers and trailing streamers left Atlanta to pick up Davis and Gordon in Montgomery. Aboard it were Howell, Hemphill, the Hill Monument Committee, and Grady, as inconspicuous as he could make himself in the midst of an event that he was stage-managing to perfection.

Gordon had not yet announced his candidacy, but Grady started the campaign with newspaper reports of his speech and activities in Montgomery. Affairs were well underway when the train pulled out of the Montgomery station for Atlanta on April 30 with the Atlantans and the ailing former president aboard, his hair now white, the pupil over his left eye appearing to have a film, his always spare face gaunt. His tall body was erect, although frail and weak.[52]

The train stopped at Opelika, Alabama, and the feeble Davis appeared on the observation platform at the rear, put his hand on the shoulder of Gordon beside him, and, in a line much quoted afterward, said: "This is my Aaron; let him speak for me." Gordon spoke. "He is our president and we intend to call him so, as long as he may live, and we can speak to say it."[53]

The train crossed the Georgia line; at West Point bands played and a crowd of thousands cheered itself hoarse. Davis bowed left and right from the rear of the last car as Gordon, his arm around Davis's shoulders, said: "My friends, I simply come to say in behalf of this dear old chief of ours, that we have positively forbidden him to speak. His heart, as well as his tongue, is full of eloquence, but his years are almost gone, and it is enough for us to look upon his face."

This scene repeated itself as the train rolled toward Atlanta. In LaGrange, home of Senator Hill, Davis said a few words, impelled perhaps by the memory that Hill had helped him as the Confederacy faded. The train stopped at Hogansville, Grantville, Newnan, Palmetto, Fairburn, and at East Point just outside Atlanta, where a tremendous crowd waited. At some stops, Davis was too weak to appear at the rear of the train. Gordon apparently never was absent from the platform while Davis was on it.

When the train pulled into the Atlanta station, Governor Mc-
Daniel entered the special car, named the "Atlanta," and emerged a
short time later with the guest. A carriage waited at the Wall Street
entrance, hats came off gray heads, bent forms stood erect, and a gigantic cheer split the air.

Davis tried three times to stand up in the carriage but was too
weak. Finally, Governor McDaniel and Dr. R. D. Spalding, chairman of the Hill Monument Committee, helped him to his feet and
told him that he could respond by removing his hat and bowing.
Gordon was standing up in another carriage behind Davis, bowing
almost the whole way from the Kimball House to the residence of
Mrs. Hill on Peachtree Street, where the former president would
stay.

The streets were swept clean, the schools turned out, and six
thousand school children, black and white, cast flowers into the path
of Davis's carriage as it approached, far enough in advance not to
frighten the horses. Nearly every building was decorated, from the
baggage room in the railroad station, which displayed bunting,
flowers, and large pictures of Lee and Davis, to the Kimball House,
covered with red, white, and blue.

When Grady managed an event, it was seldom for local consumption only. Trains brought in hordes of visitors at cheap rates, and
hotels and homes overflowed with guests. People who needed to
could sleep on the sidewalks. Perhaps fifty thousand visitors were
present. From Macon, where the Georgia Press Convention had
been meeting, the editors came in a body, not every one of them
happy. W. H. Hidell, former secretary to Stephens and now the
owner of the Rome *Daily and Weekly Courier,* saw through Grady's
plan and it angered him. Hidell wished to see Davis as a courtesy,
but his temper got away from him. In a fit of indignation, he
stormed out of the Kimball House and was almost hit by the train
bringing Davis and the Atlanta party into the station. He was furious at the Atlanta Ring. "It is not the State vs. Atlanta . . . but it is
the people of the whole State *vs.* the most corrupt ring *in Atlanta*
that has ever disgraced any State Capitol in the U.S."[54]

Grady's plans were indeed transparent, but he knew his Georgians. Emotions would overcome reservations. He saw to it that his friends did not dominate the statue ceremonies. Black, of Augusta, whom Grady and Colquitt denied a seat in the United States Senate, was principal orator. He was no member of the Atlanta Ring.[55] In the cleverist stroke of all, Gordon was not on the platform at all during the ceremonies. Rank entitled him to a place there, but when the procession started, he took a place in the ranks with the common soldiers of the Confederacy.

At the statue, located where Peachtree and West Peachtree streets join, Grady was master of ceremonies, one of his rare public appearances in those days. A memorable moment occurred which probably was not scheduled. Just before Black started the main address, a solitary horseman, wearing the uniform of a lieutenant general in the Confederate army, rode up. It was General James Longstreet, now a Republican, long estranged from Davis and from many other former Confederates. Longstreet got off his horse, approached Davis, and the two men clasped each other in embrace. Presenting Davis to the crowd, Grady said: "[T]ell Jefferson Davis that he is at home among his people."[56]

Davis's response was brief, and with the drapes of the statue pulled, the ceremony ended. Cries were heard for Gordon but he could not be found. Later in the day, a demonstration for him at the Kimball House infuriated some of Bacon's people. Gordon appeared and spoke a sentence or two, and Grady, witnessing the scene, turned to a friend and said: "Confederate money will be good before midnight!" Others saw the proceedings in uncomplimentary terms. "It is calculated that Atlanta made $50,000 out of the Davis reception and no end of advertising. Big town," said the Augusta *Chronicle*.[57]

The following morning, Davis left Atlanta for Savannah. On his way, seventy-five thousand persons greeted him, and in Savannah, Gordon was everywhere in his company. From there came the first real word that he was running for governor. He would announce after returning to his home in DeKalb County. The *Constitution* meanwhile denied absolutely that Davis's visit had anything to do with Gordon's plans. The general had taken a modest place at the dedication of the statue, and if he were called for when unavailable, the people were responsible. "The people speak when they feel like speaking, and they are responsible to themselves for what they do."[58]

Gordon entered the race on May 8, calling upon Bacon to join him in promoting primaries, something Bacon would have been insane to do. Caucuses were already delivering delegates to him. The contest was to be a two-man race. Judge Simmons was a candidate briefly, and there were minor entries who got little notice outside their counties. Grady reproduced a letter in Gordon's handwriting asking for support and distributed it all over Georgia.

When Gordon announced, no one knew how long the campaign would be; the date for the Democratic convention had not been fixed. As it developed, the campaign was short, a disadvantage for Gordon and Grady. Only fifty-nine working days elapsed between Gordon's announcement and the date when the result was clear. Grady created a three-part plan: slow down the caucuses, get Gordon into the counties to campaign, and cause primaries to be held in as many places as possible. Veterans would be the key.

One of Grady's friends described the activities with amazement and admiration: "[O]ne day, Grady would have the widows of Confederate veterans on the platform with General Gordon; another day, orphans of Confederate veterans; the next, one-armed Confederate veterans; and the next day, one-legged Confederate veterans."[59] Grady concluded correctly that only veterans and their families could thwart the Bacon organization, and they could do nothing unless organized and directed, so he set up Gordon headquarters in a storeroom near the *Constitution,* put together a staff, and took charge.

Soon, Grady heard that Lee County in southwest Georgia had been fixed for Bacon but that the decision was not final. Gordon and Bacon converged simultaneously on the courthouse at Leesburg. They held a joint discussion, and when the vote was put to the caucus, Gordon won it eighty-four to fifty-seven, taking his first county. "Let the people speak and their voice will be heard," said the *Constitution,* hitting the theme that became the refrain for the election.[60]

Even before the victory in Lee, Gordon had shown his mettle. He arrived by train in Americus, in Sumter County, and entered town in a splendid phaeton. A band in a bandwagon preceded him. Behind Gordon were the veterans, one-legged ones on this occasion, riding in a wagon pulled by an ox. One veteran held a banner aloft: "One Leg Only, But Will Get There All The Same." In enormous good humor, Gordon sent his "love" to the Macon *Telegraph,* a powerful voice for Bacon. "I am dead in love with the *Telegraph,*" he said. "The Atlanta Ring? Why I don't even live in Atlanta; I live in another county. I am a plain countryman."[61]

Some fifteen hundred well-placed politicians, working for Bacon with all their might, were the main opposition. Grady had two blessings: a splendid candidate and an opponent who made mistakes. Bacon and Gordon agreed to a series of joint appearances, with Patrick Walsh working out the details for Bacon and Evan Howell doing the same for Gordon.

The candidates presumably would debate issues, for technically they existed: the status of the State Railroad Commission, the leasing of convicts, the lease on the state-owned railroad. Finally, issues counted for little. Character and honor mattered, and the race descended to near-slander. The speeches started in Eatonton on Monday, May 17, and moved on to Sparta, Augusta, Lexington, Greensboro, and Conyers. Grady sent Clark Howell to cover these appearances.

Bacon got off to a bad start at Eatonton. Colonel Rufus Nisbet, presiding over the event, introduced Bacon acceptably until he said: "He comes to us a Georgian, and has the right to run for governor as many times as he pleases." Anger rose in Bacon and once upon his feet, he said he had hoped he would be introduced in a way not indicating the preference of the introducer. Nisbet rose and tried to speak, but Bacon pointed at him and said: "I beg that you will be seated." Bacon wanted Nisbet removed as presiding officer, and he called for someone else to preside. When Gordon rose to try to quiet the audience, Bacon told him to sit down.[62]

Bacon and Nisbet made an uneasy truce and the discussion went on, but an ugly tone was set. Two nights later in Augusta, the debate hit bottom.[63] Just as the Eatonton audience had belonged to Gordon, the one in Augusta was Bacon's. Both factions of Richmond County politics were behind him, the dominant Patrick Walsh wing of the Democratic party and the Arcadians, who usually were against anything that Walsh wanted. The Arcadians, however, said they were against all cliques including the Atlanta Ring. To them, said Howell, the Ring "pivoted on the left hand horn of the devil."

At 5 P.M., many of Bacon's supporters gathered at Clara Hall to warm up. They moved on to the opera house, and at 8 P.M., the candidates entered accompanied by delegations of prominent citizens. Gordon was the first speaker, and because his resignation from the United States Senate was a character issue, he asked one of his supporters, Judge H. D. D. Twiggs, to read a statement on the subject. The judge was harassed with hisses and boos, and when Gordon tried to speak again, he did so with difficulty.

J. C. C. Black introduced Bacon to enormous cheering. Bacon thought that Gordon's resignation as senator was an appropriate matter for discussion. He said that he was pledged to no mudslinging, but General Gordon had abandoned the high trust to which he had been elected under circumstances that were open to criticism. He developed that line, always pleasant, nearly unctuous. Howell, furiously making notes, wrote that Bacon "affirmed and reaffirmed with each of the insinuating thrusts of bargain and sale [of a Senate seat], that he meant nothing whatever by it derogatory to the general's character." Bacon sat down to vast applause.

Few in the hall had ever seen Gordon with his temper aroused. The general was entitled to fifteen more minutes, but he could hardly claim them for the uproar. He knew that he was in a strong position, however, for he was not the only candidate on the stage that evening who had abandoned a trust. Bacon had been adjutant of the Ninth Georgia Regiment in the Confederate army, had gotten a doctor's certificate saying he was sick, and had gone home to recover. He spent the rest of the war collecting taxes in kind, mostly farm supplies for the troops, a job it was later said that boys and old men could have done. When Gordon finally got the floor, he summarized Bacon's argument against him: "John B. Gordon, for the purpose of money-making, abandoned a high public trust."

> Now, there are other offices than governor that are also public trusts, and are also important. For instance, the adjutancy of the Ninth Georgia regiment. [Great applause.] That was a public trust. [Applause.] It was an important trust, but it was a good one to lay down. [Laughter and applause.] [Hurrah for the adjutant!]. . . . I didn't intend to refer to it any more. But my friend continues to impugn my fidelity to the public interest. . . . I think I may claim, without much egotism, that there was one time that I did not turn my back on a public trust—from '62 to '65.
> [Tremendous applause.]. . . .
> I don't wonder you seek to drown my voice by shouting "Bacon! Bacon!" for it is the best defense you can make of your candidate. [Laughter and applause.] Where was he when his heroic brothers of the Ninth Georgia, footsore, hungry, ragged and— I won't say—you understand—[loud laughter] and sick, [laughter] stood on the lonely picket or marched through mud, snow, and slush to the battle's front? Where was he when proud Patriotism piled her monuments in the dead bodies of liberty's sons? [Loud cheering.] What sort of monuments was he piling? Beef, pork, beans, sheep, sorghum, potatoes, eggs, and goobers. [Storms of laughter.]

This rebuttal was interrupted by applause, laughter, cheers, hisses, boos, groans, and cries of "chestnuts" and "put him out." A South Carolinian who had crossed the river to see the show thought that Gordon had destroyed Bacon. He was never more incorrect. The Augusta *Chronicle* hit upon the truth. Gordon had suffered a Waterloo in Richmond County because Bacon would still get the delegates.[64]

That fact framed the dilemma that Grady and Gordon faced. Only hard work and good luck could nominate Gordon. Outside of Atlanta, not a daily newspaper was helping and few weeklies were.

They saw the operation of the Atlanta Ring in the background, and they were utterly opposed to it. Grady probably wrote most of the political editorials in the *Constitution* during the period, although they are unsigned. One that appeared after the Augusta meeting has both the sound and the philosophy of the managing editor. "In politics, as in everything else, it is work that counts and words are idle. . . . General Gordon's fight is not won—and it is not lost. Every county in this state has been promised to Major Bacon by a crowd of small politicians who assert that they carry the county vote in their pockets."[65] Each time a caucus delivered delegates to Bacon, the action stood, for it was legal. Therefore, the courthouse meetings had to be thwarted or at least slowed down. Bacon's supporters analyzed matters in the opposite way and set out to speed them up.

Grady's activities in one county give the picture of the 1886 election, certainly the supreme effort of the decade for the Atlanta Ring. The county is Hart, located next to South Carolina along the Savannah River above Augusta. The county seat is Hartwell and the courthouse party was Bacon's. So was the weekly newspaper, the Hartwell *Sun,* edited by John H. Magill. Magill, a South Carolinian by birth, had joined the Confederate army at thirteen, and he had a battle wound on his cheek much like Gordon's. Now a vigorous thirty-seven, he had been stockholder and editor of the *Sun* for ten years.

Magill was sure that Bacon was capable of being governor, and he admired the candidate's open approach to seeking the post. The Gordon campaign claimed that the general offered himself for governor only after a public outcry demanded that he do so. Magill believed that claim was a lie. He was sure that Bacon had been the people's choice in 1883 when the Ring produced McDaniel. "[W]e want to be on the winning side this year." And when Patrick Walsh said that "the time has come to decentralize Atlanta and let the world know that there are other cities in Georgia deserving recognition," Magill agreed, reprinting the words.[66]

Bacon's political leader in Hart County was A. G. McCurry, a thirty-four-year-old lawyer with excellent family connections. His wife, the former Fannie Benson, was the daughter of Hartwell's pioneer merchant. McCurry had an important law practice in Hart and nearby counties, and he was active in the Democratic party. When the campaign began, the party had no executive committee in the county, only a chairman, but a committee was shortly elected, and McCurry became the member from the 1112th militia district.

The chairman was Thomas N. McMullan, a man badly used in the scandalous events that followed. One cannot be sure what his sentiments were, but he went along with the Bacon strategy of calling an early caucus. The caucus would choose delegates to cast the two votes of the county in the state convention. The county caucus was set for Tuesday, June 1, and the notice calling it ran in the *Sun*.

Gordon had support among veterans but his campaign had no effective leadership. Gordon needed to speak in the county and to see if anything could be rescued for his campaign. The earliest feasible date was Thursday, May 27, five days before the caucus.

Gordon arrived in Hartwell by train at six in the morning. He was met and taken to the Bobo House, where he rested and welcomed callers, many of them veterans. At 11 A.M. a large crowd gathered at the courthouse and listened to the Hartwell brass band. W. B. Dortch of nearby Bowersville introduced the general: "I have the honor now of introducing to you the soldier, statesman and patriot General John B. Gordon, candidate for governor, who was elected in 1868 and counted out." To much applause, Gordon answered: "I am going to be elected in 1886 and counted in." He dealt with allegations made against him, then criticized Bacon who was to speak in the same place two days later. The speech was a success and a good many people wore blue badges, symbols of the Gordon campaign.

More important was what the veterans were beginning to say. J. W. Harper, a local man, had been shot in the war and had slogged through mud about as far as he could when General Gordon rode up behind him on a horse. Gordon saw that Harper was doing poorly and asked what was the matter. "I told him, and he dismounted and at once placed me in his saddle and said: 'You ride. I'll try the mud. . . . ' General Gordon was no candidate then; did not know he would live another day." Harper knew how he would vote.[67]

These developments alarmed McCurry and the Bacon supporters, for they might not be able to control the caucus the following Tuesday. Magill's compositors were putting together the Friday issue of the *Sun* when McCurry and a political ally, J. D. Matthewson, appeared with a notice canceling the caucus. They took no time to check the notice with Chairman McMullan but wrote it over his signature without his permission.[68]

Complications followed. The cancellation notice arrived at the newspaper at the last moment, and in getting it into the paper, the compositor failed to take out the original notice calling the Tuesday meeting. The next day, it appeared on the same page with the cancellation.[69] Voters did not know which to believe. Gordon supporters thought that, at best, the Bacon people put the meeting off to buy more time for the courthouse ring to "re-fix" the caucus. There was an even more damaging possibility. The party bosses might go ahead with the event; a legal call for it still stood, and if they had the votes, they would elect Bacon delegates.

The *Sun* containing the double notices was widely read on Saturday, the morning that Bacon arrived in Hartwell. He came in over the narrow-gauge railroad from Bowersville. In a carriage pulled by four white horses, Bacon went around the courthouse square to the hotel where he spent two hours meeting supporters. He then spoke at the courthouse to about 350 people. As Bacon rose, someone shouted "Three cheers for Bacon," and they were hardly given when someone else called three cheers for Gordon. The visit was a modest success but no more than that. The *Sun* reported that the candidate spoke to the minds of the people but missed their hearts.

About this time at headquarters in Atlanta, Grady was worrying about counties other than Hart. The possibility of carrying it was poor, and there were problems needing attention in Screven, Haralson, Clarke, and others. Probably the *Constitution* correspondent in Hart alerted Grady to the existence of the double notices, raising the chance that Hart might be salvaged.

No delay stood between Grady's thought and his action. He did instantly what he did so often during the campaign. He turned to the Atlanta business community and borrowed a bright young man and sent him off to Hart County on an emergency mission.

The person was a lawyer, Frank M. O'Bryan, twenty-two or twenty-three years old then, working for the firm of King and Spalding. Alexander C. King was secretary of the Gordon campaign, and the other partner, Jack J. Spalding, inclined toward Bacon, a rather usual arrangement. Law firms customarily put partners on all significant sides of political contests so that the firm would have entree no matter who won. O'Bryan, a native of Walterboro, South Carolina, was a man of burly build with a round face. He had black hair and rather shallow eyes set wide apart.[70] He was a person who would make an impression in any group. Grady entered the King and Spalding office and threw O'Bryan into action without notice but with exact instructions:

> Frank, here's a pass to Toccoa. The Air Line Bell leaves here in about fifteen minutes. You go to Toccoa, and the train on the branch road will have left, but George Shefer is running a compress there and has a switch engine. The steam will not be dead in this engine when you get there, so take him this note from me, and he will send you down with his engine to Hartwell junction [Bowersville]. When you get there, it will be night. You go down the railroad about one hundred yards, and on the right hand side you will see a one-story house, covered with honeysuckle. You wake old man Bowers up and tell him that Henry Grady said to get his construction crew and send you over on a handcar on the narrow-gauge to Hartwell.

Grady knew that in waking up Bowers, O'Bryan would rouse the man who could order a crew and a car for the trip to Hartwell. William F. Bowers was an organizer and director of the narrow-gauge. Grady had instructions for O'Bryan once he got to Hartwell: "Here are two letters: one to McCurry and the other to Proffitt, the leaders of politics in Hart County. I am afraid McCurry is for Bacon. If he is don't bother him, but give this other letter to Proffitt. If he is not, give McCurry his letter." Grady obviously had written Hart County off earlier, for he assumed rather than knew who was supporting whom; but everything he knew assured him that L. C. Proffitt would be on the side opposite from McCurry.

Once in Hartwell, O'Bryan was to take over a cotton warehouse, empty at that season, and was to see several men whose names Grady supplied. On Tuesday morning, they were to send Confederate veterans to the forks of every road into town, and the veterans were to tell voters on the way to the caucus to go to the warehouse before they went to the courthouse. Grady gave O'Bryan a letter to the owner of the warehouse.

"Now, here's a speech I have written. You learn it on the way up and make that speech to the crowd at the warehouse. When you go up to the convention which has been called, if you have the crowd, nominate Gordon; if not, raise the cry of 'snap judgement,' and that there ought to be a primary so as to give every voter a chance to express his opinion. Move to put the meeting off."

Everything worked. O'Bryan caught the train to Toccoa and "got the switch engine; went to [the] junction; got the hand-car; went to Hartwell; found McCurry was for Bacon; gave the letter to Proffitt; arranged for the warehouse; sent the pickets out to the forks of the roads; held the meeting at the warehouse; and made the speech Grady wrote." An hour later at the courthouse, the Bacon supporters became alarmed and adjourned the meeting. They called a primary for July 6, but to save honor continued to say it was a mass meeting and not a primary. Magill said that the crowd at the courthouse numbered between three and four hundred people, or about half the white electorate. The voters, he said, had been "warned by courier."[71]

The executive committee made plans on June 14 for the election. Whether called a meeting or a primary, the election was an ordinary one except in one particular. There was only one polling place, the courthouse. That fact made no difference. The county had fewer than 800 registered voters, and 717 of them voted in the governor's race. Blacks were barred from the polls. "So far as the Gubernatorial candidates were concerned," said Magill, "the minds of the people were fixed, and there was absolutely no need for electioneering."

Gordon got 508 votes and Bacon 209, a victory of more than two to one for Gordon.[72] Grady understood correctly how victories could be won in 1886. Of all the primaries held in Georgia that year, Bacon won only three.

July 6, the date that Hart voted, was the last effective day of the campaign. Decisions were made in many counties that day and Gordon thereafter had enough delegates to nominate him. In fifty-nine days, Grady, with the help of a splendid candidate, had derailed a campaign that was all but won and put in its place another one that was created almost from dead start, except that it was not from dead start. Jack Spalding said that Grady knew every county in Georgia the way he knew Hart. All the work that Grady had ever done, and everything and everybody he had ever known, went into winning the race.

The *Constitution* later said that defeat in 1886 would have disgraced Gordon at home and dishonored him abroad, for his honor was at stake. "Then it was that the *Constitution*, with the mighty arm of Henry Grady, was put under his shoulder and stood by him, at the sacrifice of all else in the way, until his election. No such a contest was ever seen in Georgia, and no such a master hand as that of Grady ever piloted a canvass as he conducted that."[73] Insofar as is known, Grady never told anyone what he did in Hart County; the accounts come from others who saw them at close range. He probably did not consider his performance there outstanding, for dispatching people such as O'Bryan upon urgent business was his practice. The Augusta *Chronicle*, unhappy to see these young men coming, said they took part for the glory of it.

The *Chronicle* said that the *Constitution* also sent out a great many paid workers, "whips and organizers, the strikers who hire the wagons and pack the conventions and pay the money and do the yelling at the meetings. These are the men whom everybody sees and nobody knows, who ride the county day and night and fix it on a grand scale and call it the people's will."[74] Campaign manager Grady did his work well.

On July 28 the State Democratic Convention met in Atlanta and nominated Gordon for governor. On November 9, he was inaugurated.[75] The Ring now had two members in the Senate and one in the governor's chair, plus an array of lesser offices.

More important than the power exercised by these men was what their elections said about Atlanta. The city got what it wanted. It was a place with a future. The statement that the Ring thus made to both state and nation was one of confidence in Atlanta, a confidence it would thereafter be hard to discount.

$20,000.00   New York, May 8th 1880.

Twelve months after date I promise to pay to the order of Cyrus W. Field Esq: at the National City Bank in this City the sum of twenty thousand dollars for value received, with interest at six per cent payable semi-annually in New York. — Left as collateral two hundred shares of the par value of $100 each in the Constitution Publishing Co. of Atlanta Georgia.

Henry W. Grady.

Due 8/11 May 1881.

Grady Buys One-Fourth of the Atlanta *Constitution*, 1880. In May of 1880, Henry Grady borrowed $20,000 from the New York financier, Cyrus W. Field, to buy a fourth of the Atlanta *Constitution*. Once he became a substantial part-owner, he also became managing editor, a position he held as long as he lived. It was alleged, though never proved, that Grady and the *Constitution* supported Fields's brother to be president of the United States as a hidden condition of the Fields loan. (Henry W. Grady Papers, Special Collections, Robert W. Woodruff Library, Emory University)

Grady   Hemphill   Howell

The Principal Partners at the Atlanta *Constitution* in the 1880s.
From left to right: Managing Editor Henry W. Grady, Business Manager William A. Hemphill, Editor in Chief Evan P. Howell. (Grady photograph courtesy of Henry W. Grady Papers, Special Collections, Robert W. Woodruff Library, Emory University; Hemphill and Howell, courtesy of the Atlanta Historical Society)

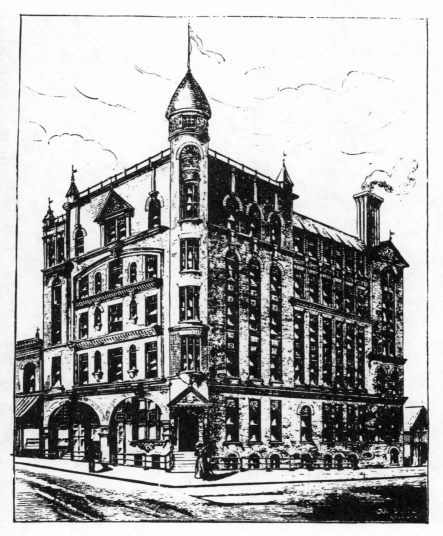

The Atlanta Constitution Building, 1884. In 1884 the *Constitution* occupied a new building at the corner of Alabama and Forsyth streets in Atlanta. The presses were in the basement, which also was the first floor. The second floor housed the business offices. The news offices, the responsibility of Grady, were on five and six, along with some editorial page functions. (Henry W. Grady Papers, Special Collections, Robert W. Woodruff Library, Emory University)

Five of Grady's Closest Editorial Associates. Clark Howell, Grady's protégé, son of Evan P. Howell, and managing editor of the Atlanta *Constitution* after Grady's death, is seated at left. Joel Chandler Harris is seated at the right. Standing, left to right, are Wallace P. Reed, the editorial writer who read and marked the exchange press for Grady; City Editor J. K. Ohl, and Frank L. Stanton, popular poet and columnist who joined the *Constitution* just before Grady died. This photograph probably was taken in 1890. (Henry W. Grady Papers, Special Collections, Robert W. Woodruff Library, Emory University)

The Grady Home on Peachtree Street, Atlanta. Henry and Julia Grady built a Victorian home to their own specifications on Peachtree Street, occupying it in 1881. In it, they entertained a procession of interesting and useful visitors. In it, Grady died at Christmastime, 1889. The house was demolished in 1921. (Henry W. Grady Papers, Special Collections, Robert W. Woodruff Library, Emory University)

Henry Grady and His Family in 1888. Henry Grady married his childhood sweetheart, Julia King of Athens. They had two children. The son, Henry King Grady, changed his name to Henry Woodfin Grady, Jr., after his father's death. The daughter, Augusta King Grady, was called Gussie in the family. (Henry W. Grady Papers, Special Collections, Robert W. Woodruff Library, Emory University)

Grady's Amateur Baseball Team about 1880. Grady was an avid sportsman who had his own private gymnasium. About 1880 he played on an amateur baseball team in Atlanta, whose members in this photograph are identified only by initials. Grady is at the right. In 1885 he helped to organize a professional team in Atlanta and became the first president of the Southern Baseball League, in which teams from eight Southern cities contended. (Courtesy of the Atlanta Historical Society)

A Scandalous Swim-Suit Picture, 1883. In the summer of 1883, a party of about forty-five persons including the Gradys went to Cape May, New Jersey, for a holiday. Grady lured two of his female companions into an area where a cameraman lay in wait and this picture, regarded as shocking in its day, was taken. At left is Mrs. Bessie Johnson, daughter-in-law of former President Andrew Johnson. At right is Estelle Cuyler Smith (Mrs. Henry H. Smith), Grady's close friend. Mrs. Smith is trying to break away from Grady. Her young son, Telemon Cuyler Smith, was the photographer. (Henry W. Grady Papers, Special Collections, Robert W. Woodruff Library, Emory University)

The Prohibition Campaign, 1887. The major partners of the Atlanta *Constitution* disagreed in public on an important issue only once. In 1887 there was a referendum on prohibition in Atlanta. Grady was a leader of the drys. Howell led the wets. The Macon *Telegraph* hugely enjoyed the spectacle and published a cartoon on November 13, 1887, satirizing the dilemma. Grady pours ice water on the people. Howell pours bourbon. Business manager Hemphill, technically a dry, blesses both sides and makes money from the advertising. Liquor won. (Henry W. Grady Papers, Special Collections, Robert W. Woodruff Library, Emory University)

The Elected Members of the Atlanta Ring. All three members were governors of Georgia and senators of the United States from Georgia. From left to right: John B. Gordon, Joseph E. Brown, Alfred H. Colquitt.

(Gordon photograph courtesy of John B. Gordon Papers, Special Collections, Robert W. Woodruff Library, Emory University; Brown and Colquitt, courtesy of Atlanta Historical Society)

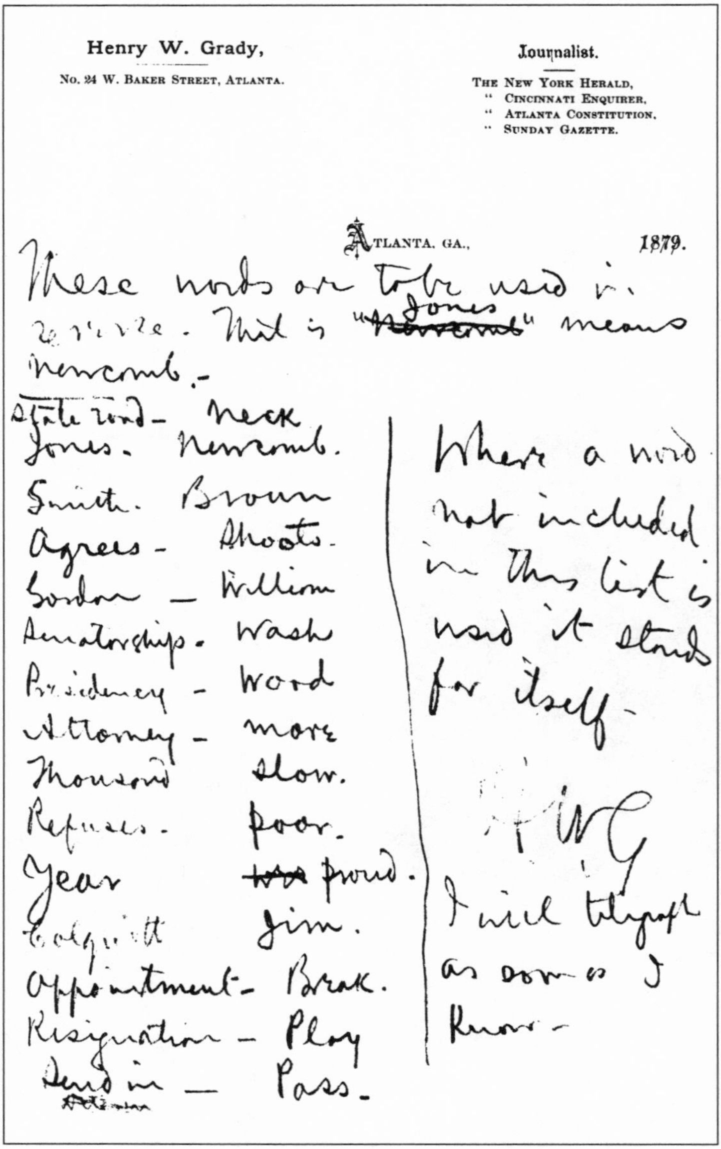

Henry W. Grady,

No. 24 W. Baker Street, Atlanta.

Jourṇalist.

The New York Herald,
" Cincinnati Enquirer,
" Atlanta Constitution,
" Sunday Gazette.

Atlanta, Ga., 1879.

[Handwritten note in Henry Grady's hand, a secret code list of word substitutions, largely illegible. Left column pairs include: State road — neck; Jones — Newcomb; Smith — Brown; Agrees — Shoots; Gordon — William; Senatorships — Wash; Presidency — Word; Attorney — more; Thousand — slow; Refuses — poor; Year — too proud; Colquitt — Jim; Appointment — Break; Resignation — Play; Send in — Pass. Right column: "Where a word not included in this list is used it stands for itself. — H W G. I will telegraph as soon as I know —"]

Henry Grady's Secret Code, 1880. To make arrangements for the appointment of Joseph E. Brown to the United States Senate in 1880, Grady composed a secret code based on word substitutions and had it delivered to Brown in an envelope. Where *Smith* was used, it meant *Brown*, and so forth. Using the code, Grady and Brown passed secret telegrams. (Joseph E. Brown Papers, Hargrett Rare Book and Manuscript Library, University of Georgia, Athens)

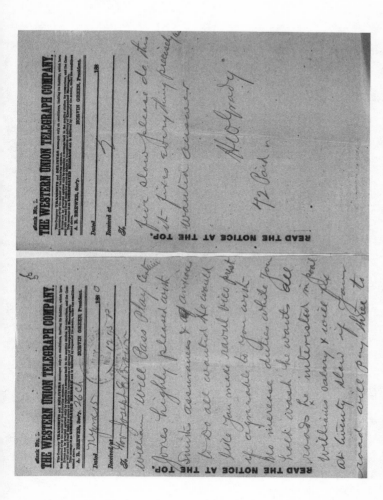

Grady Tells Brown that Gordon Will Leave the Senate, 1880. In a coded telegram, Grady tells Brown: "William will pass play certain," meaning, "Gordon will send in resignation certain." Later in the telegram, Grady discusses how many "slow," or thousands of dollars, Brown's railroad should pay to Gordon. (Joseph E. Brown Papers, Hargrett Rare Book and Manuscript Library, University of Georgia, Athens)

Atlanta Georgia
May 15th 1886

My Dear Sir;

The Campaign before us is so short that I am compelled to rely largely on the organization of my friends in the counties which I am unable to reach. My advices from all parts of the state leave no room to doubt that the people by an overwhelming majority are with me in this fight. My competitor has a compact & trained following in every section. This must be met immediately by similar organization of my friends.

I rely on you to guard my interests in your county & to aid in securing prompt organization in every militia district. If I can possibly reach your county I will meet your people face to face & rest my case there. If I can not, I rely on you & my other friends to see that I get a fair hearing & that a fair issue is made between my opponent & myself. A few earnest & devoted friends in each county can secure this & I ask for no more.

Faithfully yours

J. B. Gordon

Gordon's Mass-Produced Campaign Letter, 1886. Grady learned to mass-produce handwritten letters so that each looked like an original, and he used the technique repeatedly after 1880. In the 1886 race for governor, Grady reproduced one of Gordon's letters, asking for help in overcoming the advantages enjoyed by the opposition. He distributed it broadly. Gordon's opponent, Augustus O. Bacon, held a copy of this letter aloft at a joint rally at Greensboro and denounced it as a fraud. Gordon seized the letter from his hand and read it aloud to the audience. (John B. Gordon Papers, Special Collections, Robert W. Woodruff Library, Emory University)

The Maturing of an Editor, 1878, 1889. In 1878 (photograph at left), Grady was a twenty-eight-year-old writer for the Atlanta *Constitution*, two years away from becoming managing editor. In 1889 (right), he was a self-confident newspaper executive, orator, and national figure. The photograph was taken on the steps of Evan P. Howell's home on the day that the State Capitol Commission accepted the new building from the contractors. Grady stood nonchalantly to the right of the Commissioners as their rather formal picture was taken. The picture above, extracted from the larger photograph, was said to look very much like Grady. (Henry W. Grady Papers, Special Collections, Robert W. Woodruff Library, Emory University)

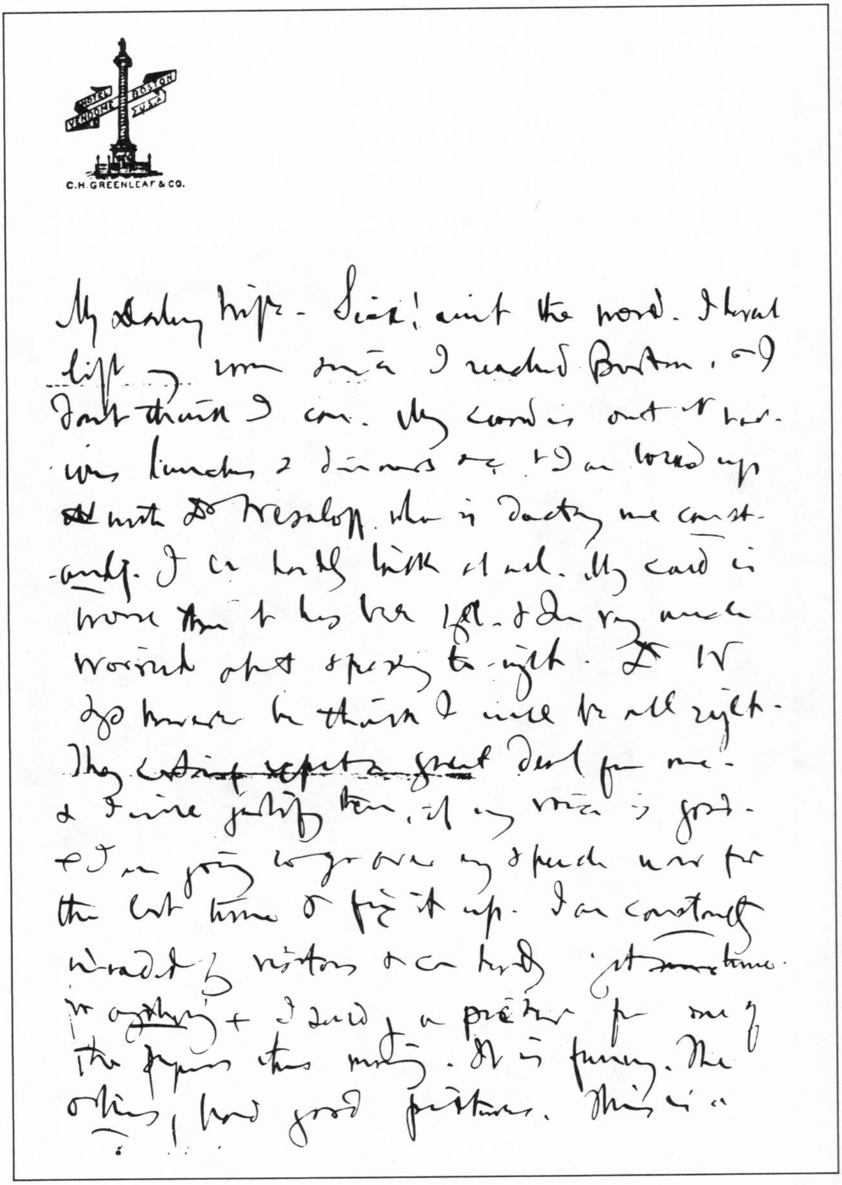

My darling wife — Sick! ain't the word. I haven't left my room since I reached Boston, and I don't think I can. My card is out at recep-tions lunches & dinners &c. & I am locked up with Dr Wesseloff who is doctoring me constantly. I can hardly talk at all. My cold is worse than it has been yet. I am very much worried about speaking to-night. Dr W says however he thinks I will be all right. They ~~expect a great~~ deal for me — & I will justify them, if my voice is good — & I am going to go over my speech now for the last time & fix it up. I am constantly invaded by visitors & can hardly get time for anything & I send you a picture from one of the papers this morning. It is funny. The others have good pictures. This is a

Grady's Final Letter to His Wife, December 1889. From Hotel Vendome in Boston, Grady wrote that his sickness was worse. That letter, of which the first page is shown, gives an idea of his handwriting, which was atrocious and which was always a problem for typesetters. There is no sign that Grady ever learned to type, but after 1885, he had a secretary, James R. Holliday, who sat behind a typewriter and took his dictation. Holliday also took shorthand. (Henry W. Grady Papers, Special Collections, Robert W. Woodruff Library, Emory University)

4
Politics and the Farmers

Virtually every spokesman for the New South Movement had an agricultural component in his plan, for common sense said that prosperity would elude the region unless farmers shared in it. Henry Grady was no different. His farm program, promoted through the Atlanta *Constitution* and elsewhere, sounded sensible on its surface, and at the outset he surely hoped that it would produce what it promised.

In 1887, however, after seven years of advocacy, his plan was a failure. He and his colleagues switched from farm policy to farm strategy in order to protect their political influence and that of Atlanta. The saga of that changeover is the story of this chapter.

Grady and the *Constitution* were not the authors of the farm concept they advanced, nor were they its sole supporters. Daily and weekly newspapers, agricultural societies and journals, other New South leaders, some businessmen, and some officers of state government backed it. It was widely discussed. Gilbert Fite concludes that if a farmer had not heard of the benefits that derived from it, he was dead, deaf, or illiterate.[1]

The program is summarized as follows: Farmers should plant cotton because it would sell for cash, but they should not plant only cotton. Secondary cash crops should be raised to bring in extra money. Prosperity was within reach if farmers also grew foodstuffs for home consumption. They could keep at home the money they once spent feeding themselves and their animals. If farmers also bought less commercial fertilizer, whose quality could not be known in advance, more money would stay at home.

The *Constitution* recommended this plan to every farmer regardless of condition—to the comfortable planter, to the white man who owned and tilled a few acres, to the white farmer who rented land, to the white tenant or sharecropper, to the little group of black farmers who owned their land, to the black man who rented, and to the huge number of black tenants and sharecroppers. One shoe fit them all.

While possessing the power found in simple ideas, these precepts lacked the struggle and joy of life, so Grady supplied the missing drama. Wherever Georgia farmers were found who did all or much of what he recommended, those persons were flattered with attention and publicity. Men unknown twenty miles from their doorsteps were discovered and, after a newspaper article was prepared and the presses rolled, enjoyed what in rural Georgia passed for fame.

The technique of producing letters so that each copy looked like an original, learned in the Colquitt gubernatorial campaign, was an important tool. Grady made mass mailings from his office. Packets of letters went out to leading citizens in all counties asking them to give the names of the most successful farmers they knew and to tell why they were successful. As answers came back, they or excerpts from them were printed provided the farmers used the recommended methods. Reporters, editors, and special correspondents also searched the state for people worth recognizing.

Jim Butler lived in Bibb County near Macon and in the blazing summer of 1887 was visited by a *Constitution* writer. In front of Butler's house, a cotton patch of twenty-six acres opened its bolls under the hot August sun. It seemed that the field would make thirty bales when Butler finished picking and ginning in the fall. One stalk had 260 bolls. Butler fertilized this remarkable spread inexpensively. He bought some guano but made a great deal of it from stable manure and other common ingredients.

Other fields grew foodstuffs for him, his family, and animals. A fine crop of corn tossed its head nearby, and Butler would surely harvest 1,000 bushels of peas and fifty tons of peavine hay. His oat lands carried forty bushels to the acre. Fruit weighted down about 250 LeConte pear trees and another 1,000, planted the season before, would produce in a year. His orchard had 1,800 wild goose plum bushes and 1,000 grapevines. What the Butler family and their animals did not eat they would sell.[2]

Such comfortable reports by staff writers numbered in the thousands during the 1880s. In six weeks in 1882, the newspaper printed the names of one thousand successful farmers. But not even the letters and the staff work supplied material in the quantity wanted, so Grady turned to the weekly press. Editors in rural counties, ever eager to identify successes in their midst, filled their columns with items about local farmers doing well. Many of these were short paragraphs, but often a full article appeared. Grady's editorial colleague, Wallace P. Reed, read these papers, clipped suitable items, and sent them to the composing room to be set for reprinting. For one issue of the *Constitution* in 1882, Reed prepared material from twenty-one county newspapers.[3]

An article of faith in the *Constitution* offices insisted that farmers were prosperous. With few exceptions, prominent persons who said to the contrary got no sympathy. Robert Toombs and Alexander H. Stephens, by virtue of their eminence, might say that each time the sun came up, it rose on poorer farmers, and Bill Arp could write about the sad state of agriculture and be published in the *Constitution*, but he was a humorist and not to be taken seriously.[4]

John T. Henderson, commissioner of agriculture for Georgia, learned not to be so frank. On July 2, 1884, the Savannah *Times* quoted him as saying that farming did not pay. When the *Constitution* noticed the offending piece, it administered a rebuke: If Henderson really thought such a thing, he should keep his mouth shut. "[T]here is no state in the union where farming pays better." In quick order, a reporter left the *Constitution* to find Henderson and within hours an explanation and partial recantation was in hand. Henderson explained: "Men that eat and indulge themself three hundred and sixty-five days in the year must not expect to do this on four months' labor." In other words, farmers did not work hard enough, a satisfactory statement affirming that failures were human shortcomings, not imperfections in agriculture as an institution.[5]

For a time, the *Constitution* shaped reasonable conformity to the proposition that farming was profitable. Whenever dissent appeared, and even when it did not, the newspaper paraded a phalanx of successful agriculturalists through its columns. There was, however, an embarrassing edge to the farm policy for which public support was missing, and which became troublesome. Almost every Georgia farmer believed from his cradle that the protective tariff was bad. Grady and the *Constitution* were vocal supporters of industry, wanting the South industrialized, they said, to balance the economy. To them, the tariff would help the process; but they had to convince farmers that the tariff was good for agriculture, a formidable task.

Making the best of the situation, they argued as follows: Tariffs helped farmers because factories supported people who bought farm products without competing with agriculture. When the South had factories, there would be home markets for farm goods; but few people would build factories without the right kind of protection.[6] Bad company and antic corollaries attended that argument. A bitter enemy, John Fletcher Hanson of the Macon *Telegraph*, made the same points, as did Patrick Walsh in Augusta. Grady and the *Constitution* considered themselves standard-bearers for the Democratic party in Georgia, yet their argument was nearly a Republican one. To lessen their vulnerability, they avoided saying what kind of tariff they wanted but supported judicious protection without being specific.

About the total farm program, Georgians would form opinions after seeing whether it succeeded. For a few people, it worked well enough; but for the overwhelming majority, it did not. Farmers who succeeded tended to be planters, capitalist/managers with resources, methods, and viewpoints similar to those business and industrial entrepreneurs whom Grady applauded.

That being so, what should one make of the thousands of items about successful farmers? Urban editors decided which evidence to print and which to discard, and those editors had preconceived notions of what it all meant. As for the "successful farmers" themselves, a person once lauded as a success is unlikely to correct the impression, human nature being what it is.

As plausible as the program sounded, impediments doomed it from the start. The credit system was one bar. Only the rare Georgian had money to finance his crop. Those who needed help seldom turned to banks, always slow to make loans on land, but went instead to a furnishing merchant who advanced supplies that were needed, always at staggering interest. Merchants disliked advancing credit on anything except cotton, which could sell for cash. The system almost forced the farmer to plant cotton to get credit. It cut the attention that he could give to foodstuffs and secondary crops. Late in the decade, Grady acknowledged that merchants told farmers that if they cut their cotton, they reduced their credit.[7]

Farmers in debt could not change merchants. No one would take them except as cash customers if someone else had a lien on their cotton. They paid merchants' prices. When the year ended and the crop did not cover what was bought plus interest, the merchant carried the farmer over for another year. Many farmers stayed in debt, chained to one store: "Few are the years that from 50 per cent. to 75 per cent. of the farmers who thus bought supplies did not come out in debt," said a contemporary writer. These people often did not even know what they owed. If they asked during the year, the merchant might say, "You are all right," and they took that as reassurance.[8]

No relief was in sight. Usury laws covering merchants' transactions were unconstitutional in Georgia, and cash purchases were not the answer. If a farmer had cash, he did not need credit. The *Constitution* said high interest rates were bad except in one respect: They proved absolutely that agriculture paid. "Were this not the case our farmers would soon be crushed to earth under their heavy burdens."[9]

The system thus forced farmers to plant much cotton, and its cultivation went up in the 1880s. Between 1880–1881 and 1890–

1891, acres planted in Georgia increased from 16,000,000 to 20,000,000; bales ginned from 6,600,000 to 8,500,000, and the value of the crop from $356,000,000 to $429,000,000. Stephen J. DeCanio, studying the economics of production and supply, finds little to support the advice given about cotton in any event. "[C]otton culture was more productive in value terms than the alternatives, other things being equal."[10]

Farmers thus demolished one part of the program by planting more and more cotton, even as they wrecked a second part. Despite exhortations to grow more foodstuffs, they grew less. During the 1880s, Georgians produced less cereal grains than their forebears grew before the Civil War. Between 1860 and 1889, wheat production dropped from 2,544,913 bushels to 1,096,312. Decreases occurred in rye, Indian corn, and barley. As cereal grains went down, so did livestock production. Smokehouses were emptier of locally grown meat in 1890 than in 1860. Production of hogs, sheep, and cows other than milk cows declined.[11]

Farmers also ignored advice about buying less commercial fertilizer. There was almost a buying craze. In 1880 Georgians bought 119.6 thousand tons of commercial guano; by 1890, the figure was 288.1, rising almost in a curve.[12]

Georgia farmers were conservative and slow to change, so it is remarkable that a number of them actually followed one tenet of the program. Some people actually grew secondary crops, especially fruits and vegetables. The climate and soil were ideal, Grady declared, and great profits lay in vegetables and in melons, especially watermelons, and in peaches, apples, pears, and grapes. The *Constitution* opened itself to ridicule by saying that if one farmer in five were a success at truck farming, it would still be a great thing but claimed that the success rate was better than that.[13]

By 1883 Grady asserted that truck farming was an established activity in Georgia despite the absence of a home market, and he was confident that railroads could get the produce to northern markets. Nevertheless, there were problems. Fruits and vegetables spoiled in ventilated cars, and Georgia railroads had almost no refrigerated ones. Under state law, freight trains parked on Sundays, leading to further spoilage. Even so, the *Constitution* said profits were "simply wonderful" and truck farmers were privileged because they had no guano bills to pay and no liens to unsettle the mind.[14]

Less than five months after these reassurances, the newspaper surveyed the railroads about their truck-transporting capacities. Responses from the Central Railroad and Banking Company of Georgia and from the Savannah, Florida, and Western showed that neither line had a refrigerator car. Neither knew how long produce would keep in a ventilated car without spoiling.[15]

Some Georgia fruits and vegetables actually reached northern markets, proving that people were working on the problems, but anxiety remained. Railroads might raise their rates and endanger the business. That began to occur at once, with the *Constitution* predicting that the lines would do better once they understood the facts. Disillusionment set in, and by 1888 a shocking story told of twenty-seven carloads of watermelons shipped to one of the best houses in New York and sold for $4,678. The railroads got $3,345.63; the growers, $1,332.37.[16]

The sad condition of the farmers must not be laid to the advice they got, especially since they took so little of it. Farmers were in the midst of what historians call the Long Depression, a difficult time lasting from 1865 until around 1900.[17] The program should not be criticized because it failed to rescue these people. What one seeks to understand is why Grady and his newspaper insisted until late in the decade that their program worked when it did not. Like so much about the New South Movement in Georgia, the answer lies in politics.

On any statewide election day, angry farmers entering the political mix could change the Ring arrangement. For that reason, farmers were more to Grady than tillers of the soil, even more than patrons of the newspaper. They were voters. The *Constitution* knew that their numbers were such that they could control the state whenever they put their minds to it.[18] Grady and his colleagues flattered them, assured them that they were prosperous and happy, and advocated a program that, if it worked, would make them more so.

In rare moments the *Constitution* agreed that all was not well. In

1883, after studying the Census of 1880, the newspaper admitted that prosperity had overlooked Georgia. In New England the average farmer kept $342 at the end of his agricultural year; in the Middle States, $454; in the West, $389, but in the South, $185. Fearful that disaffected farmers would organize and upset matters, Grady closely watched all agricultural clubs and groups. Some were conservative and safe, such as the State Horticultural Society, the Georgia Fruit Grower's Association, and especially the State Agricultural Society. Their members were mostly planters, not interested in shaking up the political arrangement. Grady himself was head of the Poultry and Bench Association, rendering it entirely benign. Other groups were dangerous, and for all groups the *Constitution* had a policy. "Keep the club out of politics. Never let a politician ride it to death. Never let it have a candidate for office."[19]

Had farmers really been prosperous, tame organizations functioning as social groups and discussion circles might have satisfied them; but by 1887 the troubles were such that they had to be addressed, and Grady wanted to be sure that the right people addressed them. The time had come for a cautious move.

Encouraged by Grady, Agriculture Commissioner Henderson called a convention of farmers from ten southern states to discuss common problems. Governors appointed delegates to the Intra-State Convention to meet in Atlanta in August 1887. Henderson hoped that a new and continuing organization would be born there. Each person paid his own expenses, assuring that almost all the delegates were planters. The *Constitution* helped to arrange the meeting and raised money for it.

On August 16, 1887, about four hundred delegates and their guests arrived at DeGive's Opera House in Atlanta. Randolph Dennis Werner, analyzing the appointees from the Augusta area, finds a delegation of prosperous men and not a single humble tiller of the soil. The agenda could have been written by Grady: the dangers of an all-cotton program; the need for diversification of crops; commercial fertilizers; industrial education for farmers, which meant seeking better ways to do things; farm labor, which meant dealing with Negroes; credit; and relations between agriculture and the

government, which meant the tariff.[20] Governor Gordon, temporary chairman and first speaker, said that farming no longer paid,
an assertion that earlier would have gotten him criticized. He then
introduced Grady. Grady entered the hall directly from an exhaust-
ing schedule at the newspaper and with no speech ready. He began
with a damaging admission that passed for humor, probably because there was truth in it. Referring to Governor Gordon, he said:
"I am the only living man who knows less about agriculture than he
does." Grady then launched into an extemporaneous talk with such
speed that he panicked the stenographer, who got down only part
of what he said.

Enough was transcribed to show that Grady made first use of a
device he would later employ with effect. He gave an eloquent talk
on a serious topic, but a talk that had little to do with reality. He embarked upon a ridiculous rhapsody to the cotton plant. Grady made
some references to manufacturing, then the overwhelmed stenographer stopped transcribing and summarized.

In the Opera House sat three men of real interest to Grady. One
was Senator Colquitt, member of the Atlanta Ring, a supposed ally
and friend. Problems were developing with Colquitt in great part
because of the tariff. A portion of his most loyal constituency lay
with the planters, and they would be astonished if he endorsed a
high tariff. Yet Grady, his political ally, was committed to one. In a
speech that grated on some ears, Colquitt pleased the planters by as-
sailing the tariff. In the editorial rooms of the *Constitution,* heads
turned away. Editorials mentioned neither the senator's name nor
his speech.

Dr. C. W. Macune, a delegate from Texas, also interested Grady.
He was definitely not a member of the planter class but was the
dominant figure in the Farmer's Alliance of Texas, an organization
of unhappy people convinced that the system abused them. The Alliance was exactly the kind of combination that Grady feared. It had
made 150,000 converts in Texas and sent out organizers to all of the
cotton states. As the convention began, Macune's men were planting seeds of trouble in Heard, Troup, Greene, and Carroll counties
of Georgia.

A third delegate was W. B. Miles of Mississippi. The *Constitution* had arranged his presence. Miles gave a vigorous protectionist speech, and to him went the editorial applause withheld from Colquitt. Miles was held up as an exemplary farmer. Before the war he owned 400 slaves and raised all the supplies used on his plantation. He never even bought a mule. At the end of the war, he owed $200,000 and paid it off in twenty cotton crops. Even better, he assailed Dr. Macune for leading a secret organization that did business behind closed doors.

Except for the attack on Macune, the convention was a pleasant gathering of the well-to-do. It did nothing that mattered, and Commissioner Henderson's plan for a ten-state organization died. Only Macune's organization had the zeal to attract simple farmers with hands shaped to the plow, men struggling against the depression and the system. There was fervor in these people, and Macune knew how to call it forth. Robert C. McMath, Jr., has computed that, in three years, the Alliance inducted as many white Georgians into its ranks as belonged to the Baptist Church.[21]

Grady showed what he thought of Macune's unwelcome organization by what he did. He put a chilling silence on it and all its works. For the next seven months as Alliance organizers worked miracles in the villages and along the back roads of Georgia, the *Constitution* looked the other way, allowing the most occasional of mentions, all routine or hostile.

The following November, Alliance people called a statewide organizational meeting. The *Constitution* gave them 145 words in a letter to the editor. When the meeting drew people from only four counties, one paragraph announced the next effort in Fort Valley in December 1887. Between these meetings, one of Grady's writers laid a burning attack on the Alliance at Newnan, southwest of Atlanta. The headline set the tone: "A New Scheme By Which the Farmers are to Become Rich. The Organizers' Liberal Fees. The Farmers Clashing With the Merchants." According to the correspondent, politicians were closing in, ready to go into office "upon the blinded zeal of their deluded brothers."[22]

The Fort Valley meeting came and went unremarked upon by the *Constitution*, although people from seventeen counties were there. By then, Alliance organizers had enrolled 10,000 Georgians. During the slow farm months of January and February 1888 the pace never slackened, and at the end of February there were 30,000 members even though the rules shut many people out. The Alliance had no room for bankers and their employees, cotton mill agents, grain dealers, railroad people, merchants and their clerks, or almost anyone connected with commerce. Welcome were white farmers more than sixteen years old, mechanics, country schoolteachers, country doctors, preachers, and the wives of all these people. After 1889 there was a Negro organization but little was heard of it in Georgia.

The state president was a preacher and state senator, R. H. Jackson of Heard County. Jackson's work was inconvenienced by the silence of the *Constitution*, and he was doubtless surprised in February 1888 to get an invitation to come to Atlanta for an interview. Even at that date, the *Constitution* was not happy to cooperate. It printed Jackson's views, it said, to provoke discussion, something the farmers said they wanted.[23]

The interview was a fair one. Jackson presented the rules and regulations adopted at Fort Valley. He was not sure how many members he had. Perhaps thirty organizers were in the field, and about a hundred groups had applied and awaited formation. In Jackson's home county, the leaders had called upon merchants and asked for bids for the Alliance trade. Two merchants bid and their stores were designated as "trade houses." Savings to the farmers were at least 25 percent, Jackson said. Trade houses existed in all organized counties, but the Alliance was thinking beyond that concept. It wished to set up exchanges of its own, mercantile establishments where farmers would buy at reduced prices and sell at good rates. Jackson said little about politics. The Alliance did not emphasize that.[24]

About 10,000 new members joined in the spring of 1888 as the *Constitution* continued to look askance. Its news columns were a bit more open but its editorial page was not. In Washington, Senator Brown was concerned. "There is a growing feeling among our people of opposition to all accumulation of capital, and it is becoming a crime for a man to have anything, no matter how honestly he gets it or how hard he works for it. There is an agrarian tendency among our people. I do not know what it will finally result in, but fear it does not promise well."[25]

With the Alliance on its way up, the *Constitution* characteristically would have embraced it with Grady smoothly supervising the switchover in strategy. That is what the newspaper did, although it delayed for as long as it could. The timing of the endorsement is a story in itself. After holding back for eleven months while the organization surged, the *Constitution* saw merit in it on June 4, 1888, the day that the Alliance said that its next statewide meeting would be in the House of Representatives chamber. The Alliance had not yet taken over the state government but was about to borrow its quarters. The newspaper still worried about its "merchant friends," but it was too late for them to protest. Without criticizing the merchants, the *Constitution* said it had always reported the facts about the farm situation. "The merchants might easily have taken the cue."[26]

Up to that moment, Grady and the *Constitution* had understood the Alliance in terms of membership and political potential but had not realized that participation was nearly a religious experience for some members. Grady soon grasped the point. Farmers usually did not work on Saturday afternoons, and the Alliance held many of its meetings then. Grady gave his version of one of them in Elbert county, and he said that similar things were happening all over Georgia:

> At Saturday noon in any part of this county you may note the farmer going from his field, eating his dinner thoughtfully and then saddling his plow-horse, or starting afoot and making his way to a neighboring church or school-house. There he finds from every farm, through every foot-path, his neighbors gathering to meet him. What is the object of this meeting? It is not social, it is not frolic, it is not a picnic—the earnest, thoughtful

faces, the serious debate and council, the closed doors and the secret session forbid this assumption. It is a meeting of men who feel that in spite of themselves their affairs are going wrong—of free and equal citizens who feel that they carry unequal burdens . . . and that the sweat of their bodies, shed freely under God's command, goes to clothe the idle and the avaricious in purple and fine linen. This is a meeting of protest, of resistance.[27]

That spirit brought ninety-two delegates from fifty-two counties to the House of Representatives chamber on June 27, 1888. They entered under a shower of praise from the *Constitution,* but among the persons thrown out of the meeting was Grady's reporter. The session was secret. The reporter saw a delegation depart the House chamber to go for Governor Gordon, who appeared in short order. Through the door, the reporter heard the governor endorse the Alliance. He was running for reelection and the Alliance had 60,000 members. The *Constitution* bowed to the obvious: The Alliance could be a power any time it wished. Forgetting earlier advice to keep agricultural clubs out of politics, the newspaper said it was time that farmers took care of themselves. "They have furnished the music for the demagogue and the tricksters long enough, and it is high time that some one else should fiddle while they dance." By November 9, more than 100 counties were organized, and between 75,000 and 80,000 people were members.[28]

The year 1888 was an anxious time of reassessment for Grady and his colleagues, a critical time. There were terrible strains with and among their principal friends. Brown, always cool to Gordon, was now furious with him. Gordon and Grady were miffed with one another, although neither said so in public. The tariff and other considerations caused problems between Colquitt and Grady. Howell sided with Grady in all disagreements. One might wonder whether the Atlanta Ring was coming apart.[29] The public saw little of the friction.

Little could be done about damage to old friendships and alliances, but much must be done about the farmers if Grady, Howell, and the *Constitution* were to continue their influence. No record exists of the conversations that the owners surely had, but a clear record remains of what they did.

When President Jackson's Alliance interview was published, he said who the enemies of the farmer were: the furnishing merchants, the banks, the oil mill trusts, the railroads, the manufacturing trusts, and the syndicates, in a word, the commercial allies of Grady and the *Constitution* in the New South Movement.[30] The newspaper had lightly criticized some of them in the past, but each was important to the Movement. A general assault upon them to show solidarity with the farmers was out of the question.

The problem solved itself. A safe villain, deserving attack, suddenly appeared in the guise of the jute trust, an aggregation that hardly had a friend in Georgia. Grady could assault it to his heart's content without repercussions and be applauded by farmers for doing so. Jute is a tough fiber from the East Indies which, made into sacking, encases a bale of cotton on its way to market. In the summer of 1888 the jute interests met in St. Louis and formed a trust. Speculators cornered the market and the price of bagging doubled. The trust delayed making its combination until the middle of 1888 when it was too late to make other provisions. Relief for the farmer was at least a year away.

For a year, hand in hand with the Alliance, the *Constitution* attacked the trust, using many of the printable expletives in the language. The combination cut deep "into the quivering flesh of the farmer." The trust was vicious; its members were robbers; it was villainous, infamous, and a plunderer. Moreover, jute people were cormorants, said the *Constitution*, certainly sending scores of Georgians to their dictionaries to learn that a cormorant is a repulsive seabird with a voracious appetite and a horrid appearance. Some of the people wanted to boycott jute but the *Constitution* opposed that idea, especially after a boycott occurred. Unless farmers sold a large portion of their crop, they could not pay off the furnishing merchants, and if those merchants collapsed, the debacle would stretch backwards to the wholesale suppliers in Atlanta. The newspaper was sure that sensible farmers would meet their obligations, and it urged them to find substitutes for jute bagging. The *Constitution* had some amazing recommendations: nailing cotton up in pine boards, encasing it in bagging made either of pine straw or the inner bark of the cornstalk, or bagging it in cotton cloth, something that actually took place.[31] The newspaper suggested that each farmer mail in a dollar to build a cotton-bagging factory in Atlanta, advice that few heeded. In time, the jute trust lost its grip on the market, and after a year the price began dropping.

The *Constitution* also demonstrated solidarity through a huge campaign in its columns. On December 2, 1888, in a Sunday editorial, the newspaper assigned itself the job of finding out why farmers were not more prosperous. "Wherever it is, the *Constitution* is going to find it if it can be found. And whenever found we shall stand by the farmers' side in breaking down that barrier to his success and prosperity, no matter where it carries us."

Grady wrote and mailed out another load of his famous letters asking Georgians in every county to send back ideas. A week later a three-month campaign began. Each Sunday a full page, more or less, dealt with the problems of farmers: relations with merchants, cows and dairy farming, hogs, cotton, politics, plowing, grape culture, wine, pears, peaches, watermelons, strawberries, home markets, potatoes, syrup, railroad rates, the Alliance, the Alliance exchange, fertilizer, sheep-raising, fencing, Negro labor, poultry, oats, wheat, red clover, hay, mules, farm mortgages, liens, and agricultural legislation. There were a great many stories about farmers who were doing well. "Example is better than precept," said the farm page of December 23, 1888, recounting the sagas of yet another batch of successful agriculturalists.

After the Sunday pages appeared for two months, the *Constitution* disclosed its preliminary findings. After all of its work, the newspaper changed its mind scarcely one whit about the formula for success. It endorsed anew every element of the failed farm program. The campaign ran another month but reached no new conclusions. The articles, printed in 20,000 Sunday *Constitutions* and

130,000 weekly ones, were said to reach one million readers not counting the patrons of other newspapers that reprinted parts of the series.

The farm program had not changed, but the tone of the newspaper had. No longer was it hortatory. Now it was gentle and soothing as it caressed the farmer in his troubles. Now it was admitted that although there were successful agriculturalists, many people lived on borrowed money. The future was bright, however, even for the merchants. The honest ones had nothing to fear.

Grady's oratory soon personalized the campaign. Before his appearance at the Intra-State Convention, he never took agriculture as a topic, but now he turned to it seriously. Grady began speaking about the time that the Sunday farm pages ended. In a tent in Albany, Georgia, on March 28, 1889, he pleased 3,000 persons, but nothing suggests that he hit his stride.[32]

The next occasion was different. For the first time, he spoke out of doors. On July 23, 1889, he mounted a platform in a ten-acre grove of live oak trees in Elberton, Georgia, and delivered the eloquent address that people had come to hear. He was funny, he was poignant, and he said he was terrified. He was afraid, he said, to be standing in front of 5,000 people while "[o]ver there, in smelling distance, where we can almost hear the lisping of the mop as it caresses the barbecued lamb . . . is being prepared a dinner that I verily believe covers more provisions than were issued to all the soldiers of Lee's army, God bless them, in their last campaign." And there stood Grady, "a single, unarmed, defenseless man," all that barred the throng from the feast. When finally the crowd preferred barbecued hog to raw orator, it was to give him a sign and he would join it at the board.[33]

The signal apparently did not come for an hour and a half, and Grady made one of the great speeches of his life. To the folk before him, he gave such an evocation of country life that, had they believed him literally, would have made them wonder how they came to be so fortunate. This symphonic apostrophe had nothing to do with the way life was lived, but that was beside the point. It was beautiful, it was well intended, it was lovingly delivered, and that was what counted. Thereafter in his numerous farm speeches, Grady never left it alone.

> I visited a country home. A modest, quiet house sheltered by great trees and set in a circle of field and meadow, gracious with the promise of harvest . . . inside the house, thrift, comfort and that cleanliness that is next to godliness. . . . Outside stood the master, strong and wholesome and upright; wearing no man's collar; with no mortgage on his roof, and no lien on his ripening harvest; pitching his crops in his own wisdom, and selling them in his own time in his chosen market; master of his lands and master of himself. Near by stood his aged father, happy in the heart and home of his son. And as they started to the house the old man's hands rested on the young man's shoulder, touching it with the knighthood of the fourth commandment, and laying there the unspeakable blessing of an honored and grateful father. As they drew near the door the old mother appeared; the sunset falling on her face. . . . Beyond was the good wife, true of touch and tender, happy amid her household cares, clean of heart and conscience, the helpmate and the buckler of her husband. And the children, strong and sturdy, trooping down the lane with the lowing herd. . . . And I saw the night descend on that home, falling gently as from the wings of the unseen dove. . . . [T]he father, a simple man of God, gathering the family about him, read from the Bible the old, old story of love and faith, and then went down in prayer, the baby hidden amid the folds of its mother's dress, and closed the record of that simple day by calling down the benediction of God on the family and the home![34]

Grady departed Elberton, leaving behind an audience ecstatic and well fed. He and his party moved to Anderson, South Carolina, and he repeated the feat there before 12,000 people, half of them Georgians who crossed the Savannah River to hear their orator. After Anderson, the party boarded canopied boats and went down the river on a floating house party, stopping for Grady to speak to throngs of farmers assembled for him by his new Alliance friends.

After returning to Atlanta, Grady appeared at Americus and probably spoke in Stewart County.[35] He kept a heavy schedule although the *Constitution* stopped reporting on him because he was repeating the Elberton speech with local references added. Joel Chandler Harris said that Grady spoke in many places of which no record remains.

As Grady worked, a bread-and-butter matter was resolved in Atlanta. The Alliance was ready to set up its state exchange and the question was where. A four-man committee, led by a former mayor of Macon, would decide. Savannah and Griffin bid for the facility, and other cities wanted it, but on August 27, 1889, the *Constitution* said that Atlanta should have it. It put up a thousand dollars and urged Atlanta businessmen to loosen their pocketbooks. Hemphill, business manager of the *Constitution,* was a negotiator for Atlanta.

The Alliance exchange struck no fear in the hearts of Atlanta merchants. Walk-in business was not its forte. It would buy up goods needed on farms, mostly from Atlanta wholesale merchants; then it would mail bulletins to the counties saying what its price was on the items. Farmers would buy those things from local merchants for the Alliance price plus freight if they could; if not, the exchange would try to fill orders. Cash was the basis for all purchases, which meant borrowing from Atlanta banks. Atlanta got the exchange, the issue no longer in doubt after the *Constitution* gave it a building at Hunter and Forsyth streets. It opened in November, 1889, and was acclaimed a success.[36]

The store was a nice prize, snatched from the hands of other localities that wanted it, but a bigger prize was on the horizon, one that Grady always coveted. A new governor would be chosen in 1890. Gordon could not run again. This time, a Ring candidate would not do. If the *Constitution* were to have a candidate, he must carry the farm vote while feeling an obligation to the newspaper. He must be quietly friendly.

The Alliance did not ordinarily endorse candidates by name, but it stirred up the farmers and urged them to vote their interests. Farmers had no reason to love Atlanta. Most of their enemies were creatures of urban areas, and Atlanta was home to a full share.

Grady began a search for a candidate with a farm background, thinking of William J. Northen, president of the State Agricultural Society, a former legislator, and a member of the Alliance but not one of its leaders. Northen lived in Hancock County in middle Georgia.

In the minds of some people, especially his own, Leonidas F. Livingston was also a candidate. Livingston had followed Jackson as head of the Alliance. He had been a legislator as well as president of the State Agricultural Society, but that organization was too conservative for him. Of the two men, Northen was safer.

His cultivation began. On February 14, 1889, the *Constitution* reprinted a speech he made to the State Agricultural Society, and the next day an editorial declared it broad, statesmanlike, practical, sensible, and an excellent platform upon which to run for governor. It was too early to endorse anybody, but a signal had been sent.

Grady turned personal attention upon Northen, writing him for advice on agricultural matters. The men were not strangers. Grady considered Northen under a mild obligation to him, although he never said what it was. A second letter from Grady arrived at Northen's home and it was to the point. Grady told Northen how to be elected governor. Line up with the movement to bring peace between the farmers and the commercial interests, he said. "The farmers have the sympathy of the commercial community in their efforts to organize and co-operate, but there is a danger that these two interests will find themselves in hopeless opposition unless somebody smooths the friction. The man who does it will be master of the situation."[37]

The situation was dangerous. If white farmers left the Democratic fold they would go to a third party, dividing the white vote. If Negroes swung behind the Republicans, they could win or influence elections, compromising the influence that Grady and the newspaper had contended for and won. What white farmers might do was uncertain and worrisome in 1889, and Negroes were potential trouble.

From the North came news of the Henry Cabot Lodge bill in the House of Representatives, and from Boston came the fateful invitation that sent Grady on his last trip. Agriculture obsessed him, and in the last months of 1889, his mind worked compulsively on the subject. He asked an employee in the composing room to find a farm for him to buy. The farm was not bought, but Grady began fantasizing that he owned it. He described the old-fashioned spring and oak grove, the meadows of grass and clover, the herd of Jersey cows, the frolicking colt, and the green barley in front of the house. The imaginary farm eased his mind. When pressures grew too much, he went into his office, closed the door, and ordered the office boy to tell visitors he had gone to his farm.[38]

In this state of mind, Grady went to Boston. Following his address to the Merchants' Association and the ill-advised visit to Plymouth Rock, Grady appeared for the last speech of his life before the Bay State Club, a Democratic organization in Massachusetts. The degree to which the farm issue worried him was apparent. He was hoarse and doubtless running a fever, but the professional in him took charge, and he made a beautiful talk using parts of old speeches now burned into his memory. The stenographer who took down those extemporaneous remarks must have been surprised when Grady began his well-worn hymn to the southern farmer. Politicians from rockbound New England must have marveled that Grady's art made the central part of the Elberton speech somehow fit the occasion. The southern farmer came to life for that group, which knew or cared little about him: the knight of the field with no lien on his property; the son of a loving father; the husband of a devoted wife; the father of beautiful children; the master of an immaculate home; the son of a beaming mother; and the contented beneficiary of the kind of life not found this side of the New Jerusalem.[39]

Grady did not see the election of 1890, but he had laid its groundwork and would have been satisfied with the results. Friends of the farmer seemed to take over just about everything, but the *Constitution* in fact preserved much of its influence. Governor Northen was friendly as were many Alliance members and sympathizers who controlled both houses of the Assembly. They would recall that Grady and the *Constitution* spoke well of farmers and gave money

and a building for the exchange. Such considerations were important, for men friendly to the Alliance occupied 32 of 44 seats in the
state Senate and 160 of 174 seats in the Georgia House of Representatives.[40] Men of similar views held all 10 Georgia seats in the United
States House of Representatives. The new Atlanta-area congressman was Livingston, persuaded to leave the race for governor to
run for Congress supported by the *Constitution*.

Governor Gordon became a United States senator again. Many
legislators allied with the farmers were not happy about him, for he
was identified with New South interests. The *Constitution* was not
happy either for reasons that were personal.[41] He, nevertheless,
would help Atlanta.

Most amazing of all, twenty-seven-year-old Clark Howell, Grady's protégé and his successor as managing editor of the *Constitution,* was the new Speaker of the Georgia House of Representatives.
He got the enthusiastic endorsement of the Alliance caucus in the
House, and it put him into office. With Howell in the chair and with
other friends to help, nothing bad would happen to Atlanta. The
voice of the *Constitution* would be powerful.

History records that the Alliance and the farmers' organizations
that followed it in the 1890s fell upon bad times and finally failed.
Their difficulties and circumscribed successes have been studied by
many scholars: Robert C. McMath, Jr., Michael Schwartz, Lawrence
Goodwyn, Donna A. Barnes, C. Vann Woodward, Lala Carr Steelman, Barton C. Shaw, and William F. Holmes, to name a few.[42]
Grady did not contribute to the final failure of the farmers' movement in Georgia. Before June 1888 he tried to damage the movement by refusing it publicity; but after that date, he sought not to
destroy or to thwart, but to use. Use it he did.

The farm program became a farm strategy, protecting the influence of Grady as long as he lived and the influence of the *Constitution* after his death. Atlanta continued to have an important voice in
the affairs of Georgia. Nothing suggests that Grady advanced the
plan in the first half of the decade entirely for those purposes. He
and his newspaper colleagues surely hoped that it would work.

By 1887 most Georgians knew that, except for a few people, the program did not work. It was then that Grady and the *Constitution* modified their approach. Flogging the jute trust did little for the man behind the mule, the show-cased reexamination of agricultural problems supplied nothing useful, and Grady's speeches were more entertainment than guide. After 1887 the program was not a plan but a tool, with few of its benefits devolving upon the farmer for whom it allegedly was made.

5
The Politics of Race

Racial policy was as much a part of Henry Grady's New South as the farm program but was harder to handle. Dealing with farmers, Grady faced one constituency. In matters of race, he faced three, each fractious and seeking different ends. As in so much else, politics was at the heart of Grady's program, and each of his three constituencies was a potential threat to its success. Pleasing one group, he was likely to outrage one or more of the others.

To make this awkward arrangement work, Grady had to balance the constituencies shrewdly. The opinion of Georgia whites must be deferred to. Northern opinion must be satisfied, or at least neutralized. Black Georgians, whose acquiescence was needed, threatened the balance to the extent that their plight was understood, cared about, and acted upon in the North.

Presumptions that white southerners held monolithic views about race are incorrect. Joel Williamson defines three mind-sets on the subject.[1]

A few white southerners were liberals who thought Negroes had potential but did not know what it was. They wanted black Americans to grow as far as their abilities would take them. In Georgia, Atticus G. Haygood most aptly represented liberal thought. President of Emory College, Haygood was a distinguished clergyman and later a bishop in the Methodist Episcopal Church, South.[2] The liberal group was too small to influence politics in Georgia in the electoral sense.

Grady disagreed with Haygood about race, believing that Negroes had little capacity for development. Grady's views were what Williamson calls conservative. This conservatism was both literal and figurative and involved "saving" or "conserving" the Negro by finding a place for him in society. Negroes were inferior, conservatives believed, and would remain so.

Grady never hid his low opinion of them. When he married Julia King in 1871, the couple took a wedding trip to Philadelphia to visit a bridesmaid, Julia Hart. Grady laughed at the troubles the Harts had with their white servants, unreliable pests full of pretenses, likely to throw up their jobs with little or no notice. "They put to shame the good natured laziness and stupid incapacity of our own precious ethiopians." Grady believed that about nineteen-twentieths of the intelligence in the South belonged to white people.[3]

To him, slavery had provided a not-altogether-bad place for Negroes, even though he said he was glad that a wise Providence overruled the Confederate army and ended it. To Georgia audiences, he said slave life made the plantation Negro the happiest worker in the world. The goodness of southern masters made the system tolerable, and Grady suspected that Negroes would never see such contentment again.[4]

In the space of about four minutes, he once told a white audience that Negroes were a people of proven incapacity; that they were simple, credulous, and impulsive. Their credulity was easily played upon, their cupidity tempted, their impulses misdirected, and their passions inflamed. Whites were the superior race, Grady said. "This is the declaration of no new truth. It has abided forever in the marrow of our bones, and shall run forever with the blood that feeds Anglo-Saxon hearts."[5]

These views did not in his own time mark Grady as an intolerant man. Many people held such ideas, and Grady held them more moderately than most. Even some black people thought he was a kindly person.

Grady's ideas were mild indeed compared to the ones held by a third category of southern whites whom Williamson calls radicals.

Radicals believed that when the federal government freed blacks, they began to turn into barbarians. Some radicals doubted whether there was even a place for them in America. They believed that only stringent discipline could control the new barbarians, therefore they endorsed lynchings and beatings. Grady was aware that many Georgians held these views, but neither he nor anybody else knew how many. Williamson says that all across the South, radicalism began increasing about 1889. It increased in Georgia that year, causing Grady no end of problems and helping to send him to his death.

Grady fashioned a policy to fit all of his constituencies: white Georgians, black Georgians, northerners. The fit was awkward and seldom in balance, and it always had him on edge, but it was the best he could do.

Local liberals were not a worry, but both white conservatives and radicals must believe that neither he nor the Atlanta *Constitution* wanted changes in the social order. The coverage of the newspaper and its editorial voice depicted the inferiority of the Negro race, while saying that some Negroes were doing well.

Black Georgians had a passive role so threatening that they could unhinge his plan, a possibility never far from his mind. Grady expected blacks to submit to the social order and to work like dervishes to improve their lots individually if not as a race. He knew that many northerners were concerned about their well-being, and bad treatment, publicized in the North, could produce northern interference in southern affairs. Blacks thus had the power to call down troubles. Although circumstances forced many black citizens to go along with Grady's scheme, many Negro leaders never accepted the arrangement and said so.

In the North, the mainstream of the Republican party was committed to civil rights for Negroes, particularly the right to vote. Perhaps Republicans were sincere, but they were also self-interested. When Negroes voted in the South, they often voted Republican. If the white vote split on issues or personalities and Negroes voted in numbers, the collapse of Grady's political system was more than a possibility. Unscrupulous white politicians could buy or seduce the black vote, Grady believed, making the outcome of every election uncertain. The black vote, swinging violently between one faction of whites and another, would wreck the system. "[I]t is the loosed cannon on the storm-tossed ship."[6]

Paul M. Gaston notes a phenomenon common to most New South leaders, who liked to claim that objectives were accomplished long before they were. Grady announced prosperity in agriculture while farmers still lived in fear of the lien collector, and he and others proclaimed the industrialization of the South by 1886, an inappropriately early date. In that same year he notified the world that the South had kept faith with the black man. "Faith will be kept with him in the future, if the South holds her reason and integrity." Three years later, Grady removed the qualification in that assertion before a national audience in a speech widely reprinted: "[W]e treat the negro fairly, measuring to him justice in the fullness the strong should give to the weak." The *Constitution* proclaimed that southern Negroes were satisfied. No racial troubles or agitations existed in Georgia, or anything bordering on them, the newspaper said, unaware that blacks and white radicals would soon create scenes making liars out of people who said such things.[7]

Apparently Grady felt he must explain why southerners treated black people so well:

During the Civil War, slaves could have disbanded the Confederate army by rioting at home. Threats to families and properties of southern soldiers would have done in an instant what northern military effort took four years to do. Slaves did not riot. Instead, they were loving and caring custodians of the dependents left behind. The South must now treat Negroes justly to repay the debt.[8]

Many white southerners liked what Grady said, and many northerners were impressed by it, but Negroes saw it differently. The Cleveland *Gazette*, a black newspaper in Ohio, said that Grady depicted the Negro as the most wonderful creature of the age, but that his pictures were unreal. "If eulogy and praise were all that is necessary in the restoration of man to his rightful and normal state, then Mr. Grady has carried his point, but deeds only will do this, and this has not yet been done." A black publication in Augusta, Georgia, was more direct. "In the future the intelligent Negro will not accept gushing platitudes for friendship. He'll know his friends by their deeds; he has had enough of hypocritical professions, he now demands something substantial." To Editor W. B. Townsend of *The Advocate,* a black newspaper in Leavenworth, Kansas, the faithful slave probably was a good custodian, but if so, the Negro never had anything for it. "[A]ll we have ever received for our care of these women and children is curses, denunciation, pilfering and murder."[9] These objections went mostly unheard in white Georgia, and Grady never swerved from his interesting interpretation of history.

In a campaign to show that the southern Negro fared well, the *Constitution* fastened upon all signs of mistreatment in the North. When whites in Felicity, Ohio, shut blacks out of white schools, the newspaper leapt upon the story, as it did when white barbers in Auburn, New York, refused to shave a black clergyman.[10]

The newspaper could say with truth that a few Negroes were thriving. In 1888 blacks in Georgia paid taxes on property worth nine million dollars, and the *Constitution* said that if they had cheated on taxes as white people did, twelve would have been a true figure. Black people acquired some land, fulfilling for a few a deeply felt need. By 1880 they had 586,664 acres, or 1.6 percent of what was available. In Atlanta in 1889, Negroes controlled 287 firms or organizations. In 1887 in Augusta, they controlled more than one hundred. The city directory of Macon in 1882 lists Negroes in forty-seven occupations.[11]

A famous study of South Carolina blacks shows that positive changes occurred during this difficult period which were not reversed by the unsympathetic nature of the times. Negroes possessed theoretical equality before the law although they were unable to enjoy it fully; yet it stood as a beacon. Reconstruction brought free public schools, and although full of imperfections, every southern state had them. Education opened future opportunities to some Negro children. The Negro church became a permanent institution.[12]

Yet despite spotty progress for a minority and Grady's protestations of fair and just treatment, the plight of Georgia Negroes was poor. White Georgians generally disapproved when they got together for a meeting or convention unless it was a church affair concerned only with religion. Breasting disapproval, Georgia blacks met three times in six years to state their grievances in uncowed terms.[13] The grievances matched exactly what actually was happening in Georgia, an inconvenient fact that convicts Grady of disrespect for truth when he claimed that whites kept faith with the Negro and meted out justice. Confirmation that the grievances were true was published over and over in Grady's own newspaper.

Two black leaders stood out at the Georgia conventions of protest. The Reverend William J. White was pastor of Harmony Baptist Church in Augusta but was more than a clergyman. He was the son of a white planter and a black-Indian mother, born in Elbert County in 1831. By the 1880s he had made a mark as an educator. In Augusta, he founded the Augusta Baptist Institute; it moved to Atlanta and became Morehouse College. He was president of the Georgia Baptist Sunday School Convention. After 1880 he was editor of the *Georgia Baptist,* published in Augusta in its own printshop, a paper on a sound footing that lasted until 1913. He was a delegate to the Republican National Convention in 1888. White was reasonably militant and during the 1880s was important at all three of the statewide gatherings of blacks.[14]

William A. Pledger possibly was more militant than White. Born a slave near Jonesboro, Georgia, to a planter father and a slave mother, he attended Atlanta University but dropped out for lack of money. He was first noticed as a waiter in the dining room at the Kimball House in Atlanta. He moved to Athens where he was coeditor of the Athens *Blade* and later was associated with two other black newspapers in Atlanta. Although his formal education was incomplete, Pledger was a superb orator and an effective writer. He was influential in the Georgia Republican party. Pledger was a significant figure at the 1888 and 1889 protest conventions and organized the latter.[15]

As a citizen of Augusta, White knew Martin V. Calvin, a white politician who was a former principal of the Augusta Free School, a sometime principal of Houghton Institute, and a powerful man in the Augusta school system. In 1882, the year before the first protest convention met, Calvin was elected to the Georgia House of Representatives and upon entry became chairman of the House Committee on Education.[16] Instantly, he was a power in education all over the state and without delay struck terror into the hearts of black people.

In the House, he sponsored what became known as the Calvin Division Bill. The Georgia constitution of 1868 created free public schools and the constitution of 1877 continued them. Possibly one-fifth of the school money went for black schools, whereas black Georgians owned only about one-fortieth of the taxable property in the state. Calvin wanted to allocate money to black and white schools in the proportion collected from each race. One-fortieth would stretch thin over 95,800 black students. The remainder would spread thicker over 165,200 white children.[17]

To Martin V. Calvin goes credit for the first black protest meeting of the decade. White called delegates to meet in Atlanta on December 12, 1883, to talk about schools. Four hundred black men answered the summons, and a rigorous convention ensued. The delegates asked Gustavus J. Orr, state school commissioner, to appear to shed light upon conditions.[18] Orr could reassure the convention but little.

Uncompromising facts had to be faced. All over Georgia, schools were supposed to run six months a year but usually ran three. County school commissioners decided how much each teacher was worth and paid him or her two-thirds of the sum, leaving the teacher to get the rest from parents who often did not pay. The system was said to drive off the best teachers. The convention asked the legislature to make the whole system free and to give black schools money in proportion to their numbers of students. It also asked for federal help.[19]

The Atlanta *Constitution* took the 1883 convention lightly. Grady's reporter had an eye for bizarre occurrences and unusual or undignified behavior. White rapped a stick with a ram's horn handle to call the meeting to order. Singing the Doxology as part of opening devotions, 400 black males raised their hats as they sang the last sentence, "Praise Father, Son, and Holy Ghost." An unholy row developed over electing a temporary chairman. Disagreement broke out over calling the roll and over which roll to call. A two-hour wrangle occurred over committee appointments, and officers were elected amid a tumultuous scene. "They yelled and howled and tore the air, stamped and beat on the desks, and it seemed that there was blood on the moon, but at last quiet was restored." The *Constitution* said its readers got a realistic account of the proceedings "as far as there were any proceedings."[20]

Petitions to the General Assembly for proportional division of school funds fell upon deaf ears, and little came from the federal government, but the Calvin Division Bill never became law. Blacks knew such measures could come up again. "A man might just as well say he wont die next year because he has lived to see this one," said a black citizen in Augusta. Some people believed that white people were not interested in black education. They were never more penurious than when called upon to help a fund to benefit black children.[21]

When a second protest convention met in Macon in 1888, public school grievances had expanded to include Atlanta University. The university was a private institution for blacks founded by northern money, chartered in 1867, and opening classes in 1869. In the 1870s, the legislature appropriated $8,000 a year for it, half the interest on the grant received under the Morrill Act of 1862. The University of Georgia in Athens also got $8,000. Year after year, the legislature continued the allocations. The governor regularly appointed a Board of Visitors to inspect Atlanta University, and over the years, the Visitors gave it favorable evaluations.

In 1887, however, they noticed a few white students going to school there, seven to fourteen of them, all children of professors except one. Governor Gordon notified the legislature, and the reaction was predictable. Representative W. C. Glenn of Dalton presented a bill to cut off the money and to punish the teachers. The black press said that the teachers were about to go to the chain gang, and the measure was amended to remove its harsher provisions. The money itself was no token. Operating expenses were $32,000 a year, of which $16,000 came from tuitions and fees, $8,000 from the state appropriation, and $8,000 from northern benefactors.[22]

Representative Glenn never was ranked among the demagogues in the Georgia House. He was a moderate and thoughtful man from the high hills of Georgia where the black population was thinner than in other parts of the state. The *Constitution* occasionally praised him.²³ His restrained speech and demeanor suggested that he reflected the thinking of moderate white persons who would entertain no integration of the races, even in private schools. The Glenn bill passed the House with two dissenting votes from black members. It passed the Senate in amended form and was signed by Governor Gordon.

Black reaction was vigorous. Horace Bumstead, a professor and financial officer of Atlanta University and after 1888 its chief administrative officer, set out for the North to raise the lost $8,000. John H. Deveaux, editor and business manager of the Savannah *Tribune,* assailed the Glenn bill, calling it infamous, a disgrace, unconstitutional, unnecessary, iniquitous, a destructive blow, and a monstrosity. "It is a step backward for Georgia and she will receive merited contempt for her action." Atlanta blacks spoke through their church publications. "We have stood the partiality of the laws of Georgia long enough. We are taxed to support a school of technology for the white children of the State [today the Georgia Institute of Technology], which will not allow a colored tax-payer's child to enter, and yet the Southern people are the Negro's best friend. We want no such friendship."²⁴

Black people were divided about the value of integrated schools, and many supported segregation until such time as Negroes could enter white institutions as equals. Even so, the Glenn bill was offensive on two counts: it affronted Negro people generally, and the money belonged to blacks, reserved for them by the federal government. Even the state government of Georgia knew that: it withheld the $8,000 until Atlanta University put the white children out, something it never did; then some three years later the state transferred the money to the Industrial College for Negroes in Savannah, a segregated institution created in part to receive it.

The black grievances catalogued at the Macon convention comprised a long list and included bad treatment on public accommodations, especially trains. The convention reproved "in unmeasured terms" the practice of selling first-class tickets to Negroes, then forcing them to sit in inferior seats. The Federal Civil Rights Act of 1875 forbade the separation of the races on railroads, but eight years later the Supreme Court declared the act unconstitutional. Grady applauded the court, saying that Negroes desired their own carriages as long as they were protected from disorderly persons.[25]

Georgia law mandated separate but equal coaches for blacks, but the requirement was expensive. Four coaches were needed to serve both races: two first-class cars and two second-class ones. Georgia railroads seldom compartmentalized cars in those days. Railroads often ignored the law and sometimes put blacks holding first-class tickets into the smoking car, where no white women were present but where people complained of foul odors. More often, conductors put Negroes with first-class tickets into second-class coaches. If they complained too much, they were put off the train.

Grady told a national audience that such occurrences were not general. With a few exceptions, railroads lived up to the law. "Where they fail," he said, "they quickly feel the weight of public opinion, and shock the sense of public justice." Grady's comment drew hoots of derision from a black newspaperman familiar with Georgia. To him Grady told "as unqualified a falsehood as an honest man, zealous to justify a bad cause, ever voluntarily swore to. The accommodation given to colored travellers in the South is as infamous an outrage as was ever tamely submitted to by any class of people in any civilized community."[26]

Instance after instance indicates that the black newspaperman was correct. The Savannah, Florida, and Western Railroad was one of the better roads from the black man's point of view, yet black travelers were never sure what to expect. In mid-July 1887 a well-dressed Negro woman and her son got aboard a train in Jacksonville, Florida. Holding first-class tickets, they took seats in the only first-class coach on the train. At Waycross, Georgia, white men ordered her into an all-black car. She refused to budge. At the next station, a white man telegraphed ahead to Jesup, Georgia, and when the train got there, seven or eight people got aboard and ordered her farther back into the train. She refused again but got up to look for the conductor, who had disappeared. The men, calling themselves the "committee," dragged her toward the door as she called for help. She held onto the door and at that moment the train started moving and the "committee" scampered off, vowing to get the "damned wench" some day. Other white men in the car did nothing. "[W]here was the conductor during this outrage on one of his passengers?" the Savannah *Tribune* wanted to know. The *Tribune* said the incident disgraced the "New South." Such occurrences had counterparts throughout the decade, with white people who took notice saying they were atypical.[27]

Delegates in Macon were well aware that white people restricted black participation in government at almost all levels. For the most part they were shut out from jury service. Blacks had served routinely during Reconstruction and the years following, but in the 1880s, county governments blocked them openly. Federal officials were more likely to call Negroes for jury service than were state officials. In 1885 Grady made a wild claim. "[T]he last remaining prejudice against him [the Negro] in the jury-box has passed away." The Macon convention saw matters differently. Of 137 counties in Georgia, blacks did jury service in fewer than seven. They served mostly in urban counties although there were problems even there.[28]

They were crudely rebuffed in rural areas. In Dodge County [Eastman] in 1888, jury commissioners got a petition from Negro citizens asking that their names be included in a forthcoming revision of the lists. On the evening of August 23, 1888, between 11 P.M. and midnight, forty or more armed white men beset the clerk of Superior Court and demanded the boxes, the jury list, and the jury book. They started a fire a few hundred yards from the courthouse and burned every scrap of paper, leaving the county temporarily without any jury.[29]

Two other factors reduced participation in government. Negroes were virtually shut out of the legislature, and during the latter part of the decade, only two served there. Worse, white men found ways to discourage blacks from voting in all elections except a few local ones. The process worked increasingly well for whites. Approval of the Reconstruction amendments gave Negroes the ballot, and they used it heavily for a time, but the 1880s marked the transition between heavy black voting and slackened participation.

Whites used an ingenious mechanism to assure that blacks voted in fewer numbers. The state constitution of 1868 created a poll tax of one dollar per year, but its collection was suspended for a time while black voting built up. The constitution of 1877 continued the tax but made it cumulative. It cost one dollar a year to vote, and even in years when there was no election, the tax accumulated. If a man were six years behind, he paid six dollars before he could cast a ballot. The cumulative tax was the most effective bar to voting ever devised short of blocking blacks from the polls entirely. It also reduced voting by poor white people. Colquitt's gubernatorial election in 1880 was the last in Georgia for eighty years in which a majority of blacks voted.[30]

J. Morgan Kousser has charted the changes in voter participation in Georgia in the 1880s. The degree to which the low numbers are due to the poll tax cannot be stated, but the figures tell a story of decline. In the 1880 presidential election, 48.8 percent of the total Georgia electorate voted compared to 65.4 percent in the rest of the South. By 1888 the turnout in Georgia was down to 37.3 percent while rising slightly in the rest of the South. Decline in black voting was dramatic. In 1880, 39 percent of the black electorate in Georgia voted. Eight years later, 19 percent did.[31]

Blacks believed that even when they voted their ballots did not get a true count. Pledger acknowledged that white men could argue that Negroes still had the vote. There were no recent outrages to point to. What had happened, he said, was that blacks abstained except in rare instances or in local elections on such subjects as prohibition or fence laws. They knew the consequences of taking part in other contests. In addition, white candidates broke promises to black voters, lessening their appetite for the process. A black man in Savannah wrote: "[L]ike 'our best friends' always do when elections are over the Negro like Rip Van Winkle, is soon forgotten."[32]

The grievances troubling black Georgians most heavily were those involving safety of life and limb. Nine of ten people confined in the penal system of Georgia were black, and confinement was regarded as living death. The system used in Georgia was found in every southern state and was controversial everywhere.

General Sherman on his march to sea had wrecked the Georgia state penitentiary, a facility that never held blacks in large numbers in any event, since punishment under slavery was usually done on plantations. After the war, the state found a new method of dealing with criminals. It leased them to bidders for whom they were a bargain. Grady figured that it cost $22 a year to keep a convict whose work was worth at least $100. Grady conceded that sometimes convicts got into the wrong hands but said that the system was probably the best one available. If the state had regular penitentiaries, he said, Negro convicts would not be better off. The *Constitution* said it favored any plan to improve matters, but that abuses tended to be errors in management rather than faults in the system. Penal laws, after all, were made to protect society.[33]

Edward L. Ayers says that lease convict labor became a symbol, perhaps even a cliché, of the New South. To blacks and some whites, it symbolized injustice and inhumanity. Whereas the activities of mobs might be explained as temporary aberrations, the death and suffering caused by the lease system had the approval, or at least the acquiescence, of the "leading men" of the South.[34]

Horrible brutalities occurred in convict camps, usually situated in isolated places out of public view. They drew protests from President Haygood of Emory College, from the leader of the Independents, Dr. Felton, and from other people. One case involved Robert Watson, a seventeen-year-old white boy convicted of a stabbing. He was in Dougherty County, in southwest Georgia, in one of the smaller camps. Watson became sick and unable to do strenuous labor, so he was put to chopping cotton, working around young cotton stalks with a hoe. His work was poor, so he was beaten first by a white supervisor, then a second and third time the same day by a Negro whipping boss. Watson was in critical condition when his mother arrived to visit and to bring food. She was turned away and the food destroyed. Watson died. The facts are authentic, supplied by guards and the whipping boss.[35]

The question of the convicts was sensitive in the editorial offices of the *Constitution* because two members of the Atlanta Ring had made money from them. John B. Gordon had leased convicts for his farm on the Flint River in Taylor County, although he got out of the convict business and thereafter denounced it. Senator Brown, one of the richest men in Atlanta, used convicts in his numerous enterprises, attracting the scorn of black leaders: "[W]e fail to understand why even a United States Senator should be allowed to swell his millions by such a hideous traffic."[36]

A mutiny took place in Dade County in 1886 at Brown's Dade Coal Company, which tells something about how the camp was run, how prisoners were treated, and what the attitude of the *Constitution* was. The Dade camp never was accused of being one of the worst in Georgia.

Dade Coal was in the northwestern corner of Georgia in the mountains, so inaccessible that to get there from Atlanta a person took a train to Chattanooga and worked downward. Some of the convicts labored in mines and others worked in the coke plant. Some time before the mutiny broke out, Grady described the camp. The men were grouped together in squads shackled to one chain watched by a guard who was armed. At night they were in a sleeping room in the stockade. The chain, with ankle shackles locked to it, stretched from bunk to bunk. The prisoners ate well and had a good health record.[37]

On July 12, 1886, about 120 convicts at the coke oven refused to work, shutting themselves up in their dormitory. The coke plant was in a valley between mountain ridges, along with machine shops, the oven and dumping chutes, and the sleeping room. The stockade stood eight feet high with fifteen or twenty guards atop it. The guards had shotguns loaded with buckshot, repeating rifles, and heavy navy pistols. Once the mutiny was underway, a telegram went to Governor McDaniel in Atlanta, and McDaniel sent three supervisors, including John R. Towers, the senior state penitentiary official, with orders to starve the prisoners out. A fourth man also went, one of Grady's reporters.

Three days later as Grady's man sat at a pine camp table writing his account, the air rang with the sound of the anvil as a blacksmith fastened the last prisoner to the squad chain. The mutiny had just been broken. While it was going on, the prisoners, nine-tenths of them black, passed notes from the dormitory to camp supervisors. The convicts wanted whippings and floggings stopped, better food, and the replacement of some of their disciplinarians. Towers would hear none of it.

At length the prisoners surrendered, coming out of the dormitory one by one, the leaders coming last. As Grady's correspondent wrote his story, the camp waited for the leaders to be whipped. The reporter was apparently bemused, calling the whippings a "special matinee" which would disturb the atmosphere of the camp considerably. The leaders screamed and begged as they were flogged. Other matinees were forthcoming on following days.[38]

Discussion of leasing became so general that on September 8, 1887, the state began an investigation. Governor Gordon got credit for the inquiry, and it won approbation for him among black Georgians. The hearings went on for two months under two Atlanta lawyers, Hoke Smith and George Hillyer, the prohibitionist and former mayor. Gordon attended and presided over some sessions, which became interesting as he questioned some of his former partners in the leasing business. Among those interrogated was Senator Brown. Relations between Gordon and Brown were never more icy. Gordon certainly enjoyed the senator's discomfiture, but Brown returned as good as he got, pointing out that every whipping boss was approved in advance of appointment by the governor; therefore they were state officials. Whippings were state business, not his.[39] The claim was too facile to be taken seriously, but Brown had shown he should not be tampered with.

When the investigation was over, some abuses had been discovered and Gordon fined the companies. The system itself was not disturbed, and conditions remained about as they had been. The legislature authorized the governor to reduce the sentences of some convicts under a formula. Blacks continued to see the system as brutal and weighted against themselves. "The poor hungry colored man who steals a piece of meat to satisfy his appetite, is an atrocious villain and should be sent to the coal mine. The white man who steals a thousand dollars belonging to the widows and orphans, is a highly respectable citizen and should be sent to the legislature."[40]

Grady and the *Constitution* occasionally showed compassion for individuals under sentence of law, but their approach to both the concept and the practice of criminal justice ranged from the flippant to the draconian. When Grady was twenty-seven years old and a reporter, he covered about a dozen hangings one spring and summer. He viewed them lightly as he wrote the headlines that went over his stories: "Jumping Jack"; "Nicked in the Neck"; "The Aerial Waltz"; "The Latest Noose." His admired mathematics professor at the University of Georgia, Williams Rutherford, wrote Grady a sober letter: "No man ever yet gained a reputation for a writer and established a character for greatness who wrote in the style which I am now criticizing. . . . My young friend you are making a grievous mistake."[41]

Grady did not cover hangings after that but apparently remained fascinated by them. As managing editor, he sent reporters or arranged correspondence to cover almost every hanging in Georgia and a good many elsewhere. Between December 15, 1885, and December 15, 1889, four years of Grady's greatest maturity as managing editor, he printed accounts of approximately one hundred.

Sometimes criminals broke down emotionally on the gallows; the rope broke or the feet of the condemned person hit the ground, bungling the job; and once, an excited mob broke through to the gallows and clipped the fingernails of the hanged man for souvenirs. Whatever happened, the *Constitution* reported it under headlines as bad as the ones Grady wrote personally: "The Rope Necklace"; "Dacey's Drop"; "By the Neck"; "Nathan Mosely's Taking Off"; "Through the Trap"; "Neck Wringings." "[P]eople still believe that a painful and disgraceful death is the proper penalty for a murderer," said the *Constitution*. The purpose was to make an example so terrible that others would avoid crime.[42]

Most of the people executed legally in Georgia were black, and

Negroes had grave doubts about the courts, but they were more horrified by lynchings where no due process existed. Pledger said that Negroes had been murdered by lynchers from one end of the state to the other, and the Macon convention denounced the practice as "unlawful and inhuman."[43]

The practice spread in the 1880s. Grady's newspaper makes it clear not only that lynching was common but that a great part of the white population justified it in some instances. Some New South newspaper editors disapproved of it. In Charleston, Dawson had grave doubts and in Augusta, Walsh was ahead of his readers in opposition.

Editorially, the *Constitution* was mostly silent. On rare occasions when it denounced lynching, it did so in such qualified form that it was unconvincing. A case in point involved Henry Pope, twice convicted of raping Minnie Kendrick, a sixteen-year-old white girl living near Summerville in Chattooga County. Governor Gordon delayed legal execution because Pope possibly had a late-appearing alibi. Nevertheless, a mob took Pope from his jail cell and hanged him on a banister of the Chattooga County courthouse. "[W]hile a great many good people of the county regret the triumph of mob law, yet nearly all feel that Henry Pope deserved his fate," said Grady's reporter. Editorially, the *Constitution* said that it disapproved of lynchings, but if there ever were justification, the Pope case was it. "[L]et every man think for a moment what he would do, under similar circumstances, if one of his own kindred or neighbors was in the condition of Miss Kendrick." The Savannah *Tribune* was infuriated. If Pope were guilty, he would have been hanged legally.[44]

Scholars studying lynching have suggested a number of causes for it, but Ayers, after much investigation, believes that the "triggers of lynching, for all the attention devoted to it by contemporaries, sociologists, and historians, are still not known," a conclusion that seems justified. Jacquelyn Dowd Hall believes that "the mysterious recesses of sex and race" provided the fuel but not the spark for lynching.[45] Not all instances avenged the alleged crime of rape, but in the 1880s in Georgia, they were the ones receiving most attention.

While the editorial page of the *Constitution* remained mostly quiet, its news columns did not, nor were they opinion free. Staff copy condoned the practice. Occasionally, the newspaper identified a person to be killed, sent a reporter to interview him and witness the event, then printed an account.

Mrs. Sarah Bush, a farmer's wife living near Redan, a village of seventy-five inhabitants in DeKalb County, was raped by a black man who at first was not identified. "Lynching Too Good For the Black Miscreant Who Assaulted Mrs. Bush," said the *Constitution* headline. "He Will Be Lynched." Reuben Hudson was captured in the closet of a train bound for Covington and taken back to Redan. The *Constitution* reporter saw the mob assemble in front of Jones and Johnson's store at Redan, ready to hang Hudson when W. P. Johnson, one of the proprietors, insisted that Mrs. Bush be brought to identify the suspect. She said Hudson was the man. Johnson tried to insist that Hudson face trial by law and was making progress when Dr. George Goldsmith of nearby Stone Mountain came up on a horse, took control and led the mob to a grove. Hudson died there on a hickory tree. Throngs of people appeared to see the corpse, including the county coroner who assembled a jury on the spot. No witnesses were found, although the *Constitution* reporter said persons on the jury helped do the lynching. The verdict was suicide. "The black fiend . . . has had justice meted out to him," said the reporter.[46]

Incendiary headlines were common. "Ready For Lynching," said one in 1887, referring to Ross Griffith of Lexington, Georgia, a black printer at the Oglethorpe *Echo*. Griffith was accused of raping a spinster, aged about forty, after slipping into her room in the dead of night. "The people are very indignant, and it is thought that he will be lynched tonight," said the *Constitution*. A mob seized Griffith and whipped him with a buggy trace until he no longer felt the blows; it took him to the steeple of the courthouse, put a rope around his neck, and was about to throw him off when the sheriff appeared and took him to jail. A *Constitution* reporter interviewed Griffith just before another mob killed him. A leading white citizen of Lexington, a member of the state legislature who normally disapproved of such things, thought killing Griffith was all right.

"Such administration of justice is almost a necessity in the country and small towns where our men are forced to leave the women more or less exposed."[47]

Coverage reflects the relative frequency of lynchings, and the news copy, especially the headlines, seems frivolous. Many of the latter make light of, acquiesce in, suggest, or condone the practice: "Lynching At Millen. A Negro Brute Taken from a Train and Hung"; "The Triple Trapeze. Three Negroes Hung to a Limb of a Tree"; "Lynched for His Crime. The Merited Fate of a Black Villain"; "Two Minutes to Pray Before a Rope Dislocates Their Vertabrae"; "This One Ought to Swing." A delegate in Macon wondered why white men bothered to lynch. "They had the court house, the law, the judge, the lawyers, the handcuffs and the rope, and I don't see why they didn't hang us by law."[48]

In every way, 1889 was the worst year of Grady's life. Worried about money and Mrs. Grady's miscarriage, exhausted by efforts to mollify the farmers, affected by strains on old friendships, he also had race to torment him. If Grady were not to be regarded as a liar, the Negro in the South must be understood as content; but the Atlanta and Macon conventions, and especially the latter with its dignified statement of grievances, showed that blacks were anything but happy. The *Constitution* could and did produce occasional blacks who said that everything was all right, but their testimony was unconvincing. Some blacks were militant, including White and Pledger, but most did not know what to do. The editor of the *Weekly Sentinel* at Augusta was unhappy but thought that hotheads should cool down. "The colored people are not in a position to win by brute force. . . . The weak must be more diplomatic than the strong. 'Tis better to conciliate, than to force."[49]

Grady had long known that "every mistake made and every error fallen into" damaged the reputation of the South. Men in the North were ready to turn upon the region, not faceless and unknown men but persons of ability and reputation in Congress. Some of their names were awesome: Nelson W. Aldrich, William B. Allison, James G. Blaine, Henry W. Blair, Joe Cannon, William E. Chandler, George F. Edmunds, George Frisbie Hoar, John J. Ingalls, Thomas

B. Reed, John Sherman, and John C. Spooner. They also included a semidistinguished United States senator named Benjamin Harrison who, as president-elect of the United States, said enough about Negro rights to suggest that Republicans meant business about voting. Harrison's words encouraged Henry Cabot Lodge. Blacks expected a great deal from Harrison,[50] and they came to expect much of Lodge.

Lodge was a dandy, thirty-six years old when he entered the House of Representatives in 1887, member of a wealthy Massachusetts family, and a former history instructor at Harvard. He entered the House with his eye upon the Senate seat once held by Charles Sumner, and he needed a reputation quickly. Blacks in the South were counted in the population that determined how many seats in the House of Representatives each state got, although few voted in House races. Lodge produced figures showing that two votes cast by southerners, virtually all white, were worth five cast in the North. As chairman of the Elections Committee of the House, he worked on a corrective measure, and his bill appeared likely to come up in 1890.[51]

By February 1889 alarm was hitting the editorial offices of the *Constitution,* and there was talk of federal soldiers at the polls to supervise federal elections in the South, the kind of action that could wreck politics.[52] Grady's national reputation was at risk; because he proclaimed that race relations were excellent, his credibility depended upon circumstances beyond his control. Racial troubles would embarrass him.

Bad problems were about to begin. Newspapers began carrying accounts of Negro riots, many of them on trains. An occasional story told of Negroes organizing to ask for better conditions. During the summer of 1889, a near-lunatic in Liberty County on the Georgia coast claimed to be the Messiah, causing black people to leave their work in droves in order to ascend with him into heaven on August 16. In a panicky lapse of judgment, the *Constitution* said that these black people had fallen into barbarism as a matter of choice. The newspaper said that of all the black people in Georgia whom it knew, only one realized his duty and responsibility as a citizen.[53] Grady did not write those comments, but they undercut his larger argument that blacks had both justice and a place in the South.

Embarrassments arose in Grady's backyard. On June 28 President Harrison appointed John R. Lewis as postmaster of Atlanta. Lewis was well respected, a white Republican and a former officer of the Union army who lost his left arm at the Battle of the Wilderness. He settled in Atlanta after the war and established the Atlanta Rubber Company.

Exactly one week after Lewis's appointment, a black man named C. C. Penny passed a civil service examination and applied for a position in the post office. Atlanta University had recently graduated Penny. Lewis had two places to fill, one in the registered mail department and the other in money order. Only two qualified people had applied, one black and one white, so Lewis put the white person in money order where there was frequent contact with the public, and Penny went to registered mail where there was little. In registered mail, however, Miss A. V. Lyons worked with her father and supervisor, Nathan Lyons. The Lyonses were white. When Penny appeared for work, Lewis took him into the registered letter room and introduced him, whereupon Lyons took Lewis by the arm and led him into an adjoining room in great anger. He did not wish Penny to meet his daughter at all, and he asked that Penny's installation be delayed a day so that he and Miss Lyons could depart. Lewis refused, later saying that he did not write the civil service act but that he had to follow it.

Word spread that a black man was assigned to work with a white woman, and during that first afternoon, two hundred of Lyons's friends came to the post office with advice and condolences. A reporter told how Penny looked: "All descriptions of the negro have not painted his skin black enough—once he would have been called a greasy black." Editorially, the *Constitution* said that Lewis had made a mistake. "The appointment is the only one in the entire office in which the appointee was brought into intimate and direct association with a young white lady."[54]

The matter was discussed in the streets and in hotel corridors, and mail carriers on their routes were hectored by citizens who wished there were two post offices so they could avoid the one where Penny worked. Lyons and his daughter resigned. The *Constitution* said that Lewis was the most unpopular man in the city.[55]

The unpopularity grew and a few evenings later produced a street demonstration against Lewis and A. E. Buck, principal Republican dispenser of patronage in the area. A leader in the demonstration was George Daniel Hall, a hotheaded Atlantan who had spent most of his life working for his family's tobacconist business on Luckie Street, but who for a time had worked for the Railway Mail Service.

Shortly before eight on the evening of the demonstration, a scaffold went up near the corner of Marietta Street, and people gathered, eight to ten thousand of them out of a population of 65,000. Straw effigies of Lewis and Buck swung on the scaffold and were set afire. The Salvation Army appeared to conduct a missionary service, and it was remarked that the Army had not been complimented by so large an audience in quite a while.[56]

The crowd went away leaving the *Constitution* worried that the incident was one of the damaging errors of which Grady had spoken. The postmaster general in Washington would hear of it from Lewis, and word would move out through the Republican network. The newspaper deplored the demonstration and expressed the belief that attempts to make it a sectional issue would not succeed.[57]

The matter would not die, however. One of the things that the leaders of the demonstration wanted was the expulsion of Lewis from the Capital City Club, a prestigious organization made up of leaders in the Atlanta business community. Few of the demonstrators had credentials enough to get them past the front door at the club, but a move nevertheless started to put Lewis out. A committee of five looked into allegations against him.

At length, Lewis wrote a twenty-page defense and answered questions orally. He had once ridden in a carriage with a Negro but he was a black professor to whom he had given a ride on a stormy day. Asked about social equality, Lewis reportedly rose from his chair and said with emphasis: "There is no man living, even though

he be southern born and bred, who is further from believing in social equality between the races, in any shape or any form, than I
am." The committee concluded that the charges against Lewis were
unproved. The full club accepted its report by a vote of thirty-nine
to seven with Grady not voting, doubtless absent and worried about
a more serious matter.[58]

About the time the Capital City Club began looking into the
charges against Lewis, a Negro named Warren Powell was lynched
in East Point, a suburb of Atlanta. Powell allegedly had raped or attempted to rape a white schoolgirl. Hanged to a post oak sapling, his
body was on view for many hours with crowds of people, white and
black, milling about. At length the body came down, an inquest said
Powell was killed by persons unknown, and the corpse was reportedly sent off to a medical school.

Blacks in East Point had no plan of action, but some of them gathered in groups on the streets where one of their number, Jake Conley, urged that the mayor and two bailiffs be killed and that the town
be burned. The mayor sent to Atlanta for a stand of Winchester rifles, and arriving by train, they were set up in the railway station.
The blacks began to disperse.

Rumors said that in the dark of night, they would reassemble in a
Negro church or schoolhouse but by 10:30 in the evening, nothing
had happened. A few minutes thereafter, a gawky white man approached E. C. Bruffey, one of Grady's three news reporters on the
scene and a veteran at the *Constitution*, and said: "Them negroes is
never coming here and we won't have any fun. If you want to see
some fun, however, just come with me." Five or six white men took
off to find Conley's home and beat him.

Coming upon a house, the leader pounded the door and threatened to kick it in. He entered the house holding a rifle in one hand
and a pistol in the other, demanding to know where Conley was.
Two Negro men and several women in the room denied knowing,
and the men were taken into the yard. "Sam, bring that buggy whip
here, and bring it quick," the leader said. A limber whip was produced, and the leader began to flog one of the men, who was bare to
the waist. The beaten man screamed in pain. "Make that noise again

and I'll kill you." A pistol was shoved into the man's face. The second Negro was also whipped.

The group moved away from the house, whipping all Negroes encountered in the road and dragging other men from their homes. They wore out two buggy whips during the evening.[59] Some Negroes hid under houses or in the weeds, but the white men beat at least fourteen people.

Bruffey's account appeared in the *Constitution* the following morning and was the talk of Atlanta and East Point. Governor Gordon arrived at the State Capitol virtually prostrated by a toothache to find a delegation of distraught Negroes awaiting him. Gordon offered one hundred dollars for the arrest of each whipper with the evidence needed to convict. Senator Colquitt appeared at the governor's office much worried. As a Christian layman, the senator had often spoken to black church groups and was sympathetic, and he also knew that if the Lodge bill came up in the Senate, he would have difficulty explaining the whippings. After a long conference with Gordon, he went off to find the judge of Superior Court of the county.

Bruffey's story misled the public in one way. It made it appear that almost everybody in Atlanta and East Point disapproved of the lynching and the whippings. The House of Representatives, in session a few doors from the governor's office, defeated the idea of disapproving the actions sixty-six to twenty-two. The Fulton County grand jury questioned people who were supposed to know about the incidents, but all professed ignorance. At the *Constitution*, Grady was convinced that one of his employees was involved, and he discharged the man.[60]

The newspaper said that what had happened was disadvantageous to the South but also outrageous. "That a half a dozen white men should . . . go about a neighborhood, rousing peaceable and innocent negroes from their sleep and whipping them, is almost incredible."[61] The confidence of the North could not be held if the East Point whippings went unpunished.

The newspaper itself was criticized for Bruffey's account. "Your political aspiration is gone to hell, on account of your article," said one citizen. At the State Capitol, a senator arose and justified what had happened. Negroes should get out of the South; he would stand with white people no matter what they did. "[A]s a member of the legislature, if you please, I proclaim that I approve of what the white people did at East Point."[62]

Grady was in a dilemma. He had spent years explaining that Negroes had rights and opportunities, yet within six miles of his office, a seven-and-a-half-minute train ride, a lynching took place, the body was displayed, and black men were dragged from their homes and beaten for no cause. For the sake of his reputation, he needed the incidents denounced.

W. P. Hill, a close friend of Grady's and president of the Young Men's Democratic League of Fulton County, called the league together to decry what had happened. For one of the few times in Grady's career, arrangements went astray with humiliating results. Hill called the meeting on an evening when Grady was out of town, possibly by design. Shortly before it met in the basement of the courthouse, George Daniel Hall appeared, marching at the head of a grim line of men walking two abreast. Hall, having successfully tormented postmaster Lewis, was now ready for Grady. Many of the men with Hall probably were not members of the league but were there to vote, and nobody challenged them. Somebody introduced a resolution denouncing the *Constitution* for printing an inflammatory account of the East Point events, for failing to say that a sick white man and a white woman had been beaten by two Negroes, for failing to give full facts about the wreck of a railroad train in East Point a short time before, and for other omissions. It criticized Grady by name.

Hall wanted to know whether the managing editor had instigated the league meeting. "I ask you the direct question. Didn't Henry W. Grady insist that you should call this meeting?" President Hill responded: "I am not here to answer your questions." Speakers endorsed the beatings and at length, the resolution criticizing Grady and the *Constitution* passed. The newspaper responded that it had never heard of white people being whipped by Negroes, that the train wreck was too remote from the subject to discuss, and that it was glad it printed the story. "And lastly, Mr. Grady will take care of himself when he returns to the city—probably this morning."[63]

In an unsigned editorial, Grady did as well for himself as he could. He said that relations between whites and blacks were strained and that any incident could produce unfortunate results. "A white man may whip a negro. The negro may retaliate by another outrage. The friends of both may become involved." Grady spoke of the need to prove false the charges by which enemies in the North poisoned the atmosphere against the South. "We are standing for the sacredly pledged word of the south that justice shall be done to the negro race."[64]

The following Saturday evening, a band of fifteen or twenty black men set upon and beat three white men on the streets of Atlanta. Some of the whites were carrying home their groceries for the week. The next evening, a white soldier at nearby Fort McPherson was returning to the fort after visiting his wife and was shot by a Negro. The soldier appeared likely to lose his left arm.[65]

Black newspapermen gave Grady's role in these events a mixed reaction. A Louisiana editor thought that Grady and the *Constitution* were courageous to stand up to the meeting of the league and wished that white editors in Louisiana would do the same. An editor in New York had no such notions. Lawlessness among black people was an outcropping of the past teachings of the *Constitution*, he said; that point should not be forgotten.[66]

The East Point occurrences and their aftermath put a new edge on militancy for some Georgia blacks. Pledger was furious and acted accordingly. Nine days after the whippings, he posted a call for a convention to meet in Atlanta on November 12, 1889, the third of the black protest meetings of the decade. He chose the date easily. The Piedmont Exposition of 1889 opened on October 7 and closed on November 10, and Pledger did not want his delegates in town with its mostly white visitors. "It was only a few days ago the colored Odd Fellows of this place invited their brethren from abroad to take part in their anniversary exercises, and while the evening repast was going on white men patroled the streets with Winchester rifles, without interferences by the city authorities, menaced and committed assault and battery upon a number of our people."[67]

Pledger denounced the East Point events, pointing out what was already known: that a contingent of Atlanta policemen, upon the call of the mayor of East Point, hurried there by train. Pledger said they went to help with the whippings. He denounced whites who drove black teachers from their work, who burned black homes and churches, and who cheated black tenants.

Then Pledger did the unpardonable, the thing that white Georgians concerned with politics would never overlook. He called upon the black convention to send delegates to President Harrison and leaders of Congress to insist that the number of congressmen from Georgia be cut from ten to five or six following the 1890 census. Negroes were not represented in Congress, Pledger said, but were counted as though they were. For this enormity and for calling the protest meeting, the *Constitution* led the attack: "If this wretched agitator had ever done one real service to his race, or had even set it the example of a busy and industrious life, we could look with more patience on this last flagrant and miserable outrage."[68]

The convention met on November 12, sitting for a few hours in a church that was shortly closed to it, then moving to a hall on Broad Street. A Committee on Outrages set about making a record of abuses for the final report of the convention. If any person were afraid to have his name used in reporting an outrage, the name could be withheld. The convention also dealt with reducing the number of congressmen. When the census taker came, black people should dodge him as the fox dodges the hound.[69]

Events now had momentum of their own. In Washington, President Harrison endorsed the principles in the Lodge bill. Supporters called it the Elections Bill of 1890 and opponents called it the Force bill. With the president's endorsement, it had a good chance of becoming law.

The Lodge bill was not the drastic proposal its opponents said it was. Congressman Lodge wished to extend the Federal Supervisory Act of 1870 to every congressional district in which one hundred citizens petitioned for the law to be in effect. Lodge would have federal supervisors oversee all registration and balloting in federal elections in those districts. Even though the bill was not stringent, its sponsors believed that it would lead to a stronger law. Even in the form that Lodge offered it, it would begin to undermine Grady's political structure by rebuilding the practice of black voting.

In the South, the proposal was seen as an assault upon honor as well as the system, and white southerners reacted with horror. An antic Republican congressman said: "I firmly believe that if we were to strike out every word in this bill and insert three of the Ten Commandments: Thou shalt not steal; Thou shalt not bear false witness; Thou shalt not kill—the whole Democratic party would declare it an assault upon the South, subversive of the Constitution, and an infringement of the reserved rights of the States."[70]

Then from Boston came the invitation for Grady to speak. He was to talk about race relations in the South, a perfect time and place to say that the Negro was well treated, that the South was just, and that the Force bill was unnecessary. President Harrison influenced the form of Grady's speech by asking a set of skeptical questions.[71]

Carrying illness within him and a multitude of problems upon him, Grady made the speech, praising New England and the generous invitation that brought him at last to her soil. He vowed to tell the truth, withholding no essential element. There was no personal sacrifice he would not make to remove the imputation that the South was unfair.

Its existence depended upon a right solution of problems connected with race. The truth was, he said, that the Negro was happy. There were Afro-American agitators, said Grady, not mentioning White, Pledger, or Jake Conley by name, but for each one, there were a thousand blacks happy in the contentment of their cabins, "at night taking from the lips of their children the helpful message their State sends them from the schoolhouse door." Negroes worked freely in trades, trades shut to them in the North. Although the penitentiaries were mostly black, Negroes had their place on southern juries. The North was ever quick to affix blame for incidents involving race, he said. "Lawless men may ravage a county in

Iowa and it is accepted as an incident—in the South a drunken row is declared to be the fixed habit of the community."

President Harrison had asked when the Negro would cast a free ballot. "When ignorance anywhere is not dominated by the will of the intelligent . . . when the strong and steadfast do not everywhere control the suffrage of the weak and shiftless—then and not till then will the ballot of the negro be free." Whites were right to unite against the Negro vote, he said, citing instances of suppressed black votes in the North. "You may pass force bills, but they will not avail. . . . We wrested our State government from negro supremacy when the Federal drumbeat rolled closer to the ballot-box and Federal bayonets hedged it deeper about than will ever again be permitted in this free government. But, sir, though the cannon of this Republic thundered in every voting district of the South, we still should find in the mercy of God the means and the courage to prevent its re-establishment!"

President Harrison had asked whether the South was at work on racial problems. "We simply report progress and ask your patience. . . . Meantime we treat the negro fairly. . . . We open to him every pursuit in which he can prosper, and seek to broaden his training and capacity." Grady said that the South loved black people and was indebted to them. "[W]e shall give them uttermost justice and abiding friendship." The Georgians who sat with him that evening at the Hotel Vendome were typical southerners, Grady said. "These gentlemen . . . never saw, I dare assert, an outrage committed on a negro! And if they did, not one of you would be swifter to prevent or punish. It is through them, and the men who think with them—making nine-tenths of every southern community—that these two races have been carried thus far."

Never before, said Grady, had any people been asked to solve such a problem as the South had—two races, approximately equal in number, carried within the same society. Americans had brutally cut down the red man "as a weed" and had shut the yellow man out. "But the black man, affecting but one section, is clothed with every privilege of government and pinned to the soil, and my people commanded to make good at any hazard, and at any cost, his full and equal heirship of American privilege and prosperity." The South, assigned the problem, must be left to work out the solution alone.[72]

Although a part of this speech was uncongenial to the ears of many northerners, its delivery triumphed, for the response of the audience in the hall was enthusiastic, and the reaction of the white press ranged from respect to enthusiasm. The black press was mostly hostile. Within days, however, the speech was no longer judged upon its merits, for Grady's early death caused it to be seen in other lights.

The South saw him as a brave warrior who wore himself out on the field of battle; the North remembered a brilliant man who, though ailing, stood up to argue the case for his countrymen. The Boston address, whatever the violence it committed upon truth, was seen as the apotheosis of a young, beautiful, and prematurely dead knight. Consensus said it was a great utterance.

It was soon alleged that Grady's work was unfinished, although that seems unlikely and his mother doubted it at the time. He could have done little more that was not a repetition of past triumphs. The atmosphere in his own Georgia and in the South was changing and he could not control it. In a short time, men, women, and newspapers who earlier disapproved of lynchings and brutalizations accepted or encouraged them, having convinced themselves that black people chose barbarism.

Grady's views were middle-of-the-road for his time, not in the least adventurous. One might inquire whether he could have done more to seek real justice for blacks without destroying himself as a political power. He could not have advocated institutional changes without loss of local influence.

Grady could have made contributions in two fields in which he held back. He could have taken more interest in education for blacks. Instead, he was satisfied for Haygood to do it. He could have taken a four-square stand against lynchings and the physical mistreatment of blacks. He never did so until the last four months of his life following the East Point events, and he did so then when his reputation was imperiled.

Grady's New South policy on race never had much to do with justice. It had to do with misleading the North while leaving the South free to do as it wished with blacks, a course most southern whites considered essential and proper. The policy freed Grady to continue manipulation of Georgia politics without external interference. In the meanwhile, most of what black people received or were denied, outside of what they did for themselves, depended upon the white man's whim.

Grady died at the right moment to avoid sights that he would have disliked. Ugly scenes had slipped up on him in 1889 in ways he could not ignore. He was intelligent, but he never was an intellectual who examined his ideas for inconsistencies. One can never know the degree to which he realized that the justice he said was at hand for Negroes was false justice, an arrangement made by white men to suit white men, subject to change without notice.

6
Development and Reconciliation

Efforts in politics, agriculture, and race relations helped to produce the atmosphere in which the development of Atlanta could go forward. Competition with other cities, especially with Augusta and Macon, was brisk, at times fair, at times underhanded.

Atlanta could justify this mixed approach. Other cities never gave it anything voluntarily, with one stunning exception. Other localities unintentionally created Atlanta, not as a rival but as a railroad junction, a crossroads that might support a few stores and a tavern or two. The junction first took the accurate if unexciting name of Terminus. Augusta and Savannah both wanted rail access to the center of Georgia, little realizing that anything important would happen at the point of convenience where tracks came together.

Augusta seized proprietary interest in one of the inward-bound lines, the Georgia Railroad, which eventually ran from Augusta to Atlanta. Augusta snatched the line from Athens where the idea for it was born. An embittered Athens, stranded miles from the trunk, grumbled along with an inferior branch of plate rail over which, for several years, mules and horses pulled small cars. The Georgia Railroad pushed through to Atlanta, and the first train passed over the line on September 15, 1845, amid rejoicing.[1]

Savannah embarked upon another enterprise. Every large American city at that time was a seaport or was on deep water, and leaders in Savannah believed that a rail line to the interior would pour traffic through their excellent harbor. Savannah and Macon embarked upon a railroad between their cities, 190 miles long and called the Central of Georgia. The road was chartered in 1833 and finished in 1843. Another company built from Macon to Monroe and then on to Atlanta, and by 1847 trains ran from Atlanta through Macon to Savannah.[2]

Three years after these lines were chartered, the legislature set the state of Georgia to work on a northwestern line, believing that private money could not be found to build it. This famous effort, the Western and Atlantic, was criticized and involved in politics, but on balance, became the most important example in American history of a state-owned railroad. Its track ran 138 miles from Atlanta to what is now Chattanooga, Tennessee. By 1851 trains ran over it. Planters and farmers of the antebellum era, like those of the 1880s, grew only a part of their foodstuffs, and down the Western and Atlantic, southeast from Chattanooga, the remainder of what they needed poured in huge quantities: wheat, oats, corn, bacon, flour, hogs, and sheep, and finally, whiskey. By then, what started as little Terminus was on its own with railroads going in three directions.[3]

The growth of Atlanta gravely disappointed Augusta which had foreseen no such eventuality. Macon, left with the second best railroad connections in Georgia, found its own growth less than desired, and Savannah, which had hoped for great profits from its port, saw with dislike the rise in Georgia of a new phenomenon: an inland rival without water transportation, its life's blood pouring in over the rails.

A fourth railroad shortly came the way of Atlanta, the Atlanta and West Point over which trains ran from East Point just below Atlanta to West Point on the Alabama line, then on to Montgomery.[4]

For its day, the system was a marvel. By the beginning of the Civil War, five through routes served ten southern states. Three of them passed through Atlanta.[5]

The railroads brought problems as well as opportunities, but energy and creativity made the problems endurable. Atlanta had the roads but did not control them. Rate discrimination victimized the city. Rail companies fixed through charges according to their own schedules, giving favorable tariffs to cities where water transport competed: Augusta, Charleston, Savannah, and Macon. In 1858 a man spent $1.50 sending a hundred pounds of lard from Nashville, Tennessee, to Atlanta; he could send the same lard from Nashville through Atlanta and on to Augusta for sixty cents; to Macon for fifty cents; and to Savannah for eighty cents. People believed that the lines, controlled in competing cities, scheduled passenger trains to pass directly through Atlanta or to come and go in the dead of night so that wayfarers had little chance to get off the train and spend money.[6] There was no immediate way to redress the grievances.

Atlanta had one advantage. It was so new that it had little inherited aristocracy. Shrewd, energetic men carved their niches without inquiry into their ancestry, and the problems brought by the railroads led such men, especially the merchants, to act in audacious ways. Banking in Atlanta was rudimentary before the Civil War, so credit was a problem. Local merchants embarked upon a practice that seemed suicidal. They offered cash-only business to farmers for about a hundred miles around the city, and these men drove in their wagons loaded with meat, fruits, and vegetables, sold what they had in a public market that opened an hour before sunrise, then bought for cash in Atlanta stores. Because transactions were mostly cash-only and were done on a small profit margin, Atlanta always sold 25 percent below prices in other cities, and sometimes 50 to 60 percent. The plethora of wagons and carts created a traffic problem, but the "wagon trade" became the economic backbone of the city. With this thriving market to build upon, Atlanta became a trading center with many wholesale and retail stores offering a variety of goods, including northern goods not available in many parts of Georgia.[7]

Atlanta recovered quickly from the Civil War, and the "wagon trade" continued to pour in. Railroads, for all the problems they brought, were recognized for their true value, and Atlanta set about acquiring a new one for itself, a line to open unbroken track from Atlanta to New York and the American cities of the East and Northeast. A good line already existed from Charlotte, North Carolina, to those cities, and only the gap to Charlotte needed closing.

The value of the Charlotte connection was appreciated before the Civil War, and the city council subscribed $100,000 for it, but there was virtually no progress. In 1868 agitation began anew. Promoters arranged a tenuous financing, and the first contract for construction was let in 1869. Trains ran over the line, called the Air Line, in 1873.

Although the opening of the Air Line was of vast value, Atlanta was disappointed. Financiers from elsewhere had majority control, although Atlantans had a substantial interest. Rather quickly, the importance of the connection was clear. The track opened not only a long and convenient commercial route but improved the trade value of the hinterland. Between Atlanta and the South Carolina border, a string of towns and cities was created or augmented along or near the roadbed: Buford, Norcross, Gainesville, Lula, Toccoa, and so forth. These fell naturally into the trade area of the city.

In other Georgia localities, the Air Line was understood correctly, and apprehension set in. The Augusta *Chronicle* assured its readers that Augusta was not a "finished" city and urged work and vigilance at home. Augustans commented with envy upon the Atlanta spirit. Of $7,950,000 needed to pay for the 265 miles of track, Atlantans had produced about $800,000.

By then, salesmen for Atlanta wholesale and retail houses, commonly called drummers, swarmed the state, using the rails to full advantage, invading any territory they could enter. The *Chronicle* said: "Charleston, Savannah, and Augusta merchants should not permit Atlanta to wrest from them the trade of the country tributary to their respective cities. . . . [I]t behooves our people to wake up and drive these irrepressible Atlanta drummers back into their own territory." In 1888 one of the prominent and powerful leaders of Macon correctly analyzed matters in a speech. Atlanta had fought Augusta and his own Macon for every inch of ground and had done so with "marshaled battalions," referring to drummers. With Grady sitting behind him on the platform, this astute critic suggested a brusque and insulting motto for Atlanta: "Get There Somehow."[8]

Atlanta needed a railroad to the coalfields of Birmingham, Alabama. In 1881 John B. Gordon became president of Georgia Pacific Railroad, and two years later, the first trains ran between the cities. About the same time, the East Tennessee, Virginia, and Georgia put together a combination that opened a new route to the ocean at Brunswick, Georgia, and which extended toward the North, giving chastening competition to the Western and Atlantic.[9]

The value of these lines was appreciated, especially as each trunk was augmented by feeders, or branches, going off into the countryside. The short lines carried produce, timber, and minerals into the market, "and this means bringing them in one sense or another to Atlanta."[10]

Grady and Evan P. Howell followed railroad developments minutely, and Howell had a financial interest in some of them. Railroads, however, were only one concern. The New South Movement meant manufacturing to many people, usually cotton mills. Before the Civil War, Atlanta had had no cotton factory of significance. It lay north of the best of the cotton belt, although fertilizer, speeding up the growth of the plants, later moved the belt some forty miles northward. Atlanta traded in cotton more than it manufactured it.

In 1881 the Atlanta spirit took hold of the possibilities of cotton manufacturing, and in a great civic effort the city staged what C. Vann Woodward calls the "inaugural ceremony" of the industrial part of the New South Movement.[11] The International Cotton Exposition of 1881, put together in 108 working days mostly by a group of Atlanta businessmen, tells a great deal about the civic spirit and leadership of the city, as well as what the city fathers wanted. The leadership, which included the Atlanta *Constitution*, took a leap involving great risks and almost landed in trouble.

The exposition, touted all over America, was unready to receive guests when the doors swung open on October 5, 1881. Buildings were unfinished and many exhibits were not in place. The director general of the exposition, H. I. Kimball, assisted by John C. Peck, director of construction, drove building crews without mercy to achieve even partial results. Exhibitors arriving early to set up exhibits suffered attacks of nerves. One of them beset Kimball who calmly told him: "My friend, the lumber that is to go in the building in which your exhibit is to be made is not sawed yet." Kimball told the astonished man that he could set up in ten days.[12]

The exposition had first been suggested by Edward Atkinson, a Boston economist and inventor regarded in the New South as a friend. History suggests that his motives were mixed. Atkinson was an important member of the New England Cotton Manufacturers' Association and at various times was treasurer of several mills in New England. The association was disturbed about the quality of cotton coming from the South, much of it badly ginned and dirty. New Englanders proposed schemes to get around the problem, including the impractical idea of shipping raw cotton North for ginning. A better plan involved an educational program to show southern farmers that they were better off when their cotton went north in good condition.[13]

Writing to the New York *Herald* in the summer of 1880, Atkinson suggested that persons interested in cotton get together for discussions. He also suggested holding an exposition devoted to cotton production and manufacturing, although he did not have in mind creating southern factories to compete with those in his own region. Atkinson visited Atlanta and addressed local leaders. New York and New Orleans wanted the exposition, but the *Constitution* declared that Atlanta would have it.[14]

When the *Constitution* made that statement, the 1880 presidential election was the subject of the hour. Most white southerners hoped for the election of Winfield Scott Hancock, a Democrat. When James A. Garfield became president instead, some southerners decided it was time to stop looking for national political solutions for southern problems and time to go to work at home.

In Atlanta on November 26, 1880, two men from Philadelphia, publishers of the *Textile Record,* visited the offices of the *Constitution* with messages from businessmen in the Northeast who manufactured cloth and made machinery for cotton mills. They encouraged the idea of the exposition, and one of the visitors, J. W. Ryckman, played a role in the events that followed.

Governor Colquitt became chairman of a committee to organize the exposition, and he and others created a formal structure, "The

International Cotton Exposition Association." Senator Brown was president, Samuel M. Inman treasurer, and Ryckman was secretary. The board of directors included Howell. Grady had no official post but was a figure behind the scenes, using all his abilities to develop regional and national publicity, and serving as a host for visiting dignitaries. Brown, who had illness in his family, resigned as president and Colquitt took the post.

The association set out to sell $100,000 worth of stock but increased the sum to $200,000. Atlantans were to subscribe $33,333, which they did in six hours on March 15, 1881.[15] The state gave no money, but word came that General Sherman, who had burned a large part of the city in 1864, was pledging $2,000. The Associated Press flashed word of this generous gesture over the nation, stimulating sale of the rest of the stock in the North and elsewhere.

The exposition was to open on October 5, yet the executive committee of the association never met until May 3, and Kimball was not in office until May 5. Expositions took three to six years to organize, and Atlanta was proposing to do it quickly.[16]

The promoters made two important decisions. The exposition would devote itself to cotton but not confine itself to that product. Commercial machinery, commercial products, and raw materials would be on display. The promoters also decided that the principal building would be a model cotton factory. After all events were over, it would become a working mill. The structure went up rapidly.

The fair finally had twenty-seven buildings on nineteen landscaped acres. The facilities housed 1,113 exhibits with six foreign nations represented, justifying the international claims of the sponsors. Cotton from four nations grew in patches around the halls.

The organizers had projected that thousands of visitors would be present simultaneously and that many would come from out-of-town. Hotels built or leased additional space. A new hotel, the Southern, went up near the grounds, and campgrounds, with floored tents, rented accommodations nearby.

The exposition was at Oglethorpe Park, a city-owned facility two miles west of town. Western and Atlantic Railroad tracks carried first-class coaches from the heart of the city to the fair every fifteen minutes during the day. The streetcar company put on eighteen new carriages, and hacks served those who could afford them.

On opening day a theme of national reconciliation mingled with commercial development. Governor Colquitt praised the business impulse evident everywhere but bowed before a more noble purpose: to draw "the people of every section of this great country nearer and more truly together." In that spirit, the principal speakers represented North and South: Senators Zebulon B. Vance of North Carolina and Daniel W. Vorhees of Indiana. Although the fair was not in good order, opening day was counted a success.

Jealousies arose in other cities, especially in Macon and Augusta. The *Constitution* suggested snidely that they invite manufacturers visiting the exposition to their own localities to see what they had to offer. "It is much better than carping at Atlanta."[17]

There was worry behind the scenes. Crowds were slim, averaging 844 persons a day during October. The tendency to fix blame targeted the railroads. They had failed to set attractive excursion rates from other cities. The roads made adjustments. Black people in Atlanta had little enthusiasm for the fair, and white citizens usually worked six days a week. Exposition gates were shut on Sundays. Kimball refused to run the fair at night for fear of wearing out the staff. Ordinary citizens of Atlanta participated only minimally.[18]

Against the odds, the exposition finally came together. Some persons thought that October 27, twenty-one days after opening, was when it happened. The promoters had organized "Governors' Day" and asked thirty-eight American governors to be present. Six came, among them Governor Hobart B. Bigelow of Connecticut. Governors Colquitt and Bigelow went to the fairgrounds, were weighed on Howe scales, and presumably were measured as well. They were about to take part in a demonstration of what could happen when, in a slogan of the Movement, the mill was brought to the cotton.

The sun was barely up on October 27 when several persons went into the patches around the exhibition halls, picked a quantity of cotton, then began the rush to turn it into two suits of clothing for the governors to wear that evening. Hurrying technicians carded the cotton, spun it into thread, wove it into cloth, dyed and dried it, cut and sewed it into suits, and finished the buttonholes before sunset. At 8:30 that evening, Colquitt and Bigelow wore new swallow-tailed black suits to a reception at the Executive Mansion on Peachtree Street. The *Constitution* was awed. The suit fibers had "at sunrise dangled, dew-gemmed, from the stalks."

Enthusiastic crowds began coming, including General Sherman, glad to see buildings where once there had been battlefields. The exposition was solvent and finally made a small profit. From various places came requests that it stay open past December 31, but Kimball would hear none of it. On the last day of the year, Governor Colquitt signaled for all machinery to stop. Atlanta, with 37,409 residents in 1880 had held a world's fair that drew 290,000 visitors and vast acclaim.[19]

The sponsors forgot all difficulties in the euphoria of success. Kimball said that local support was a major factor in the triumph, which was true, and declared that the exposition had banished the last vestiges of sectionalism from America, which remained to be demonstrated.

Jack Blicksilver has evaluated what the fair meant to Atlanta and to Georgia. Georgia appears to have benefited by sharing in the general industrial progress of the region which began about that time. Even so, the state remained overwhelmingly agricultural. Effects upon agriculture are uncertain, although exhibitors after the fair said that a substantial amount of agricultural equipment had been sold.

Atlanta, on the other hand, benefited directly and indirectly. By modest estimation, visitors spent $2,000,000. Several merchants said they each made $30,000 from exposition business. Local manufacturing was stimulated. The main building at the fair became the Exposition Cotton Mills. Atlanta manufacturers won awards and recognition for their products: J. P. Stevens and Company for its watches; E. Van Winkle and Company for the best saw gin with feeder, and E. Clarke and Company for its cotton cleaner. The exposition probably gave impetus for the founding of several new factories: Southern Agricultural Works, producing cotton cultivators and machinery; Chattahoochee Brick Company; a cottonseed oil mill; a cotton compress; several fertilizer plants, and a new chemical works. Proprietors enlarged other shops. Grady's efforts attracted three hundred writers from northern and midwestern newspapers to the reporter's pavilion, and the publicity helped the city, although its effects cannot be measured.

During the eighties, Atlantans saw an improvement in their condition that some people thought owed something to the exposition and which certainly owed something to the spirit that brought the exposition about. The population rose from 37,409 in 1880 to 63,533 in 1890. Assessed value of real estate went up from $16,200,000 in 1882 to $41,500,000 in 1893. Atlanta paved more of its streets and sidewalks and built a satisfactory sewage system. In the North, countless businessmen and entrepreneurs who had been entertained in the parlors of the best Atlanta homes spoke well of the exposition and of the city.[20]

Twice more during the decade, the city repeated the remarkable feat. The expositions of 1887 and 1889 were organized in the offices of the *Constitution* with Grady and his colleagues behind them. Grady did much of the work on these fairs.

The 1881 exposition was the first of its scope in the South, but the fair of 1887 was in some ways more spectacular. Except for a visit from Rutherford B. Hayes in 1877, Atlanta had had little attention from sitting presidents of the United States until 1887, when Grady brought President Grover Cleveland to the Piedmont Exposition. Cleveland, the first Democrat to sit in the White House since the Civil War, was vastly popular. His invitation arrived at the White House engraved on thin sheets of gold from the Dahlonega mines in north central Georgia. Grady understood the impact that Cleveland's visit would have.

He raised what he called a "delicate" subject with Daniel S. Lamont, Cleveland's secretary, and asked that what he said be kept secret. Grady wanted Cleveland to come to Atlanta alone in the South, turning down invitations from other cities and other fairs. "If for example he is going to stop at the Carolina State Fair, and at the Alabama State Fair, and at other fairs, the people of those localities will simply stay at home, and see him there. If he comes to Atlanta alone, we will quicken travel on every road in the south, and will have such multitudes to meet him here as he can have no reasonable conception of until he sees them." Grady arranged inexpensive rail tickets to Atlanta on virtually every southern railroad.[21]

Cleveland arrived on October 17, 1887, in a drizzle of rain which continued throughout his stay. Even so, every public detail of his program went forward before immense throngs. At the exposition grounds, site of what today is Piedmont Park in Atlanta, Grady introduced Cleveland to 50,000 people. The exposition made $58,000, which was committed to another hugely successful fair two years later.

By then, such events were being held everywhere. Louisville held a Southern Exposition in 1883, and New Orleans followed with the Cotton Centennial Exposition of 1885. Smaller localities fell into line. Augusta, Georgia, staged a creditable exposition in 1888, with other cities of medium size following suit.

Just as the exposition of 1881 was an "inaugural event," a speech by Grady in New York in 1886 was the vehicle by which the North was thoroughly exposed to the southern concept of national reconciliation. The concept was immensely flattering to the North, for it said that the South wished to become like the North in many ways. It asked for help to bring about changes in the South, even though southerners did not like to acknowledge northern help when it came. They liked to say that they were improving themselves without much help and without universal approval.[22] In point of fact, they were hungry both for assistance and for praise. When praise came, it was leapt upon and reprinted in southern newspapers and referred to in speeches.

For three reasons, the New South leaders preached reconciliation. They wanted money as investments. They wanted northerners to immigrate to the South to help develop the region, something that happened to some degree. As already seen, they wanted northerners to believe that the Negro was happy and had justice to go with his freedom.

The best way to advance toward these ends was to declare the

Civil War over and to say that the South accepted its results. General Robert E. Lee started the process before he died in 1870. L. Q. C. Lamar of Mississippi adapted the line brilliantly, as did Benjamin H. Hill of Georgia. Colquitt made a pedestrian try at it at the exposition of 1881.[23] In 1886 there was reason to try harder to get the message across. Two years earlier, the Republicans lost the White House and, as people out of power sometimes do, were inclining to follow their more radical, antisouthern leaders.

Among those northern businessmen who believed that reassuring words were needed from the South was John H. Inman, a man with southern roots and a brother of Samuel M. Inman, Grady's friend and a stockholder in the *Constitution.* John Inman had invested large sums in the South and was said to be a director of every inch of railroad between Louisville and Atlanta and between Atlanta and Washington. He was a subscriber to the exposition of 1881. John Inman was also a member of the New England Society of New York, an organization whose wealthy members read the newspapers and already knew of Grady's coverage of the Charleston earthquake. Inman suggested that Grady speak to the society at its December meeting in 1886, and Grady accepted.[24]

The Society met at Delmonico's in New York City on December 22. The toast of the evening was "The New South," and Grady had credentials to respond to it, especially if the main theme were reconciliation. He had no Confederate past. He had been a boy when the war ended. Although a Democrat, he held no office, and four years earlier had made it plain that he did not want one. He declined to run for what should have been a safe seat in the United States House of Representatives.

Dangers and apprehensions attended the address. The audience was unknown. During its long history, the society had stayed clear of southern speakers. Also, Grady's message had nothing new in it. Speakers great and small and newspapers of every size and opinion had trumpeted it. Nothing suggested that the message would at last be heard in 1886.

Grady worked hard to cast what he had to say in acceptable form. He thought of a thousand things, but if he said five hundred of them, he would be murdered at the banquet table, and if he said the other five hundred, he would be slaughtered at home.[25]

When Grady finally spoke in New York, he did so technically from notes scribbled on the back of the dinner menu, but he had worked through many drafts and rehearsed the speech in his mind. In the dining room that December evening, 360 seats held some of the most influential men in America, and the walls were lined with junior members of the society unable to get dinner tickets. Horace Russell, president of the society, was host at the head table, and near him was Dr. T. DeWitt Talmage, the Brooklyn clergyman whose speaking ability and printed sermons earned him a national reputation. Guests of honor were General Sherman, Inman, J. Pierpont Morgan, H. M. Flagler, Lyman Abbott, Seth Thomas, Elihu Root, George H. Lincoln, Russell Sage, and F. Hopkinson Smith.

Talmage spoke first, talking of the typical American and how he was yet to appear. Talmage reached his high point with a description of the northern army returning to Washington at the end of the war. "God knew that the day was stupendous, and He cleared the heavens of clouds and mist and chill, and strung the blue sky as a triumphal arch for the returning warriors to pass under. . . . I heard in every step those conflicts through which they had waded, and seemed to see dripping from their smoky flags the blood of our country's martyrs."[26]

Mighty cheers greeted Talmage, and General Sherman followed him, responding to a toast in honor of President Cleveland, who was absent. As Sherman finished, the Seventh Regiment band in the balcony struck up "Marching Through Georgia."

Grady was thirty-six years old, clean shaven, and boyish, in the company of older men. He stood at the speaker's table, looking pale, and without acknowledging introducer or introduction, leaned forward and said in a clear, slow voice: "There was a South of slavery and secession—that South is dead. There is a South of union and freedom—that South, thank God, is living, breathing, growing every hour."[27] Grady told the audience that the words he spoke were uttered in New York twenty years earlier, in 1866, by Hill of Georgia and that he would make them his text, bespeaking the "utmost stretch of your courtesy to-night."

Gently contradicting Talmage, Grady said that the typical American had already come. Abraham Lincoln was the "first who comprehended within himself all the strength and gentleness, all the majesty and grace of this republic." He was the sum of the Puritan and the Cavalier but was greater than either "in that he was American, and that in his honest form were first gathered the vast and thrilling forces of his ideal government."

Talmage had drawn a picture of the returning federal armies. Grady asked leave to tell of the "footsore Confederate soldier," buttoning up his coat at Appomattox and turning his face South in April 1865.

> He finds his house in ruins, his farm devastated, his slaves free, his stock killed, his barns empty, his trade destroyed, his money worthless . . . his comrades slain, and the burdens of others heavy on his shoulders. . . .
> What does he do—this hero in gray with a heart of gold? Does he sit down in sullenness and despair? Not for a day. . . . The soldier stepped from the trenches into the furrow; horses that had charged Federal guns marched before the plow, and fields that ran red with human blood in April were green with the harvest in June.

The South "found her jewel in the toad's head of defeat," Grady said. The shackles of Negro slavery had limited development as it confined the slave. Now all shackles were gone. He then asked:

> [W]hat answer has New England to this message? Will she permit the prejudice of war to remain in the hearts of the conquerors, when it has died in the hearts of the conquered? . . . If she does, the South . . . must accept with dignity its refusal; but if she does not refuse to accept in frankness and sincerity this message of good will and friendship, then will the prophecy of Webster, delivered in this very society forty years ago amid tremendous applause, become true, be verified in its fullest sense, when he said: "Standing hand to hand and clasping hands, we

should remain united as we have been for sixty years, citizens of the same country, members of the same government, united, all united now and united forever."

From his opening sentence, Grady captured his audience. At the end, he was mobbed where he stood. Compliments and congratulations poured upon him. At length, the southerners present escorted him away.[28]

In the days following, hundreds of letters and telegrams applauded the speech, some from surprising sources. The *Constitution* made much of a message from a terrible foe, John Fletcher Hanson of the Macon *Telegraph*. The *Telegraph* itself marveled that the message at last had been heard. The New York *Times* said that Grady's was an "American" speech, and the New York *Evening Post* believed it was a perfect setting forth of what the South had not communicated and the North had not understood. The New York *Sun* thought Grady would make a good candidate for vice-president of the United States, and that he even might be presidential. The Atlanta rival of the *Constitution,* the Atlanta *Evening Journal,* went through hundreds of its exchanges and found only two newspapers that dispraised both speech and speaker.[29]

One of these was in Charleston, South Carolina, where jealousy overcame Dawson, editor of the *News and Courier.* For six days, he withheld mention of the speech, and when he finally commented editorially, he did not mention Grady's name. He denied that "among thoughtful Southerners there is any such thing as an intelligent recognition of Mr. Lincoln as a typical American." Lincoln was "coarse while kindly, vulgar though good-hearted, ill-bred while acute, awkward while amiable, and weak in act while strong in word."[30] Dawson was churlish but had hit the speech where it was weak.

Grady, as he was often accused of doing, had let facts fend for themselves. The tribute to Lincoln was preposterous. Men in the audience at Delmonico's had known and served Lincoln. They had seen much of the Puritan in the dead president, but neither they nor anyone else had seen much of the Cavalier. As for the "vast and thrilling forces of his ideal government," the government had seemed less than ideal at close range. Moreover, Hill never said the words quoted, and no record shows that Hill spoke at all in New York in 1866.

Even though the facts were askew, the result was achieved. Praising Lincoln by name, Grady bowed before a northern hero. The footsore Confederate soldier was a generic type, not an identifiable person, and he could be lauded without giving offense. Even though Hill never said the words attributed, they represented his views, and Grady successfully conjured up a warm-hearted southerner standing before a New York audience within a year of Appomattox, the hand of fellowship extended. Grady's hyperbole told much of what the North wanted to hear.

Paul H. Buck has concluded that even though reconciliation was popular in both North and South, men in both parties wanted old hatreds alive.[31] Buck primarily was referring to the years before 1880, but enough partisan advantage still attached to vilifying one section or the other to carry his conclusion forward into the eighties. Many publications and spokesmen sought out materials emphasizing the oneness of the nation, but others reacted with acrimony to almost any stimulus.

When Jefferson Davis was in Montgomery just before Grady produced him in Atlanta, the archly Republican New York *Tribune* scarcely managed its indignation. "Twenty-one years after he should have been hanged this unrepentant old villain and Union-hater gets up and whines about the 'loss of liberty' and the 'glories of the Lost Cause.' " The Chicago *Inter-Ocean* discountenanced southerners who took part in the plan to resurrect Davis. The *Constitution* referred to newspapers saying such things as "outrage mills" and occasionally answered them in kind. Usually, however, the newspaper spoke of peace, generosity, and mutual respect. Following the Charleston earthquake, it praised the efforts of northerners to relieve that damaged city. "We are one people after all." On the anniversary dates of Civil War battles, the *Constitution* gave columns of space to northern and southern veterans visiting on fields where they had been foes.[32]

The New South leadership was certain that warm and law-abiding sentiments would deliver dividends. Northern money had already played a part in developing the southern railroad network. What Atlanta really wanted now was industry, the cynosure of every southern town and city. Atlanta was relentless in pursuit of it and of all development. "She has won her promotion by constant aggression. When she stands with hands down, she loses at once her place and her prestige."[33]

Southern orators often cataloged the benefits that billowing chimneys and busy shops would bring, preceding them with an enumeration of the natural resources of the region. Most such recitations were numbingly dry. Almost alone, Grady gave pathos to an unmagical list of raw materials. Several times late in his career, he told of attending a funeral in Pickens County in the north Georgia mountains. The dead man was an ordinary Georgian, poor but proud, who in his younger years wore Confederate gray. Grady never wrote the speech down, but stenographic reporters were quick to note its elegiac quality and recorded what became some of Grady's most frequently quoted lines.

They buried him in the midst of a marble quarry: they cut through solid marble to make his grave; and yet a little tombstone they put above him was from Vermont. They buried him in the heart of a pine forest, and yet the pine coffin was imported from Cincinnati. They buried him within touch of an iron mine, and yet the nails in his coffin and the iron in the shovel that dug his grave were imported from Pittsburgh. They buried him by the side of the best sheep-grazing country on the earth, and yet the wool in the coffin bands and the coffin bands themselves were brought from the North. The South didn't furnish a thing on earth for that funeral but the corpse and the hole in the ground. There they put him away and the clods rattled down on his coffin, and they buried him in a New York coat and a Boston pair of shoes and a pair of breeches from Chicago and a shirt from Cincinnati, leaving him nothing to carry into the next world with him to remind him of the country in which he lived, and for which he fought for four years, but the chill of blood in his veins and the marrow in his bones.[34]

This speech calls for the industrialization of the South but urges the industrialization of no designated city or state. It points to a Southwide opportunity and by implication, calls for improvement of the whole region. In any town of size in the South, the city fathers already dreamed Grady's dream and in many places had organized factories or acquired them.

Internal evidence in the speech suggests, however, that Grady had Atlanta on his mind. By factories, most New South leaders meant cotton mills; yet a clear-eyed reading of the Pickens County speech shows that nowhere is cotton or a cotton factory mentioned. The reason may be guessed at. The version quoted was tucked away into the last address of Grady's life in December 1889. By then, Atlantans knew that their city would never be home to large numbers of cotton factories.

Early in the 1880s they still hoped for them. The city had little usable waterpower, so promoters developed a scheme to tap the Chattahoochee River, which ran nearby. They would cut a canal into the river thirty miles above the city, run the canal beside the city, and empty the water back into the stream eight miles below town. In the last eight miles, it was said the water would drop 225 feet. The canal front could accommodate a string of factories. The canal was never built.[35]

Atlanta in the early 1880s already had the three cotton factories with which it would close the century: the Exposition Mills, the Fulton County Spinning Company (Elsas, May, and Company), and the Atlanta Cotton Mills. The three firms together employed about 1,100 workers, an important number but not a foundation for broad-based fortune.[36]

There was some astonishment when, in 1882, the *Constitution* announced that Atlanta was not only the manufacturing leader in the state but in several adjoining states as well. The claim was regarded as a falsehood even by some Atlantans, but the census of 1880 supplied a basis for it. Atlanta had a host of small shops and factories, and city leaders alleged that Atlanta workers had more work, that more value was created locally when materials were manufactured, and that a greater variety of goods was produced. Augusta, Macon, Columbus, and Charleston protested with indignation.

Statistically, Atlanta defended the claim, even if it appeared that it had chosen the terms of argumentation in a self-serving way. In 1880 Atlanta had 196 factories and shops that employed perhaps 3,680 people; thus, an average Atlanta shop or factory had some 18.8 workers and was a small operation. In Augusta at the same time, the average operation had about 28 employees.

Instantly, the *Constitution* began proclaiming the superiority of small operations. Cities dependent upon cotton manufacturing, or some other large interest, were paralyzed when depression hit the dominant industry. Atlanta, with small and diversified shops, pursued a more even course in depression times. Workers benefited more from small industries than from big ones because every member of the family, male and female, could usually find work. The *Constitution* claimed that whole families had trouble finding employment in cities with specialized lines of manufacture.

The *Constitution* surveyed some of the factories and shops, identifying and praising many. A wagon factory had 8 employees; a stoneworks had 5; a candy and cracker factory had 125; a cutlery shop needed 47 workers but had found only 38. Businesses were making a panoply of goods: metal materials, paper products, sunbonnets.[37]

Each shred of evidence depicting an economic boom was trumpeted. Larger tax digests meant vibrancy. Increased real estate values showed the confidence the people had in the future. The opening of new businesses held bright auspices for forthcoming years. To the *Constitution*, the city was more than a corporation and was almost a person, a "living entity."[38]

Atlantans who thought otherwise and said so were a threat to progress. J. W. Clayton was a wholesale liquor dealer whose business was wrecked when the city went dry in 1886. To a friend in New York, he wrote that prohibition was ruining the city. Trade was nearly stopped, houses were vacant, and assessments of real estate had been increased to bring in revenue. Atlanta could not pay contractors for work done on its streets.

Clayton was doubtless shocked when parts of his letter appeared in the New York *Post*. A *Constitution* reporter immediately beset him, but Clayton would not hedge on what he had said. The *Constitution* believed that a blow had been struck at the city, whose growth "depends very largely on its reputation." If people thought that Atlanta was unprosperous, they would avoid it. Twelve prominent citizens, including the mayor, criticized Clayton, whose points were far from new. Each was discussed during the first prohibition campaign. They were alarming only when paraded unrebutted before alien audiences.[39]

The *Constitution* swooped down not only on its own dissenting citizens, but upon other cities, Augusta in particular. The rivalry with Augusta was in part political, for it usually was allied with Macon and other anti-Atlanta municipalities; but to that element was added pure bad feeling, based in part upon its industrial success. In the realm of cotton manufacturing, Augusta thrived in a way to gladden the heart of any disinterested New South leader. The *Constitution* never discussed its true views of Augusta, although Grady did so early in his career. He saw it as more comfortable with mint juleps in hand than with mallets. Augustans were so interested in ancestry that their required reading was the "stud-book."[40] At times, the *Constitution* protested its goodwill, but the leadership of Augusta was hard to convince.

It had reason to be skeptical. Periodically, the *Constitution* staff, at times under Grady's direct supervision, developed materials that Augustans saw as crossing their lifeline, undermining their credit. The editorial position of Grady and the *Constitution* could not be faulted on its face. They said that when any city in Georgia was improved, Atlanta was helped, and Walsh and his *Chronicle* were doing all they could for their city.

Relations hit bottom in the middle of the decade. Augusta had much to be proud of. It had a marvelous collection of cotton mills, and plants also flourished across the Savannah River in South Carolina, helping the economy of Augusta.[41] Then, in 1884, two of the leaders of the city were caught in incorrect business arrangements, and an economic slump slowed mill activity. Business failures followed.

The following year, after collapses multiplied, one of Grady's special correspondents wrote a piece published under the headline, "A Stagnant Town." A "spirit of commercial ruin" lay over the city following troubles at the Enterprise factory, the failure of Roberts and Company, O'Connell and Burke, a half dozen lesser enterprises, and the Bank of Augusta. The *Constitution* seemed to gloat. "A city may soon, by renewed and increased vigor, live down the local effects of repeated failures, but it is much more difficult to reestablish the confidence of the outside world, when that confidence has been so profoundly disturbed."

Some cities handled their affairs well, said the *Constitution*. Baltimore, Louisville, Nashville, and Atlanta did, specifying three distant and unthreatening places. Others did poorly. Augusta, Savannah, and Charleston sat on their riverbanks and watched the stream go by. Augusta was in a dilapidated condition, its buildings worm-eaten. There was not a first-class business building in town. The streets were unpaved, the sidewalks irregular, the water muddy, and no one could count on the gas supply. "The people on the streets do not rush as in Atlanta and other energetic cities."[42]

Walsh exploded. His *Chronicle* asserted that financiers had confidence in the credit of Augusta; that local managers ran the factories with faithfulness, and that the future of the city was unaffected by the troubles. Rather than choosing to do good, the *Constitution* had done ill. "To our friends their article will not have a feather's weight; abroad, the shaft may bear an arrow's barb." Walsh feared the barb. The managers of northern money markets read the *Constitution* and rarely read the *Chronicle*. The *Constitution* defended itself in a familiar way, declaring that every city in Georgia was dear to it. Augusta depicted Atlanta as an octopus trying to wrap its tentacles around the trade of Augusta.[43]

Business was better in Augusta in 1886, bringing a different problem. Workers, who had suffered during the slump, now wanted more money and better working conditions. An incident set off a strike at the Algernon Mill, workers at Riverside Mill joined the strikers, and others followed. Some mill owners locked their employees out, and the stoppage became general with three thousand people idle.

Walsh took a middle ground between workers and mill owners, urging arbitration. The *Chronicle* said: "Let the mill men . . . select a citizen, and let the operatives select a citizen . . . and these two to choose a third party, and to this tribunal let the trouble be referred."[44]

For weeks, Walsh and his associates delivered this sensible advice; but on September 12, 1886, the *Constitution* shattered the pacific character of their Sunday morning. Grady had sent a sharp-penned writer to chronicle the problems of Augusta, not the nearly anonymous hired gun who wrote "A Stagnant Town," but his own right-hand man, Clark Howell. Grady gave almost all of page two that Sunday to Howell's account. A ten-deck headline described terrible and unprecedented events. Eight thousand persons were idle and the outlook was gloomy. To reach his eight thousand figure, Howell counted in the dependents of the three thousand idle workers. All of these desperate people were on the charity of the world. The business interests of the city were jeopardized and the wheels of commerce clogged.[45]

Walsh and his associates were beside themselves, positive that the story was "calculated to do Augusta serious injury." They flailed back with limp and untuned raillery, which purported to disclose the physical ailments of Grady and Howell: nervous dyspepsia, indigestion, sick headaches, disorders of the liver, and so forth. Atlanta itself was a cesspool of disease: ringworm, milk leg, barbers' itch, to name a few.

As unhealthy as the place was, it sprang to life when a convention was in town and there were visitors to be plucked. Legislative seasons saw Atlantans rise above their environment, rallying to elect an Atlanta man governor or senator or to send a delegation to Washington to name an Atlantan marshal, district attorney, or judge.

The *Chronicle* even supplied an unflattering interpretation of Grady's coverage of the Charleston earthquake, which had just occurred. Journalists almost everywhere praised the coverage and the effort to raise money for Charleston as large-spirited and decent. The *Chronicle* thought otherwise. The coverage was a disguised blow, aimed at the economy of the already damaged city. This interpretation was interesting but not new, for it already enjoyed currency in South Carolina.[46]

Exactly one week after Howell's piece, the *Chronicle* made a substantive response, claiming that in trade, Augusta was a match for Atlanta. Almost all of page one the following Sunday was a long article titled "Augusta as She Is," an encyclopedic study of the local economy. All of page nine and part of page ten contained an article headed "Augusta's New Allies," showing that much of South Carolina was an economic tributary. In "A Parting Word to Atlanta," the *Chronicle* claimed that Augusta drummers were sweeping the field, peddling goods under the nose of the capital city, and sending carload after carload of merchandise into three states.[47]

Every New South leader knew that labor relations, and more specifically, labor peace, was a principal inducement to northern investors. "[C]otton mill strikes in the south, up to the present time, have been entirely unknown," the *Constitution* said in 1882, well before the Augusta problems began. "There is certainly organization among the laborers—organization in the direction of benevolence—but this has never yet taken the shape of antagonism to the capital that employs them."[48] Serious labor problems would help no city that had them, a fact well digested in Augusta.

During the Augusta difficulties, Grady and the *Constitution* glossed over news of a nasty confrontation in their own shop. They liked to depict labor in Atlanta as benevolent when they depicted it at all. When printers in the composing room stormed out in 1882, the *Constitution* reported it in a low-key way, and then made no further reference for three years, when those who had left began distributing leaflets.

With hostile flyers in the hands of its readers, the newspaper published its own version of events. Three years earlier, it said, union typographers became involved in a dispute concerning work stations. The union men walked out, and the Typographical Union lost power as the departed men were replaced by others willing to work on terms set by the newspaper.

Because the men now made demands concerning reinstatement of their union, and because the newspaper thought the public was being invited to damage its property, the *Constitution* asked the Knights of Labor to arbitrate. The newspaper arbiters were its principal owners, Howell, Hemphill, Grady, and Inman, the latter three experts at conciliation. They had an escape route if they did not like the results. The rights of the nonunion men then working at the paper must be respected, and no "ruinous conditions" would be accepted, a phrase open to any interpretation. At length, the arbiters struck an agreement under which the *Constitution* continued with its own work force and rules.[49]

The moral ambiguities involved in the intercity rivalries, such as selective attention to business and labor problems, never seemed to trouble Grady. He and his colleagues were too busy at their work. Virtually every civic enterprise bore Grady's stamp or that of his closest associates: the international fairs, a new building for the Young Men's Christian Association, the reorganization of the Young Men's Library, fund-raising for a Confederate Veterans Home, and many drives for relief of the poor, a hallmark of any civilized city. The claims of Atlanta as a cultural center were tenuous during the 1880s, but New South cities needed that dimension, and Grady invited southern authors and lecturers to speak, encouraged musical events, and personally sponsored an ambitious Chautauqua. All of these developments were done cleanly, harming no one and helping Atlanta.

Other aspects of intercity competition were also aboveboard. Atlanta got the state store of the Farmer's Alliance by making the best bid. The struggle over the location of what today is the Georgia Institute of Technology was fairly decided even though it left Atlanta with embittered enemies.

The fight over Georgia Tech was an extended one. Gavin Wright says that early leadership in industrialization generated cumulative advantages for regions that got a head start.[50] The South had had industrial development before the Civil War, but any cumulative advantages were difficult to identify. That fact gave the new state technological institute a special role and importance.

Grady and his colleagues thought little of classical education built upon ancient languages and liberal studies. That course of study produced politicians, lawyers, and speechmakers and did not lead naturally into business. They were enthusiastic for two kinds of schools: industrial ones and technical institutes. Industrial schools trained ordinary workers, male and female: bricklayers, carpenters, mechanics, and workers on machines in factories. Technical schools trained superintendents, foremen, and engineers. About one-half their curriculum was mathematics, grammar, and such studies, and the other half was practical training.[51]

For a time, the *Constitution* favored industrial schools in all Georgia locales which could use them, but education was headed in the other direction. From Macon came the first move for a technological institute. Hanson of the *Telegraph* had his editor, Harry S. Edwards, call for the creation of a technical school for Georgia in a powerful editorial on March 2, 1882. Nathaniel E. Harris, the Macon lawyer who, as seen, was later associated with Augustus O. Bacon, ran for the legislature pledged to the creation of the school and was elected.[52]

Harris got his measure through the General Assembly and signed into law on October 13, 1885. A five-member committee would fix the location, create the school, and serve as trustees. The city offering the best inducements would get the school, provided it was healthful and accessible.

The *Constitution* immediately coordinated the bid that Atlanta would make. Four other localities envisioned themselves as sites. Harris, chairman of the location committee, led the campaign for Macon. Athens, home of the University of Georgia, wanted to fold the new school into the University and said it could do it cheaply by hiring one professor and putting up a shop. Milledgeville, still aggrieved by the loss of the capital, wanted it as did Penfield, former home of Mercer, an institution of higher education that had moved to Macon.

Atlanta, Macon, and Athens were the real competitors. Each major partner in the *Constitution* was involved. Inman was on the site committee representing Atlanta. He, Grady, and Hemphill put up personal money, and Howell was a principal spokesman for Atlanta. He dealt roughly with Athens when that city offered its inducement, which was pretty much the facilities of the university already owned by the state. Howell thought that Atlanta might offer the Western and Atlantic Railroad, also state-owned. That road might be operated in connection with the school some day. Grady, a trustee of the University of Georgia, tried to appear impartial but was in the committee room conferring with the other representatives of Atlanta.[53]

Macon made an underhanded thrust, claiming that Atlanta was poorly drained and unhealthy. The *Constitution* struck back and accused the *Telegraph*, which had published the allegation, of an "amazing pitch of stupid hatred."[54] Upon that elevated note, the day came for a decision, and the committee took twenty-one ballots with no result. When proceedings resumed, Atlanta won on the twenty-fourth ballot with three of five votes, the Macon and Athens representatives holding out to the end. Atlanta offered $50,000 from the city, $20,000 from private citizens, one of three sites to build upon, and $2,000 a year from the city for twenty years.

Athens and Macon could not be reconciled. The Athens *Banner-Watchman* thought that a permanent rift was made and that the university and the technical school would be at daggers drawn. Some opponents argued that the act creating the new institution was unconstitutional. There was talk of repealing it in the legislature, destroying the legal footing of the enterprise. The move never took place. At the inaugural exercises, Harris spoke for himself and doubtless for his friends in Macon: "[M]y heart was almost broken."[55]

The *Twelfth Census* of the United States, conducted in 1900, was done twenty years after Grady became managing editor of the *Constitution,* nineteen years after the exposition of 1881, and twelve years after the opening of Georgia Tech. In that massive collection of data, the director, William R. Merriam, and his chief statistician for manufactures, S. N. D. North, authorized several statements expressing turn-of-the-century opinion.

The exposition of 1881 was a "great impetus" to manufacturing in Georgia. The Georgia Institute of Technology was a huge asset. Its graduates were engaged in manufacturing with remarkable success. Many cities of Georgia had made advances, including those considered the principal rivals of Atlanta; but Atlanta was the leading manufacturer and had shown the most rapid growth. Its average number of wage earners went up 17.6 percent between 1890 and 1900. The worth of its manufactures increased 17.8 percent, and its products made up 15.7 percent of all the goods made in Georgia in terms of value. Cotton mills were still the largest employers in Georgia, but Atlanta had only three. The triumph of the city lay in smaller industries.[56]

Under the bright aegis of the New South Movement, the struggle for dominance and development had gone forward. Jealousy, suspicion, and misrepresentation mixed uneasily with the spirit of foursquare, if heated, competition. Grady's work in the 1880s had helped to shape the broader reputations of several cities including his own, and by 1900 Atlanta had achieved some of the goals that he desired for it.

7
Epilogue

The Atlanta Ring began coming apart on the day in 1886 that Gordon was elected governor. From that moment until the hour of Grady's death in 1889, the estrangement of the men became more marked.[1] The reason may be guessed at. Gordon was a celebrated figure. He disliked hearing men say that Grady had elected him governor and was increasingly irritated at it. Once elected, he no longer needed Grady. As an incumbent, he could handle his own reelection.

The self-interest holding the Ring together weakened further when Colquitt flamboyantly went his own way on the tariff. Although Grady and Evan P. Howell sometimes denied being protectionists, they believed that a substantial tariff was required to encourage industry. Colquitt, with part of his political base in the planter class, was a low-tariff senator. He wanted Grady and Howell to help his reelection to the Senate in 1888, but after his talk to the Intra-State Farm Convention in 1887, he could not know whether help would come.

Rumors spread that there was trouble in the Ring, and men began to say that the *Constitution* and Gordon were now distant. The governor said nothing, but what the newspaper said could be read several ways: as heavy-handed humor, as raillery, or as saucy insult: "The *Constitution* does not need the governor. He is neither an editor, reporter, proof-reader, printer or pressman, and even if he was, our staff is full."[2] The newspaper continued to praise Gordon from time to time, and the public saw nothing of a rupture.

The first real break came with Colquitt. In 1888 President Cleveland was ending his first term and Democrats were divided on several issues. Many of them supported the Mills bill, a measure to lower the tariff, and Cleveland himself favored a lower tariff. To Grady and Howell, the Mills bill moved in the wrong direction, and the matter became divisive in May 1888, at the State Democratic Convention. Colquitt was there and to many people appeared to take over while denying doing so. It seemed that he wanted no one except supporters of the Mills bill to go to the National Democratic Convention in St. Louis. Howell was outraged that Colquitt helped to select a slate of delegates, then defeated everyone else. A confidant of Grady's sneaked the senator's choices to Grady before they were made public.[3]

Among the persons whom the Colquitt people defeated was Walsh, editor of the Augusta *Chronicle*, a protectionist like Grady and Howell and up to that moment, only a very occasional friend. Once Colquitt crushed Walsh, however, Grady and Howell threw their arms around him.[4]

"[I]n all this we will get even with Colquitt," said Howell. "Grady is outraged at his conduct. Colquitt sent Grady word that he had done as much for him Grady as he Grady had ever done for him, &c. Grady has at last found him out, and says he shall have opposition [for reelection to the Senate] if he has to make the race [himself]." Howell wrote to Senator Brown in Washington asking for a letter backing Grady for the United States Senate.[5]

The Atlanta Ring had lost its purpose when one member thought of running against another. Colquitt professed surprise that Grady's resentment reached such a pitch and said that Grady was responsible if their friendship ended.[6]

A personal rebuff of the kind not easily forgiven entered the picture. In March 1888 Grady organized the Piedmont Chautauqua, patterned after the Chautauqua Institution founded in New York in the 1870s. Grady was technically only vice-president of the enterprise but actually was its mover. The idea was to have a Summer

University at Salt Springs, Georgia, some twenty miles northwest of Atlanta, and to shuttle large numbers of people from Atlanta out to it. The University of Virginia would supply most of the faculty. Regular registrants could not make a profit for the Chautauqua, however; only special events drawing huge throngs could do that.

To draw such crowds, Grady arranged appearances by T. DeWitt Talmage, Thomas Nelson Page, himself, and Roger Mills, author of the Mills bill. Because Mills was low-tariff, Congressman William McKinley was thought a proper person to present a high-tariff viewpoint, and Colquitt was asked to invite McKinley.

He absolutely refused to help. Grady was furious. His personal money, never in plentiful supply, was invested in the Chautauqua and he worried about its financial health. Finally, Senator Brown invited McKinley, who spoke to a large audience on August 21, 1888.[7]

The November day when the legislature would elect a United States senator was approaching, and Colquitt had no idea of vacating the seat voluntarily. Reports abounded that Grady was a candidate, urged on by Howell who believed that Gordon would repay his debt to Grady by supporting him. Howell was never more incorrect. Gordon's office, if later reports are believed, was headquarters for the opposition. Grady never announced as a candidate but made an ambiguous statement which led some people to believe that he wanted to be elected. Gordon himself believed that Grady was asking members of the Assembly for their votes, and even the *Constitution* said that more than seventy legislators had agreed to support him. Gordon later told Grady that had Grady frankly avowed his ambitions, "I had not the slightest objection to your being a candidate," a far different thing from saying that Grady had his backing.[8]

During much of November 1888 the *Constitution* seemed to run a campaign for Grady in the news columns, which Grady controlled, while keeping silent editorially. When the election finally was held, the managing editor's name was not presented. Colquitt was re-elected, but irreparable harm was done to inter-Ring relationships. Grady's secretary said that Gordon's conduct hurt Grady more than the world ever knew.[9]

Senator Brown remained a friend, but no one knew what was about to happen to him. In 1888 Gordon heard Brown say that poor health might cause him to leave the Senate. From that moment, Gordon told everyone who inquired that he probably would run for Brown's seat in 1890. Apparently he did not care whether Brown was ready to give it up.[10]

Brown's health was the issue over which a total rupture occurred. In June 1889 rumors reported Brown near death.[11] On June 9 Grady wrote a short editorial for the Sunday paper saying that Brown was not seriously ill and that he had a long history of rising from sickbeds. "The administrators of his political estate may rely on this."

Gordon certainly took offense at that sentence, and the offense grew worse when people told Gordon that Grady was circulating unflattering reports about him. Grady allegedly told a son of Brown that Gordon was seeking votes in the legislature to secure his own choice as senator in the event that Brown died, which, if true, was the same as disporting oneself on the grave of a man not yet dead. Acrimonious letters followed. Gordon made unfortunate reference to Grady's "professed" friendship for him, and Grady's response was chilling. "In your letter you say that I have for years 'professed' a sincere friendship for you. You will pardon me for saying, my dear general, that this word is a poor summing up of our relations for the past fifteen years. However, I shall enter no defense to the doubt and discourtesy it carries. To the sincerity of my friendship for you, I prefer to let the record of those fifteen years bear testimony. The open record to the public; the open and sealed record to you."[12]

A few months later, when Grady made up the party to accompany him on his final trip to Boston, someone suggested that Governor Gordon be invited. Grady said that he "would not ask him if he were the last man in Atlanta." When Gordon appeared at Grady's funeral, the family acknowledged his presence but thought it "poor requital for the wrongs the governor did Mr. Grady while living."[13]

Had Grady lived and wished to go to the Senate in 1890, he probably could have defeated Governor Gordon for the seat. Such an accord had been struck with the farmers that when Clark Howell, a mere beneficiary of the arrangement, ran for Speaker of the Georgia House of Representatives in November 1890, he got the unanimous endorsement of the Alliance Caucus and became Speaker with 143 of 167 votes cast. Grady might have expected to do as well in a bid for the Senate. The Alliance was unhappy with Gordon. Nevertheless, he was elected to the Senate in 1890 replacing Brown; a heavy vote against Gordon went to a weak and scattered opposition.[14]

Service in the United States Senate for a long period probably would have been uncongenial to Grady. His life in Georgia brimmed with moment-to-moment activity—writing, arranging, manipulating, and in the final three years, speaking. In the Senate, the pace was slow with little room for the improvisation at which he excelled and in which he took pleasure. Neither could the Senate have served his New South objectives so well as did the managing editorship of the Atlanta *Constitution.*

One scholar has wondered whether it was possible for Grady to have had as much influence as surviving records suggest he had. Two factors support the testimony of the records.

First, despite what he said in his speeches and writings, Grady's objectives were local and limited. The resources he brought to bear upon them were close at hand, and the energy and single-mindedness he applied to them were marveled at in his own day. He was committed to winning elections for his candidates, to sponsoring expositions and events to benefit Atlanta, to promoting business and civic enterprises, all local goals he could accomplish.

Second, in achieving his ends, Grady often had help he could not have commanded. In his general objective of advancing Atlanta, location and demographics helped the city. The pattern of railroad development, so essential to prosperity, was in place before Grady became managing editor of the Atlanta *Constitution.* The "Atlanta spirit," which made the city such a ferocious competitor, was noted before the Civil War. He had the undivided assistance of the Atlanta business community in mounting the expositions he organized, in supplying manpower for the political campaigns he directed, and in advancing innumerable enterprises.

In political campaigns, he usually had good candidates. They would have won some of their elections without him. One thinks immediately of the bids of Governor McDaniel and Senator Brown in 1884, both strong with the power of incumbency and sure to be returned. Sometimes, as in the Colquitt campaign of 1880, Grady had help from people and newspapers who a short time later became his enemies. In his farm strategy, he finally had the all-out assistance of the Alliance, which earlier he had wished to kill by silence.

All of that being so, what does one make of Grady's activities? Judging him as one would judge a present-day politician—by how much of his plans went into effect—one observes that a great part of what he worked for came to pass.[15]

The purpose of this study, however, is to determine what the New South Movement meant to Grady. What do his activities say about the Movement as he saw it? In answering that question, his actions count more than his words, what he did and where he expended his efforts more than what he accomplished. On the surface, he articulated a vision of the New South noteworthy for beauty and consistency. Leaders in communities seeking to develop themselves in the pattern described by Grady had the same vision and in fact ascribed great qualities of leadership to him. However, Grady used the New South platform as a safe and attractive convenience, blame-free in its pure form, and mostly work-free for him. He did little about it beyond writing articles and making speeches. His committed work went into a singular local application of the New South elements— farm policy, race, industrialization, and reconciliation—each emphasized or distorted in a way to help his city.

What Grady said about the New South never matched what he did. Except for an occasional investment for profit, there is no sign that he ever helped any nuts-and-bolts plan to develop the South as a whole or any city other than his own. Occasional praise and congratulations extended to other localities had a perfunctory ring to it. When in 1888 he finally lent his oratorical skills to two other cities, one suspects interested motives. He spoke in Dallas, Texas, in October 1888, shortly before the Georgia legislature elected a senator. It was said that publicity from Dallas was expected to help Grady's senatorial chances. He also spoke on "Carolina Day" at Walsh's Augusta Exposition shortly after the Assembly reelected Colquitt. By then, he wished to please Walsh, rebuffed by Colquitt, and he also wished to be heard by the influential audience that Walsh had assembled, the state officials and legislatures of Georgia and South Carolina.

Grady's heart belonged to Atlanta, not to his region. He said that Atlanta was his "first and only love," and allowing for the exaggeration for which he was famous, his activities bore him out.[16]

Appendix
The Dissolved Friendship of Henry W. Grady
and John B. Gordon: Five Documents

Document One

[In June, 1889, rumors in Georgia reported that Senator Joseph E. Brown was sick and might die. Grady heard those reports along with others that said Governor John B. Gordon was speaking with legislators on behalf of his own election to the United States Senate in case the seat became vacant. Gordon was nearing the end of the first year of his second two-year term as governor and he could not succeed himself. Grady wrote an unsigned editorial for a Sunday edition of the *Constitution* at which Gordon took offense.]

Senator Brown Constantly Improving.

Our reporters were on Friday night led into the error sedulously spread abroad concerning Senator Brown's health, and reported that he was critically ill.

The truth is, Senator Brown has not been critically ill at all. He has steadily improved for the past two weeks, and on Friday was better than he had been since he was taken sick. He continues to improve and will soon be out and among the people.

Since Cardinal Richelieu—blessed be his dauntless memory—there has lived no man who is quite the equal of Senator Joe Brown in rising from a sick bed and with a patient smile resuming his place in the ranks of men to the surprise of those who had been speculating on his death. There is yet work for Georgia's senior senator to do, and he is going to do it. The administrators of his political estate may rely on this.[1]

Document Two
[John B. Gordon to Henry W. Grady]

June 24, 1889

Dear Henry,

Our friendship has been close & cordial & of long standing. I am unconscious of having done one act or said one word that should cause estrangement.

Mr. Julius Brown however on inquiry from me informs me that you told him that I had been engaged in writing letters predicting the early death of his Father & seeking to influence votes for myself as his successor, and that you had written or would write the Editorial which appeared in the Constitution Sunday, June [9].[2]

I request that you will answer in writing the following questions.

1st—Upon whose authority did you make such statements?

2nd—What was your motive in thus representing me to one of Governor Brown's family?

With the hope of hearing from you promptly, I am

Very Truly Yours,
J. B. GORDON[3]

Document Three
[Henry W. Grady to John B. Gordon]

[Date not given]

[Dear General,]

I did write the editorial you refer to. My reason for writing it was this: A distinguished Georgian was lying ill. Two or three newspapers, openly predicting his early death, were as openly dividing up his political estate. It was stated in these papers, repeatedly and unrebuked, that a candidate was selected for his place, not yet vacated by death or resignation, and his succession already provided for. This I knew to be an annoyance to the family and a humiliation to the senator. I thought it called for an editorial statement as to his real condition, and that it justified it.

You will see, therefore, that I wrote this in answer to what you must agree with me was an unwarranted and improper discussion in the press in which the estate of a sick man was being openly administered and divided up before his own eyes, although he had not yet vacated it by death or resignation. My editorial was proper, was called for, and I do not see how it contained an unwarranted thrust at any one. It certainly was not so intended but was an answer to what I considered an improper discussion in the press. I do not see how this answer could hurt you; it certainly was not intended to do so.

As to the other subject of your letter I take pleasure in saying, first, that I did not carry to Senator Brown's family the information alluded to. The first time I mentioned the matter was at my own house. A friend of yours, and of mine, had just told me that you had stated to him on the preceding Thursday that if there was a vacancy by Senator Brown's death or resignation, you would be a candidate for his place, and asked for his support. As this gentleman left my piazza three others came in, and the matter was discussed in a casual way. One of the gentlemen I since learn mentioned the matter to Mr. Julius Brown. Some weeks afterward—after I had heard the matter discussed from a dozen different standpoints—I met Mr. Brown on the street. He thanked me for the editorial I had written some time previous, and in the casual and brief conversation that followed, your relation to the matter was discussed. I assuredly would not have carried any such information as this to Senator Brown or his family. I regret that it ever reached them—and, indeed, I regret that I should ever have mentioned it at all.

Second, I did not intend to be understood as saying that you had written personal letters predicting Senator Brown's early death and asking support for his place. I have never seen any such letter, and do not recall any instance in which any such letter is directly said to have been written. To be perfectly frank with you, I did think you were actively in the field for Senator Brown's place. My reasons were as follows: I had received not less than a dozen letters from friends in different parts of the state stating that you were positively in the race for Senator Brown's vacancy, and that letters had been received asking that the members of that and adjoining counties be seen in your interest immediately and asked to support you. Three of these letters were enclosed back to me. These letters covered nearly every section of the state, and I took them to indicate a general and concerted canvass.

About that time a gentleman came to my office and stated to Mr. Clark Howell and myself that he had just left your office and that you had stated to him positively that you would be a candidate if a vacancy occurred, that one of the members from his county would support you, and asked him to see the other member at once in your interest, and write you the result. From these and similar indications I concluded that you were a candidate, and on the two occasions referred to, spoke of the matter.

In your letter you say that I have for years "professed" a sincere friendship for you. You will pardon me for saying, my dear general, that this word is a poor summing up of our relations for the past fifteen years. However, I shall enter no defense to the doubt and discourtesy it carries. To the sincerity of my friendship for you, I prefer to let the record of those fifteen years bear testimony. The open record to the public; the open and sealed record to you.[4]

[Henry W. Grady]

Document Four
[John B. Gordon to Henry W. Grady]

July 5, 1889

Dear Henry,

I have been unable to answer your letter because of the unusual tax upon me during the last few days.[5] In the meantime I have a letter from Mr. Julius Brown, a copy of which you have doubtless received.

In regard to the irrelevant portions of that letter, my recollection differs widely from that of Mr. Brown as to what occurred in the interview and in much that he states, his recollection is entirely at fault. Mr. Brown's information as to your bankrupting yourself on my account, and sharing in my financial ventures, &c., will doubtless be as great a revelation to you as it is to me. But all of this is irrelevant to the matter about which I complained in my first letter, and therefore is of no consequence in this connection.

But his recollection and mine are practically the same as to important matters on which I denounced the statement that I had written any such letters as the one referred to. As I had never written nor even contemplated writing such a letter, the charge that I had done so, was an outrage upon me that amply justified the [illegible] language used by me. My denunciation was intended solely for the man who had made that charge, and it was accompanied by a qualification that prevents the language used by me from applying to you if you have been misrepresented.

His statements, however, as to what you told him and others in reference to having a letter from Hon. Guyt McLendon, and Mr. McLendon's statements touching the same, will, when taken together, give you more explicitly the reasons for my first letter to you and justify my complaint that a grievous wrong has been done me.[6]

And now as to your letter in reply to mine, I accept your disclaimer of any intention to reflect upon me in your editorial referred to in my first letter, and discussed in yours which reached me a few days ago; but if I understand the general tenor of your letter, it does me almost a great injustice as did your discussion with Mr. Julius Brown and others, which I am glad to know you now regret. I will not however prolong this letter further than may be necessary to correct some other apprehensions under which you seem to be laboring.

First let me say that I think you must have misunderstood the mutual friend who told you that I "had asked him for his support"; for I have neither written letters upon the subject nor sought to influence the action of any member of the Legislature.

A year or more ago, Senator Brown said in my presence that he had some times thought that he might be compelled to [resign?] his seat on account of his declining health. This called from me the expression of my sincere hope that his health would improve and that no such necessity might arise; but I told him at the time that if living I should probably be a candidate at the end of his term, or upon his resignation if that should occur. From that time to this, I have not hesitated to make this same frank avowal to any one who felt enough interest in the subject to ask about it. In all such matters, I think it more manly, and more consistent with my duty to the people, to be candid and to make no effort to disguise my purposes.

In the next place I am sure that the friend whose name you offer [illegible] who told you of my statement that you were actively canvassing [for a United States Senate seat in 1888], will also tell you that I gave as my reasons for the belief that you were a candidate, the positive statements of many citizens of Georgia. That friend will further tell you, I think, (and if he does not, others will) that I also stated that I had not the slightest objection to your being a candidate, provided you would frankly avow yourself as such; my sole regret in the premises being the change in your feelings to ward me, the evidences of which have been manifest for some time to mutual friends as well as to myself. [Illegible] and feel that it is without any sufficient cause.

And now as to my use of the word "professed" friendship &c. Let me assure you, Henry, that the construction placed by you upon that word ("professed") is wholly at variance with the meaning intended by me, and I think on reflection you will perceive that [illegible] a strained construction. I use the word in the sense of [illegible]—"openly avowed"—an outspoken friendship. I sought to convey by the word "professed" the usual, natural, and primal meaning given to it by Webster; and I regret that you should have misconstrued me.

My sole purpose in referring in that connection to your friendship for me was to emphasize the amazement I experienced on hearing that you were a party to the wrong which I felt so keenly.

Yours truly,
J. B. Gordon[7]

Document Five

[After Grady's death, a memorial service for him was held in Atlanta at De-Give's Opera House. The speeches went on for three hours and Gordon spoke last. On their face, Gordon's remarks seem appropriate; however, they are cooler than one might expect. They describe Grady's abilities, the grief felt in many quarters, his generosity to those who needed him, and the loss sustained by the state and the nation. Nowhere does Gordon express personal regret or acknowledge a personal loss. Nowhere does he cite a recollection or an instance that passed between him and Grady, as the eulogistic style of the day usually required. Gordon's speech was brief.]

Speech of John B. Gordon

The news of Henry Grady's death reached me at a quiet country retreat in a distant section of the State. The grief of that rural community, as deep and sincere as the shock produced by his death was great and unexpected, told more feelingly and eloquently than any words of mine possibly can, the universality of the love and admiration of all her people for Georgia's peerless son.

It is no exaggeration to say that the humblest and the highest, the poorest and richest—all classes, colors and creeds, with an unspeakable sorrow, mourn his death as a public calamity. It is no exaggeration to say that no man lives who can take his place. It is no extravagant eulogy to declare that scarcely any half-dozen men, by their combined efforts, can fill in all departments the places which he filled in his laborious and glorious life.

His wonderful intellect, enabling him, without apparent effort, to master the most difficult and obtuse public questions, and to treat them with matchless grace and power; his versatile genius, which made him at once the leader in great social reforms, as well as in gigantic industrial movements—that genius which made him at once the eloquent advocate, the logical expounder, the wise organiser, the vigorous executive—all these rich and unrivaled endowments, justify in claiming for him a place among the greatest and most gifted of this or any age.

But splendid as were his intellectual abilities, it is the boundless generosity of his nature, his sweet and loving spirit, his considerate and tender charity, exhaustless as a fountain of living waters, refreshing and making happy all hearts around him, these are the characteristics on which I love most to dwell. It is no wonder that his splendid genius attracted the gaze and challenged the homage of the continent. It is perhaps even a less wonder that a man with such boundless sympathies for his fellow men and so prodigal with his own time and talent and money in the service of the public, should be so universally and tenderly loved.

The career of Henry Grady is more than unique. It constitutes a new chapter in human experience. No private citizen in the whole eventful history of this Republic ever wore a chaplet so fadeless or linked his name so surely with deathless immortality. His name as a journalist and orator, his brilliant and useful life, his final crowning triumph, especially the circumstances of martyrdom surrounding his death, making it like that of the giant of holy writ, as we trust, more potential than ever in intellectual prowess of magic of the living man—all these will conspire not more surely to carry his fame to posterity, than will his deeds of charity and ready responses to those who needed his effective help, serve to endear to our hearts and memories, as long as life shall last, the memory of Henry W. Grady.[8]

Notes

1 *Introduction*

1 Henry W. Grady to Mrs. Henry W. Grady [December 1889], written from the Hotel Vendome, Boston, in Henry W. Grady Papers, Box 1, Robert W. Woodruff Library, Emory University, Atlanta, Ga., hereinafter cited as Grady Papers. In 1880 Grady bought shares in the *Constitution* for $80 a share, and additional shares from N. P. T. Finch, associate editor of the newspaper. By 1889 Grady's 236⅔ shares were worth $500 each, or $118,330. Dennis J. Pfennig, "Evan and Clark Howell of the *Atlanta Constitution:* The Partnership (1889–1897)" (Ph.D. dissertation, University of Georgia, 1975), 9, n. 25.

2 The text of this address can be read in Joel Chandler Harris, *Life of Henry W. Grady, Including His Writings and Speeches* (New York, 1890), 158–79.

3 Henry W. Grady to Walter A. Taylor, Atlanta *Constitution*, December 31, 1889.

4 Dr. E. Guernsey to Dr. F. H. Orme, *Constitution*, December 29, 1889.

5 Grady to Mrs. Grady [December 1889], written from the Hotel Vendome, Boston, in Grady Papers, Box 1.

6 The text of the address can be read in Joel Chandler Harris, *Life of Henry W. Grady*, 180–98.

7 Most of the details of the dinner of the evening of December 12 and of the events of December 13 are taken from the *Constitution*, December 13, 14, 1889, and from Raymond B. Nixon, *Henry W. Grady: Spokesman of the New South* (New York, 1943), 316–27. Some of the details of the journey to Boston, the stay there, and the journey home to Georgia are from a memoir by Evan P. Howell, editor in chief, *Constitution*, October 21, 1891.

8 The Bay State Club address, in Joel Chandler Harris, *Life of Henry W. Grady*, 199–207.

206 | *Notes to Pages 5–16*

9 Henry W. Grady to Walter A. Taylor, December 31, 1889; Dr. E. Guernsey to Dr. F. H. Orme, both in *Constitution*, December 29, 1889.

10 Details of the arrival and of Dr. Orme's statement are from the *Constitution*, December 18, 1889.

11 Details of Grady's final days, death, and funeral, ibid., December 23, 24, 26, 1889.

12 "Subscribers to raise the Grady mortgage," copy of an undated memorandum on stationery of the *Constitution* Weekly Department, W. A. Hemphill Papers, Robert W. Woodruff Library, Emory University, Atlanta, Ga.

13 Joel Chandler Harris, *Life of Henry W. Grady*, 42.

14 Ibid., 41; Grady Scrapbook No. 1, pp. 1, 38, in Grady Papers.

15 Joel Chandler Harris, *Life of Henry W. Grady*, 26–27; Nixon, *Henry W. Grady: Spokesman of the New South*, 25.

16 Grady to Joel Chandler Harris, July [?], 1873. Letter found in 1985 in the attic of Harris's home in Atlanta and preserved there.

17 [H. C. Hudgins and Co.], *Life and Labors of Henry W. Grady: His Speeches, Writings, Etc.* (Atlanta, Ga., 1890), 42. The colleague quoted is I. W. Avery.

18 Grady to Clark Howell, September 20, 1884, in Joel Chandler Harris, *Life of Henry W. Grady*, 40–42.

19 Grady to Augusta King Grady, January 31, 1884, in Nixon, *Henry W. Grady: Spokesman of the New South*, 19.

20 Joel Chandler Harris, *Life of Henry W. Grady*, 21.

21 Mrs. William H. (Rebecca Latimer) Felton, *My Memoirs of Georgia Politics* (Atlanta, 1911), 186.

22 Nixon, *Henry W. Grady: Spokesman of the New South*, 22, 240–41.

23 Henry W. Grady, "The Atheistic Tide Sweeping over The Continent," reprinted in Joel Chandler Harris, *Life of Henry W. Grady*, 230–37.

24 Joel Chandler Harris, *Life of Henry W. Grady*, 34–37; *Constitution*, January 13, 1884.

25 *Constitution*, October 21, 22, 1891; May 25, 26, 1892.

26 Ibid., February 13, 1890.

27 Ibid., April 5, 1890.

28 Philip Alexander Bruce, *The Rise of the New South* (Philadelphia, 1905), v–vi, passim.

29 Holland Thompson, *The New South: A Chronicle of Social and Industrial Evolution* (New Haven, Toronto, London, Oxford, 1919), 1, 10–11, 130–42, 192–93, 226. This work is a volume in the Chronicles of America series.

30 Broadus Mitchell, *The Rise of Cotton Mills in the South* (Baltimore, 1921), passim.

31 See Benjamin B. Kendrick and Alex M. Arnett, *The South Looks at Its Past* (Chapel Hill, N.C., 1935), and Walter Prescott Webb, *Divided We Stand: The Crisis of a Frontierless Democracy* (New York, Toronto, 1937). These scholars questioned whether the South was as united on major issues as the New

South proponents claimed. Webb sought to undermine the idea that the Movement was a heroic effort of self-defense by valiant southerners.

32 Paul H. Buck, *The Road to Reunion, 1865–1900* (Boston, Toronto, 1937), 193–95, 305.

33 W. J. Cash, *The Mind of the South* (New York, 1941), x–xi, 103–85.

34 Nixon, *Henry W. Grady: Spokesman of the New South,* passim.

35 C. Vann Woodward, *Tom Watson: Agrarian Rebel* (New York, 1938); C. Vann Woodward, *Origins of the New South, 1877–1913* (Baton Rouge, La., 1951); C. Vann Woodward, *Thinking Back: The Perils of Writing History* (Baton Rouge, La., and London, 1986). What Woodward terms his Black Mass "blasphemy" is in *Thinking Back,* 63–64.

36 Paul M. Gaston, *The New South Creed: A Study in Southern Mythmaking* (New York, 1970); Jonathan M. Wiener, *Social Origins of the New South: Alabama, 1860–1885* (Baton Rouge, La., and London, 1978); Dwight B. Billings, Jr., *Planters and the Making of a "New South": Class, Politics, and Development in North Carolina, 1865–1900* (Chapel Hill, N.C., 1979); David L. Carlton, *Mill and Town in South Carolina, 1880–1920* (Baton Rouge, La., and London, 1982); Carl N. Degler, *Place Over Time: The Continuity of Southern Distinctiveness* (Baton Rouge, La., and London, 1977); Gavin Wright, *Old South, New South: Revolutions in the Southern Economy Since the Civil War* (New York, 1986); Michael Wayne, *The Reshaping of Plantation Society: The Natchez District, 1860–1880* (Baton Rouge, La., and London, 1983); Barbara J. Fields, *Slavery and Freedom on the Middle Ground: Maryland During the Nineteenth Century* (New Haven, Conn., and London, 1985); and James C. Cobb, "Beyond Planters and Industrialists: A New Perspective on the New South," *Journal of Southern History,* LIV (February 1988), 45–68.

37 Much of the line of argument of this book could apply in South Carolina. See E. Culpepper Clark, *Francis Warrington Dawson and the Politics of Restoration: South Carolina, 1874–1889* (University, Ala., 1980).

38 Joel Chandler Harris, *Life of Henry W. Grady,* 87.

39 *Constitution,* December 25, 1886.

40 Numan V. Bartley, *The Creation of Modern Georgia* (Athens, Ga., 1983). See Kenneth Coleman, et al., *A History of Georgia* (Athens, Ga., 1977). Part IV of this work (1865–90) was written by Charles E. Wynes. Steven Hahn, *The Roots of Southern Populism: Yeoman Farmers and the Transformation of the Georgia Upcountry, 1850–1890* (New York, 1983); Robert C. McMath, Jr., *Populist Vanguard: A History of the Southern Farmers' Alliance* (Chapel Hill, N.C., 1975); Stephen J. DeCanio, *Agriculture in the Postbellum South: The Economics of Production and Supply* (Cambridge, Mass., and London, 1974); Lewis Nicholas Wynne, *The Continuity of Cotton: Planter Politics in Georgia, 1865–1892* (Macon, Ga., 1986); Charles L. Flynn, Jr., *White Land, Black Labor, Caste and Class in Late Nineteenth-Century Georgia* (Baton Rouge, La., and London, 1983). Roger L. Ransom and Richard Sutch, *One Kind of Freedom:*

208 | *Notes to Pages 19–24*

The Economic Consequences of Emancipation (Cambridge, Mass., London, New York, Melbourne, 1977); Joel Williamson, *The Crucible of Race, Black-White Relations in the American South Since Emancipation* (New York, Oxford, 1984); J. Morgan Kousser, *The Shaping of Southern Politics: Suffrage Restriction and the Establishment of the One-Party South, 1880–1910* (New Haven, Conn., and London, 1974). James Michael Russell, *Atlanta, 1847–1890: City Building in the Old South and the New* (Baton Rouge, La., and London, 1988); Edward J. Cashin, *The Story of Augusta* (Augusta, Ga., 1980).

41 Richard C. Wade, *The Urban Frontier: The Rise of Western Cities, 1790–1830* (Cambridge, Mass., 1967), 322–36. The quotation is from 336.

42 Woodward, *Tom Watson;* Woodward, *Origins of the New South;* Carlton, *Mill and Town in South Carolina;* Wiener, *Social Origins of the New South,* Chaps. 6 and 7.

2 Grady and the Atlanta Constitution

1 Franklin M. Garrett, *Atlanta and Environs: A Chronicle of Its People and Events* (Athens, Ga., 1969, facsimile reprint of a 1954 edition), I, 788–91; Samuel W. Small, "Story of the Constitution's Sixty Years of Service to the City, State and Country" (mimeographed account), Ralph E. McGill Collection, Robert W. Woodruff Library, Emory University, Atlanta, Ga.; Thomas H. Martin, *Atlanta and Its Builders: A Comprehensive History of the Gate City of the South* (Atlanta, Ga., 1902), II, 370–71; Walter G. Cooper, *The Story of Georgia* (New York, 1938), IV, 110; Louis T. Griffith and John E. Talmadge, *Georgia Journalism, 1763–1950* (Athens, Ga., 1951), 93–107.

2 Sketch of William Arnold Hemphill, in Kenneth Coleman and Charles Stephen Gurr, eds., *Dictionary of Georgia Biography* (Athens, Ga., 1983), I, 434–35. The sketch was written by Jack Spalding, former editor of the Atlanta *Journal.* See Wallace P. Reed, *History of Atlanta, Georgia* (Syracuse, N.Y., 1889), Pt. II, 60–62.

3 Sketch of Isaac Wheeler Avery, in Coleman and Gurr, eds., *Dictionary of Georgia Biography,* I, 40–41. The sketch was written by Ellen Barrier Garrison.

4 Sketch of Evan Park Howell, ibid., 484–85. The sketch was written by Dennis J. Pfennig.

5 Isaac W. Avery, *The History of the State of Georgia from 1850 to 1881* (New York, 1881), 613–15; Griffith and Talmadge, *Georgia Journalism, 1763–1950,* 93–106; Dennis J. Pfennig, "Evan and Clark Howell," 10–11; Small, "Story of the Constitution's Sixty Years of Service to the City, State and Country," in McGill Collection.

6 *Constitution,* March 31, June 12, 1881; March 25, 1883. The *Constitution* did not discuss the quality of the "midnight edition" until a newspaper in Albany, Ga., made an issue of it.

7 When Finch retired in December 1885, he sold his stock and had no further involvement with the newspaper. He had 200 shares with a par value of $100, but his holdings, technically valued at $20,000, were worth $60,000 when sold. Howell, Hemphill, and Grady each bought $5,000 worth. Businessmen bought the remainder as an investment but had no voice in operating the company. William A. Hemphill had 271⅓ shares; Howell, 266⅔; Grady, 236⅔; Samuel M. Inman, an Atlanta cotton broker, 100; James Swann of New York, who was also president of the Atlanta National Bank, 50; Robert A. Hemphill, 37; and William J. Campbell, 20. Campbell was employed by the Constitution Publishing Company as a bookkeeper in the general business office. The stock had been worth $80 a share in 1880. By December 1889, it was worth $500. *Constitution,* December 22, 1885; Pfennig, "Evan and Clark Howell," 9.

8 What follows concerning the facilities and schedule of the newspaper is from the *Constitution,* August 17, 1884, except as indicated.

9 Sketch of Clark Howell, in Coleman and Gurr, eds., *Dictionary of Georgia Biography,* I, 483–84. The sketch was written by Dennis J. Pfennig. Clark Howell became assistant managing editor of the *Constitution* in January 1888.

10 P. J. Moran became night editor in January 1888.

11 (H.C. Hudgins and Co.), *Life and Labors of Henry W. Grady,* 59–60.

12 *Constitution,* November 19, 24, 1884; December 3, 1889.

13 Ibid., November 2, 1884; November 28, 1886.

14 Ibid., February 18, May 6, November 25, December 16, 1888.

15 Ibid., September 7, 1883; April 2, 1886. See Bill Arp's account, December 24, 1939.

16 Ibid., April 1, 1886.

17 What follows about Grady's life up to 1880 is based upon Nixon, *Henry W. Grady: Spokesman of the New South,* 25–169, except as indicated.

18 Grady to Ann Gartrell Grady, April 10, 1869, in Grady Papers; Dorothy Siedenburg Hadley, "Henry W. Grady as a Student Speaker," *Quarterly Journal of Speech,* XXV (April 1939), 205–11. Hadley has studied all surviving records of Grady's debating activities as a student. She is convinced that his reputation as a student speaker, though respectable enough, is based upon the reminiscences that his friends wrote in light of later events.

19 Joel Chandler Harris, *Life of Henry W. Grady,* 142.

20 Grady Scrapbook No. 1, p. 19, in Grady Papers; Marvin G. Bauer, "Henry W. Grady, Spokesman of the New South" (Ph.D. dissertation, University of Wisconsin, 1936), 175.

21 For an account of Grady's early ventures in journalism, see a memoir written by Avery, published in the *Constitution,* October 21, 1891.

22 Grady Scrapbook No. 1, pp. 2, 11, in Grady Papers; *United States Congress, Testimony Taken by Joint Select Committee on Condition of Affairs in the Late Insurrectionary States* (Washington, D.C., 1872), VII, 625, 634–37, 879, 886.

23 Joel Chandler Harris, *Life of Henry W. Grady*, 25, 31.
24 Nixon, *Henry W. Grady: Spokesman of the New South*, 44.
25 Joel Chandler Harris, *Life of Henry W. Grady*, 25–26.
26 Joseph H. Parks, *Joseph E. Brown of Georgia* (Baton Rouge, 1977), 478–79.
27 Joel Chandler Harris, *Life of Henry W. Grady*, 32.
28 Ibid., 32–33.
29 Bauer, "Henry W. Grady, Spokesman of the New South," 385–419.
30 Joel Chandler Harris, *Life of Henry W. Grady*, 47–52.
31 Manuscript of W. T. Turnbull, Box 1, in Grady Papers. Turnbull later was Judge of the Superior Court in Rome, Ga.
32 Grady Diary, December 1, 1878, Box 2, in Grady Papers.
33 John F. Stover, *The Railroads of the South, 1865–1900: A Study in Finance and Control* (Chapel Hill, N.C., 1955), 148–49, 226.
34 Promissory note of Henry W. Grady to Cyrus W. Field, May 8, 1880, and letter of the same date from Field to Grady, in Grady Papers.
35 *Constitution*, August 12, 1880. Grady's associate was John B. Gordon.
36 Ibid., July 27, 1888. The newspaper fired the cannon in 1960 following the election of John F. Kennedy as president, as well as in 1884 for the election of Grover Cleveland. See December 17, 1884; January 30, 1887.
37 Ibid., June 5, 1889.
38 Ibid., December 29, 1885; August 17, 1884; Joel Chandler Harris, *Life of Henry W. Grady*, 39–40.
39 *Constitution*, August 30, 1885.
40 Ibid., September 18, 1881.
41 Ibid., October 21, 1882; February 13, 1887; January 24, 1889; January 19, 1890; Savannah (Ga.) *Morning News*, July 15, 1888.
42 *Constitution*, January 14, 23, 28, 1887; E. Culpepper Clark, *Francis Warrington Dawson and the Politics of Restoration*, 140–46.
43 *Constitution*, March 13, 1889.
44 Ibid., April 13, 1883. The politician was Augustus O. Bacon of Macon. Bacon was a United States senator from Georgia from 1895 until his death in 1914.
45 Ibid., July 1, 1886.
46 Macon *Telegraph*, November 13, 1887.
47 The text of Howell's and Grady's speeches appeared in the *Constitution*, November 20, 1887. There was coverage of the campaign in almost every issue during November.
48 Ibid., November 12, 1887.
49 Ibid.; Garrett, *Atlanta and Environs*, II, 159–60.
50 Nixon, *Henry W. Grady: Spokesman of the New South*, 275.
51 *Constitution*, November 29, 1887.
52 Ibid., November 30, 1887.
53 Ibid., November 29, 30, December 1, 4, 6, 7, 8, 18, 1887; Garrett, *Atlanta and Environs*, II, 164. Atlanta municipal politics during this period was ex-

amined by Eugene John Watts, "Characteristics of Candidates in City Politics: Atlanta, 1865–1903" (Ph.D. dissertation, Emory University, 1969), 172–205.

54 *Constitution,* October 7, 9, 18, December 2, 5, 6, 1888; Garrett, *Atlanta and Environs,* II, 181–82.
55 Alexander K. McClure, *Colonel Alexander K. McClure's Recollections of Half a Century* (Salem, Mass., 1902; reprinted by AMS Press of New York, 1976), 401–402.
56 Joel Chandler Harris, *Life of Henry W. Grady,* 30.
57 McClure, *Recollections of Half a Century,* 401.
58 Thomas W. Reed, "Henry W. Grady: A Sketch Based upon Personal Recollections," *Bulletin No. 3a,* University of Georgia, Athens (February 1935), 7–8; sketch of Reed in Coleman and Gurr, eds., *Dictionary of Georgia Biography,* II, 829–31. The sketch was written by Susan B. Tate.
59 *Constitution,* September 1–8, 1886; Nixon, *Henry W. Grady: Spokesman of the New South,* 3–7; E. Culpepper Clark, *Francis Warrington Dawson,* 138–41.
60 Joel Chandler Harris, *Life of Henry W. Grady,* 30–31.
61 *Constitution,* November 4, 1884; October 4, 5, November 4, 1888.
62 Joel Chandler Harris, *Life of Henry W. Grady,* 65–66.
63 Ibid.; *Constitution,* January 23, August 30, 1885; April 20, November 28, 1886; January 1, 1888; December 17, 1889; Weekly *Constitution* envelope, postmarked August 9, 1887, with superscription claiming 118,000 circulation, in Box 1, Grady Papers.
64 Randolph L. Fort, "History of the Atlanta Journal" (M.A. thesis, Emory University, Atlanta, Ga., 1930), 1–16.

3   *Politics and the Atlanta Ring: 1880–1886*

1 Grigsby Hart Wotton, Jr., "New City of the South: Atlanta, 1843–1873" (Ph.D. dissertation, The Johns Hopkins University, 1973), 222–24.
2 Grady Scrap Book No. 2, p. 102, in Grady Papers. See Judson C. Ward, "The Atlanta Spirit in Post-Bellum Georgia," an unpublished paper delivered before the Atlanta Historical Society, October 24, 1953.
3 C. Mildred Thompson, *Reconstruction in Georgia: Economic, Social, Political, 1865–1872* (Savannah, Ga., 1972, first published in 1915 by the Columbia University Press, New York), 173–75. Also see Walter McElreath, *A Treatise on the Constitution of Georgia* (Atlanta, Ga., 1912), 146–68. See Royce Shingleton, "Atlanta Becomes the Capital: The Role of Richard Peters," *Atlanta Historical Journal,* XXVIII (Winter 1984–85), 39–50.
4 Avery, *History of the State of Georgia from 1850 to 1881,* 528. The constitution bestowed broad powers to help business and railroads, and much help was given to railroads, often connectors, which benefited Atlanta. See *Consti-*

tution of the State of Georgia, 1868, Art. III, Sec. 6, Para. 5, printed in Mc-
Elreath, *A Treatise on the Constitution of Georgia,* 330–31; also see McElreath,
169; Thompson, *Reconstruction in Georgia,* 207–17; Lewis Nicholas Wynne,
"Planter Politics in Georgia: 1860–1890" (Ph.D. dissertation, University of
Georgia, 1980), 224–25.

5 Ellen Barrier Garrison, "Old South or New? Georgia and the Constitution
of 1877" (Ph.D. dissertation, Stanford University, 1981), 100–104, 126 ff.;
William P. Brandon, "Calling the Georgia Constitutional Convention of
1877," *Georgia Historical Quarterly,* XVII (September 1933), 189–203; E.
Merton Coulter, *The South During Reconstruction* (Baton Rouge, La., 1947),
287; McElreath, *A Treatise on the Constitution of Georgia,* 169. The vote for the
convention was 48,181, with 39,057 against. There were no returns from
two counties.

6 Garrison, "Old South or New?" 160–61; Brandon, "Calling the Georgia
Constitutional Convention of 1877," 190–92.

7 Augusta *Chronicle and Constitutionalist,* February 1, 1877, quoted in Garrison, "Old South or New?" 140.

8 Garrison, "Old South or New?" 186–87.

9 Nixon, *Henry W. Grady: Spokesman of the New South,* 144. Grady's facts were
slightly awry, but he had caught the spirit. The refusal to employ a chaplain
was not so bold as it looked. The convention was trying to save a salary. Several members were clergymen and rotated opening prayers among their
number.

10 Samuel W. Small, *A Stenographic Report of the Proceedings of the Constitutional
Convention Held in Atlanta, Georgia, 1877* (Atlanta, Ga., 1877), 307–10. For
an overview of the convention and the constitution of 1877, see McElreath,
A Treatise on the Constitution of Georgia, 169–81; Albert Berry Saye, *A Constitutional History of Georgia, 1732–1945* (Athens, Ga., 1948), 279–90.

11 *Constitution of the State of Georgia, 1877,* Art. VII, Sec. 5; Art. IV, Sec. 2, 267–
69; Art. I, Sec. 2, Para. 4, 354, published in McElreath, *A Treatise on the Constitution of Georgia,* 385. The General Assembly set up the machinery to
regulate railroads on October 14, 1879, by creating the Georgia Railroad
Commission. In 1880 the commission posted a standard rate of charges for
both passengers and freight. This schedule withstood attack on several
fronts and became an effective if sometimes controversial instrument by
which rates were set. Jim David Cherry, "The Georgia Railroad Commission, 1879–1888" (M.A. thesis, University of North Carolina at Chapel
Hill, 1941), 66–69.

12 Ulrich Bonnell Phillips concludes that as much as Milledgeville wanted the
Capitol, its presence in that town had been damaging. "Its political importance and the possible advantages to accrue therefrom overshadowed the
town's commercial and industrial interests, [and] inclined the people in a
measure to look for favors instead of for opportunities." The energies of
the town were paralyzed, he says. Ulrich Bonnell Phillips, *A History Of*

Transportation in the Eastern Cotton Belt to 1860 (New York, 1908), 282. Atlanta had a different leadership and spirit and never fell into similar error.

13 Wynne, *The Continuity of Cotton*, 103.

14 Ibid., 112; Judson C. Ward, "Georgia Under the Bourbon Democrats, 1872–1890" (Ph.D. dissertation, University of North Carolina at Chapel Hill, 1947), 521; Garrison, "Old South or New?" 258–59; Charles E. Wynes, writing in Kenneth Coleman, ed., *A History of Georgia* (Athens, Ga., 1977), 219. A historian of Augusta reports that the citizens of that city were not happy with the constitution of 1877. Most of the leaders there were identified with the New South Movement. Cashin, *The Story of Augusta*, 154.

15 Augusta *Chronicle and Constitutionalist*, December 4, 1877; *Constitution*, August 28, 1877.

16 Avery, *History of the State of Georgia from 1850 to 1881*, 530. See Reed, *History of Atlanta, Georgia*, Pt. II, 73.

17 Saye, *Constitutional History of Georgia*, 283; *Constitution*, August 28, December 5, 1877. The newspaper continued its efforts at conciliation by congratulating individuals who disported themselves well while opposing Atlanta. See the commendation of Farish Furman of Milledgeville, *Constitution*, December 7, 1877.

18 James Michael Russell, "Atlanta Gate City of the South, 1847 to 1885" (Ph.D. dissertation, Princeton University, 1972), 275–81; Russell, *Atlanta, 1847–1890*, 182–207.

19 *Constitution*, July 2, 1882.

20 Ibid., June 14, 1881; June 5, 1883; Milledgeville *Union and Recorder*, May 29, 1877; Eastman *Journal*, quoted in the Macon *Telegraph*, May 16, 1886; *Telegraph*, June 7, 1886.

21 Felton, *Memoirs of Georgia Politics*, 7.

22 Grady to Joseph E. Brown, March 8, 1884, in Joseph E. Brown Papers, Box 3, Folder 69, University of Georgia Libraries, Athens, hereinafter cited as Joseph E. Brown Papers.

23 For an interesting view of both Brown and the railroad, see Derrell C. Roberts, "Joseph E. Brown and the Western and Atlantic Railroad," *Atlanta Historical Journal*, XXIX (Spring 1985), 5–40.

24 Marietta (Ga.) *Journal*, June 13, 1886, quoted in James Gaston Towery, "The Georgia Gubernatorial Campaign of 1886" (M.A. thesis, Emory University, 1930), 80.

25 A good study of the Georgia Bourbons is Ward, "Georgia Under the Bourbon Democrats, 1872–1890." Especially see the long introduction and 519–25. Ward says that the Bourbons espoused a narrow concept of government but were good conciliators who urged people to submerge personal interests for the common good, which meant keeping blacks under control and Bourbons in charge. Their government was efficient if parsimonious and was conducted under laissez-faire principles. For a more recent study, see Bartley, *The Creation of Modern Georgia*, Chap. 4. See C. Vann

Woodward, "Bourbonism in Georgia," *North Carolina Historical Review,* XVI (January 1939), 23–35.
26 Derrell C. Roberts to the author, November 6, 1985.
27 Grady Secret Code, in Joseph E. Brown Papers, Box 3, Folder 65.
28 Telegram of Grady to Joseph E. Brown, May 15, 1880, ibid.
29 Telegram of Grady to Brown, May 17, 1880, ibid. Grady's use of a code seems sinister, but codes were common. For an example involving another figure, see Stover, *The Railroads of the South,* 173–74.
30 Telegram of Alfred H. Colquitt to Joseph E. Brown, May 19, 1880, in Joseph E. Brown Papers, Box 3, Folder 65.
31 Felton, *Memoirs of Georgia Politics,* 266. Also see Ralph L. Eckert, "The Breath of Scandal: John B. Gordon, Henry W. Grady, and the Resignation-Appointment Controversy of May 1880," *Georgia Historical Quarterly,* LXIX (Fall 1985), 315–37.
32 See William Pittman Roberts, "The Public Career of Doctor William Harrell Felton" (Ph.D. dissertation, University of North Carolina at Chapel Hill, 1952).
33 Avery, *History of the State of Georgia from 1850 to 1881,* 532, 538–39.
34 Ibid., 569, 587–601.
35 Lala Carr Steelman, "The Public Career of Augustus Octavius Bacon" (Ph.D. dissertation, University of North Carolina at Chapel Hill, 1950), passim.
36 Nathaniel E. Harris, *Autobiography: The Story of an Old Man's Life with Reminiscences of Seventy-Five Years* (Macon, Ga., 1925), 316–17.
37 Bacon laid plans for a campaign well into the spring of 1882. He and Senator Brown had long been enemies. Bacon opposed Brown in 1880 when Brown went to the Senate, and Brown had opposed Bacon's election as Speaker of the Georgia House of Representatives. Nevertheless, Bacon said that they had made a truce of sorts, although little evidence supports that claim. Bacon wrote to Brown in 1882 asking for help in becoming governor. Brown politely declined to help. Augustus O. Bacon to Joseph E. Brown, May 22, 1882; Brown to Bacon, May 25, 1882, Box 1, Folder 3, in Elijah Brown Collection, Atlanta Historical Society, Atlanta, Ga.
38 Ward, "Georgia Under the Bourbon Democrats," 122–56; Grady to Estelle C. Smith, May 18, 1883, in Grady Papers, Box 1.
39 *Constitution,* March 27, 1883.
40 Grady to Estelle C. Smith, May 18, 1883, in Grady Papers, Box 1. For an account of these events, see Steelman, "Public Career of Augustus Octavius Bacon," 63–71.
41 *Constitution,* April 13, 1883.
42 Ray Stannard Baker, *Woodrow Wilson: Life and Letters* (Garden City, N.Y., 1927), I, 156.
43 Macon *Daily Telegraph,* May 10, 1886; Hartwell (Ga.) *Sun,* April 30, 1886.

44 Grady to Joseph E. Brown, February 17, 1884, in Joseph E. Brown Papers, Box 3, Folder 69.
45 *Constitution*, April 27, 1884. Cleveland was elected, and his election was riotously celebrated in Atlanta. A crowd assembled, the *Constitution* cannon was fired, and the throng marched on the capitol where the Georgia legislature was in session. Grady was marshal of the procession, his hat draped with an American flag. He brushed passed the doorkeeper of the House of Representatives, mounted the Speaker's dias, seized the gavel, and adjourned the House to celebrate. Nixon, *Henry W. Grady: Spokesman of the New South*, 218–19.
46 Grady to Joseph E. Brown, March 7, 1884, in Joseph E. Brown Papers, Box 3, Folder 69.
47 Ibid.
48 Grady to Joseph E. Brown, March 6, 7, 8, April 17, and an undated July letter, 1884; Evan P. Howell to Joseph E. Brown, March 24, 1884, ibid.
49 *Constitution*, May 13, 1886.
50 L. M. Holland, *The Direct Primary in Georgia* (Urbana, Ill., 1949), 17 ff.
51 Dispatch filed on March 31 for the Macon *Telegraph*, printed April 1, 1886.
52 *Constitution*, April 11, 1886.
53 Ibid., April 30, May 1, 1886. All that follows concerning the journey to Atlanta and the arrival there is from these issues.
54 W. H. Hidell to Dr. W. H. Felton, May 2, 1886, in Rebecca Latimer Felton Papers, Box 2, University of Georgia Libraries, Athens, Ga.
55 *Constitution*, April 9, 1886.
56 Marvin G. Bauer, "Henry W. Grady: Spokesman of the New South" (Ph.D. dissertation, University of Wisconsin, 1936), 426.
57 Samuel Guyton McLendon in the *Constitution*, May 23, 1921; Augusta *Chronicle*, May 5, 1886.
58 *Constitution*, May 3, 7, 1886.
59 Jack J. Spalding to Marvin G. Bauer, June 15, 1936. Reproduced in Bauer, "Henry W. Grady," 526.
60 *Constitution*, May 16, 1886.
61 Ibid., May 13, 1886.
62 Ibid., May 19, 1886.
63 The account of the Augusta confrontation is ibid., May 20, 1886.
64 Augusta *Chronicle*, May 20, 1886.
65 *Constitution*, May 28, 1886.
66 Hartwell *Sun*, April 30, May 14, 21, 1886.
67 *Constitution*, May 28, 1886. Also see June 2, 3, 1886. All reports of this campaign rally and of Harper's account are from the *Constitution*. The Hartwell *Sun* affirms that Gordon had a success in Hartwell.
68 *Constitution*, June 3, 1886.
69 Hartwell *Sun*, May 28, 1886.

70 *Constitution*, February 23, 1888; October 21, 1891.
71 Jack J. Spalding to Marvin G. Bauer, June 15, 1936. Reproduced in Bauer, "Henry W. Grady," 526–27. Spalding's letter was written fifty years after the events occurred and would be treated with caution unless accuracy could be established from contemporary records. The Hartwell *Sun* and the *Constitution* confirm the accuracy. Insofar as the names of people were concerned, Spalding was more accurate fifty years after the events than the *Constitution* was the next morning. One of Spalding's grandsons, also named Jack Spalding, is not surprised. He says that his grandfather never shaded facts even to improve a funny story. John William Baker's *History of Hart County* (Atlanta, Ga., 1933) has information about many of the persons involved and about the narrow-gauge railway. See Hartwell *Sun*, June 4, 1886.
72 Hartwell *Sun*, June 18, July 9, 1886.
73 *Constitution*, November 16, 1890.
74 Augusta *Chronicle*, June 29, 1886.
75 Governor Gordon appointed Frank M. O'Bryan as solicitor of the city court of Atlanta, overriding the petitions of three other qualified candidates. *Constitution*, June 30, 1887; February 23, 1888.

4 Politics and the Farmers

1 Gilbert C. Fite, *Cotton Fields No More: Southern Agriculture, 1865–1980* (Lexington, Ky., 1984), 68. In 1881 Grady wrote a long article entitled "Cotton and Its Kingdom," in which he set forth the elements of the program. It was published in *Harper's New Monthly Magazine*, LXIII (October 1881), 719–34. Late in the decade, Grady commented increasingly on farm matters in speeches, and in April 1887 he bought one-third interest in an agricultural publication, the *Georgia Stock and Agricultural Journal*. He immediately changed its name to *Southern Farm*. Grady was its editor, but its managing editor, William Louis Jones of the University of Georgia, did almost all the work, and the *Constitution* continued as the major forum for Grady's ideas. Nixon, *Henry W. Grady: Spokesman of the New South*, 262.
2 *Constitution*, August 26, 1887.
3 Ibid., April 11, December 20, 1882.
4 Willard Range, *A Century of Georgia Agriculture, 1850–1950* (Athens, Ga., 1954), 151.
5 *Constitution*, August 20, 21, 1884. James Monroe Smith, a successful farmer and sometime legislator from Oglethorpe County, made the mistake in 1885 of saying that farming did not pay. His work force was hit by measles, 300 of his hogs died of cholera, and he was under attack by the principal physician of the state penitentiary for allegedly mistreating the state convicts who worked on his farms. The *Constitution* pummeled Smith for saying

that farming did not pay. The newspaper printed a damaging series of documents about the treatment of his convicts, even though the legal proceedings concerning the matter were closed and the documents were almost a year old. As for Secretary Henderson, he apparently bore a grudge against Grady for years, although he continued to work with him. Following Grady's death, Henderson said: "I had not given in fully to the fact that Grady was a great man until he delivered his famous speech at Boston." That was on December 12, 1889, eleven days before Grady died. See ibid., December 24, 1889; August 7, 1884.

6 Ibid., September 20, 1886. For a representative sampling of the opinion of the *Constitution*, see January 2, 1884; January 9, 29, March 23, July 23, and August 24, 1886; March 16, August 21, 1887; February 18, 20, 26, 29, 1888. For a useful if polemical analysis of the views of the Georgia congressional delegation in the 1880s, see Hiram Harvie Britt, "The Georgia Delegation in Congress, 1880–1890" (M.A. thesis, Emory University, 1930).

7 Charles H. Otken, *The Ills of the South, or Related Causes Hostile to the General Prosperity of the Southern People* (New York, London, 1894), 57. Merchants were entitled to substantial interest charges, for they were making advances on an unharvested crop for which the price was unset. However, the charges were shocking. Rates of 50 percent were common, and four-month loans for corn in 1883 reached 120.9 percent, and for bacon in 1886, 127.5 percent. Ransom and Sutch, *One Kind of Freedom: The Economic Consequences of Emancipation*, 237–40.

8 Otken, *The Ills of the South*, 16–19. For a traditional view of the lien credit system, see John D. Hicks, *The Populist Revolt* (Lincoln, Nebr., reprint), 48 ff. Also see Flynn, *White Land, Black Labor*, 87–93. For an analysis of how the system bound the farmer to the merchant, see Ransom and Sutch, "The 'Lock-in' Mechanism and Overproduction of Cotton in the Postbellum South," 405–25. Thomas D. Clark has described the tone and operations of furnishing stores in *Pills, Petticoats and Plows: The Southern Country Store* (Indianapolis and New York, 1943). Robert Preston Brooks believes that before the worst abuses began, credit under the lien laws may have helped farmers who could not get loans otherwise. See Robert Preston Brooks, *The Agrarian Revolution in Georgia, 1865–1912* (New York, 1971; reissue of the 1914 edition printed at Madison, Wisc.), 32–34. For an overview of some of the agricultural problems of the period, see Harold D. Woodman, *King Cotton and His Retainers: Financing and Marketing the Cotton Crop of the South, 1800–1925* (Lexington, Ky., 1968), Chap. 26.

9 *Constitution*, May 18, 1886. For comment on interest rates and usury laws, see ibid., March 22, April 30, May 20, June 17, 1881; January 18, 1882.

10 R. T. Nesbitt, *Publications of the Georgia State Department of Agriculture for 1892* (Atlanta, Ga., 1892), 177. Adapted from Lewis Nicholas Wynne, "The Alliance Legislature of 1890" (M.A. thesis, University of Georgia, 1970), 8; DeCanio, *Agriculture in the Postbellum South*, 13.

11 Otken, *The Ills of the South,* 99–100, 125. Otken constructed the calculations from census reports. Ransom and Sutch, using modern methods, came to the same conclusions. They rest their findings upon data from Georgia, South Carolina, Alabama, Mississippi, and Louisiana. Ransom and Sutch, *One Kind of Freedom,* 151–59.

12 Grady made a campaign on behalf of an inexpensive fertilizer produced in Georgia by Farish Furman, a Baldwin County farmer and scientist. Stable manure was a major ingredient of Furman's formula. Furman's prospects were cut short by his sudden death in 1883. Lester D. Stephens, "Farish Furman's Formula: Scientific Farming and the 'New South,' " *Agricultural History,* L (April 1976), 377–90; "The Commercial Aspect," *The American Fertilizer,* I (August 1894), 101. Cited in Ransom and Sutch, *One Kind of Freedom,* 189.

13 *Constitution,* June 29, 1883.

14 Ibid., May 2, 1883; December 13, 1882; June 28, 1883.

15 Ibid., May 24, 1883.

16 Ibid., August 14, 1883; August 15, 1888.

17 For excellent analysis of the condition of Georgia farmers, see Alex Mathews Arnett, *The Populist Movement in Georgia* (New York, 1967, reprint of the 1922 edition), 49–75, and Barton C. Shaw, *The Wool-Hat Boys: Georgia's Populist Party* (Baton Rouge, La., and London, 1984), 5–16.

18 *Constitution,* June 25, 1882.

19 Ibid., February 21, September 6, 1883.

20 Randolph Dennis Werner, "Hegemony and Conflict: The Political Economy of a Southern Region, Augusta, Georgia, 1865–1895" (Ph.D. dissertation, University of Virginia, 1977), 238. All that follows concerning the convention is from the *Constitution,* August 16–19, 1887.

21 Robert C. McMath, Jr., "Mobilizing Agrarian Discontent: The Rise of the Farmers' Alliance in Georgia," Unpublished address presented at the convention of the Southern Historical Association, Atlanta, Ga., November 8, 1973, p. 1.

22 *Constitution,* November 2, 18, 22, 1887.

23 Ibid., February 28, 1888.

24 Ibid.

25 Joseph E. Brown to L. N. Trammell, May 23, 1888, in L. N. Trammell Papers, Robert W. Woodruff Library, Emory University, Atlanta, Ga., hereinafter cited as Trammell Papers.

26 *Constitution,* June 4, 1888.

27 Joel Chandler Harris, *Life of Henry W. Grady,* 160; McMath, *Populist Vanguard: A History of the Southern Farmers Alliance,* especially Chap. 5, "Brothers and Sisters: The Alliance as Community." For an interesting study of the North Carolina Alliance, see Lala Carr Steelman, *The North Carolina Farmers' Alliance: A Political History, 1887–1893* (Greenville, N.C., 1985).

28 *Constitution,* July 8, November 10, 1888.

29 The leaders of the Ring were well aware of how bad the situation was. *Con-*

stitution, November 16, 1890. Joseph E. Brown to L. N. Trammell, April 7, 1888, and Alfred H. Colquitt to L. N. Trammell, May 23, 1888, in Trammell Papers.

30 *Constitution*, February 28, 1888.
31 Ibid., August 8, 17, 22, 28, 30, September 9, 23, October 16, 26, 1888; April 4, June 9, 1889.
32 Ibid., March 29, 1889.
33 Joel Chandler Harris, *Life of Henry W. Grady*, 158–59; *Constitution*, July 24, 1889.
34 Joel Chandler Harris, *Life of Henry W. Grady*, 18–19, 176–77.
35 *Constitution*, July 25, 26, 28, August 15, 1889.
36 McMath, *Populist Vanguard*, 49–50; *Constitution*, September 26, 1889.
37 Grady to William J. Northen, February 27, March 4, 1889, Scrapbook Vol. III, Ser. 4, Box 5, 264, in William J. Northen Papers, Georgia Department of Archives and History, Atlanta, herinafter cited as Northen Papers. Grady to Joseph E. Brown, uncertain date, 1884, in Joseph E. Brown Papers, Box 3, Folder 69.
38 Joel Chandler Harris, *Life of Henry W. Grady*, 18–20.
39 Ibid., 202–203.
40 These figures are from Wynne, "The Alliance Legislature of 1890," 82. Wynne counted every legislator who expressed pro-Alliance views. Other scholars have applied more conservative criteria and have other figures, but the Alliance strength is impressive no matter how calculated. See McMath, "Mobilizing Agrarian Discontent," table; James C. Bonner, "The Alliance Legislature of 1890," 163, published in James C. Bonner and Lucien E. Roberts, *Studies in Georgia History and Government* (Athens, Ga., 1940), and Theodore Saloutos, *Farmer Movements in the South, 1865–1933* (Berkeley and Los Angeles, 1960), 111.
41 *Constitution*, November 16, 1890.
42 McMath, *Populist Vanguard;* Michael Schwartz, *Radical Protest and Social Structure: The Southern Farmers' Alliance and Cotton Tenancy, 1880–1890* (New York, 1976); Lawrence Goodwyn, *Democratic Promise: The Populist Movement in America* (New York, 1976); Donna A. Barnes, *Farmers in Rebellion: The Rise and Fall of the Southern Farmers' Alliance and People's Party in Texas* (Austin, Tex., 1984); Woodward, *Tom Watson: Agrarian Rebel;* Steelman, *The North Carolina Farmers' Alliance;* Shaw, *The Wool-Hat Boys;* and William F. Holmes, "The Southern Farmers' Alliance: The Georgia Experience," *Georgia Historical Quarterly*, LXXII (Winter 1988), 627–52.

5 *The Politics of Race*

1 Williamson, *The Crucible of Race*, 5–7.
2 Sketch of Atticus Greene Haygood, in Coleman and Gurr, eds., *Dictionary of Georgia Biography*, I, 424–26. The sketch was written by Harold W. Mann.

220 I Notes to Pages 134–137

Grady did not criticize Haygood's racial views. No profit could come from attacking this particular preacher. Grady did, however, lay burning attacks on another liberal, the author George Washington Cable, who lived in Louisiana. Cable supported political and legal rights for blacks. George Washington Cable, "The Freedman's Case in Equity," *The Century*, XXIX (January 1885), 409–18. Grady criticized Cable's views in a firm but moderate tone intended mostly for a northern audience. Grady's article is a carefully prepared version of his own ideas. Henry W. Grady, "In Plain Black and White," *The Century*, XXIX (April 1885), 909–17. His dislike for Cable was masked in the *Century* article, but the *Constitution* expressed it fully in views intended for a Georgia audience. Cable was superficial, a sentimentalist, a man of malign purposes, and a crank. *Constitution*, January 1, 7, 12, 16, 1885; October 8, 1886; June 15, 1887; March 7, 15, April 17, 1888. Grady used the same tactic on Cable that he had used on the jute trust. In this instance, he showed solidarity with white Georgians of conservative and radical views by attacking a distant liberal with few local friends.

3 Grady Scrapbook No. 1, in Grady Papers, 48–49; Henry W. Grady, *The New South: With a Character Sketch of Henry W. Grady by Oliver Dyer* (New York, 1890), 236–37.

4 Grady made these comments in a review of a stage version of Uncle Tom's Cabin at Booth's Theater in New York in 1881. Apparently he never read the book. Once in Florida, he passed the home of Harriet Beecher Stowe while on a boat trip on the St. Johns River. He avenged himself by turning up his nose. *Constitution*, January 12, 1881; Nixon, *Henry W. Grady: Spokesman of the New South*, 135.

5 Joel Chandler Harris, *Life of Henry W. Grady*, 98–100.

6 Ibid., 126.

7 Gaston, *The New South Creed*, passim; Joel Chandler Harris, *Life of Henry W. Grady*, 90, 194; *Constitution*, January 2, 1889.

8 Joel Chandler Harris, *Life of Henry W. Grady*, 97–98.

9 Cleveland (O.) *Gazette*, January 29, 1887; *Methodist Union* (Augusta, Ga.), quoted in Indianapolis (Ind.) *Freeman*, September 7, 1889. The *Methodist Union* does not appear to have been discussing any particular speech, but was referring to the kind of address that Grady was making. *Advocate* (Leavenworth, Kans.), January 11, 1890.

10 *Constitution*, August 12, 13, 1889.

11 Ibid., May 28, 1888; Ransom and Sutch, *One Kind of Freedom*, 85. These figures include every Georgia county except Camden. Indianapolis (Ind.) *Freeman*, November 23, 1889; *Weekly Pelican* (New Orleans, La.), June 18, 1887; Clarence A. Bacote, "The Negro In Georgia Politics, 1880–1908" (Ph.D. dissertation, University of Chicago, 1955), 4.

12 George Brown Tindall, *South Carolina Negroes, 1877–1900* (Columbia, S.C., 1952), 303–306.

13 The black conventions listed seven major grievances. An eighth was minor, having to do with the organization of the state militia, which was one-fourth black. The officers on the staff of the commander in chief were all white. Blacks wanted proportional representation. The first meeting drew 400 delegates to Atlanta on December 12, 1883, and dealt with schools. The second and most comprehensive meeting was in Macon on January 25–26, 1888. It set forth the eight grievances formally. About 350 black delegates in Macon came from most Georgia counties and included the two Negro members of the legislature, editors of five black newspapers, ministers and teachers, politicians, and many individuals who fell into móre than one category. The final meeting of the decade convened in Atlanta on November 12, 1889, after incidents showed that radicals were in the ascendency. The 1889 meeting was a general protest. For a catalogue of grievances described in 1888, see the Savannah (Ga.) *Tribune*, February 11, 1888. The *Tribune* was a vigorous black newspaper issued every Saturday on Market Square (Ellis Square) in Savannah. For the 1883 meeting in Atlanta, see the *Constitution*, December 13, 1883. For the 1888 meeting in Macon, see April 1, 1888; Macon *Telegraph*, January 26–28, 1888; Savannah (Ga.) *Tribune*, February 11, 1888. Reports of the 1889 meeting are in the *Constitution*, September 14, 15, November 13, 1889.
14 Sketch of William Jefferson White, in Coleman and Gurr, eds., *Dictionary of Georgia Biography*, II, 1059–61. The sketch was written by Bess Beatty.
15 Ibid., sketch of William A. Pledger, II, 802–804. The sketch was written by Bess Beatty. See Ruth Currie McDaniel, "Black Power in Georgia: William A. Pledger and the Takeover of the Republican Party," *Georgia Historical Quarterly*, LXII (Fall 1978), 225–39.
16 Charles C. Jones, Jr., and Salem Dutcher, *Memorial History of Augusta, Georgia* (Syracuse, N.Y., 1890), 16–19.
17 The figures on enrollments are from the *Constitution*, December 13, 1883.
18 Sketch of Gustavus John Orr, in Coleman and Gurr, eds., *Dictionary of Georgia Biography*, II, 766–68. The sketch is by Judson C. Ward. Orr all but wore himself out as school commissioner between 1872 and his death in 1887. Many white people were against public education and especially did not want black children educated. Orr wrote countless letters asking for support, made speaking trips, and lobbied in the General Assembly, encountering men at every turn seeking to reduce his funding. He lobbied the federal government for money and at one point was head of the National Education Association.
19 New York *Globe*, October 6, November 17, 1883; April 19, 1884; *Constitution*, December 13, 1883.
20 *Constitution*, December 13, 1883.
21 New York *Globe*, November 17, December 22, 1883.
22 Myron W. Adams, *A History of Atlanta University* (Atlanta, Ga., 1930), passim.

23 *Constitution*, February 3, 1888; December 12, 1886.
24 Savannah (Ga.) *Tribune*, July 23, 30, August 6, September 24, 1887; Alton Hornsby, Jr., "Georgia," in Henry Lewis Suggs, ed., *The Black Press in the South, 1865–1979* (Westport, Conn., London, 1983), 119–27; Atlanta *Herald of United Churches*, quoted in the New York *Age*, February 18, 1888.
25 Savannah (Ga.) *Tribune*, February 11, 1888. Grady made his comments in one of the rare editorials in 1883 that can be identified as his. Grady Scrapbook No. 9, pp. 41–42, in Grady Papers.
26 Grady, "In Plain Black and White," 915; New York *Freeman*, April 11, 1885.
27 Savannah (Ga.) *Tribune*, May 7, July 2, 23, August 6, 1887; June 2, 9, July 14, 1888. In 1883 Negroes had trouble on the Central and the Georgia lines. Savannah correspondence of the New York *Globe*, March 31, April 7, 1883; Cleveland (O.) *Gazette*, June 16, 1888. The son of Adam Morse, a Savannah black man, allegedly was mistreated by a railroad conductor in Chatham County. Morse attacked the conductor, was indicted by the grand jury for assault with intent to murder, fled to Canada, and upon return to Savannah found the black community behind him. On July 14, 1888, Morse appeared for trial, but when the state requested a delay under conditions the judge would not allow, Morse went free amid rejoicing in the black community.
28 Grady, "In Plain Black and White," 915–16; Savannah (Ga.) *Tribune*, February 11, 1888. For an interesting example in Bibb County (Macon), see the *Constitution*, March 14, 1889.
29 Savannah (Ga.) *Tribune*, September 1, 1888; *Advocate* (Leavenworth, Kans.), September 22, 1888. The *Constitution*, once moderate on jury service, took a hard line as the decade ended. In 1889 Francis W. Dawson, editor of the Charleston (S.C.) *News and Courier*, was murdered by a white doctor in Charleston. The doctor was acquitted by a jury of seven blacks and five whites. He clearly had killed Dawson. The verdict set off derisive comments about Negroes as jurors. The *Constitution* blamed the situation on northerners who forced blacks onto southern juries at bayonet point. *Constitution*, July 2, 7, 1889. See E. Culpepper Clark, *Francis Warrington Dawson and the Politics of Restoration*, 215–29. Black spokesmen defended the black jurors in the Dawson case. *Georgia Baptist*, quoted in the *Constitution*, July 14, 1889. One black editor said that there were five white men on the jury and any one could have blocked the verdict. *Advocate* (Leavenworth, Kans.), July 27, 1889.
30 Cash payments of any size were difficult to manage for most persons. In the eleven states of the Old Confederacy, estimated per capita income in 1880 was $86 per person, which included "income" not in the form of cash. Black citizens made less money than that. Kousser, *The Shaping of Southern Politics*, 214.
31 Ibid., 67–68.

32 Macon *Telegraph,* January 27, 1888; Savannah (Ga.) *Tribune,* December 3, 1887.

33 Grady Scrapbook No. 4, pp. 37–38, in Grady Papers; *Constitution,* July 16, 1881; July 10, August 28, 1887. For typical comments, see October 3, 1884; December 18, 1886; August 10, 11, September 21, 1887; May 11, 1889.

34 Edward L. Ayers, *Vengeance and Justice: Crime and Punishment in the 19th-Century American South* (New York, 1984), 185–86.

35 A. Elizabeth Taylor, "The Convict Lease System in Georgia, 1866–1908" (M.A. thesis, University of North Carolina, Chapel Hill, 1940), 60–61.

36 Cleveland (O.) *Gazette,* September 3, 1887.

37 Grady Scrapbook No. 4, pp. 37–38, in Grady Papers.

38 Events of the mutiny are from the *Constitution,* July 14, 15, 1886.

39 Ibid., October 2, 1887.

40 Quoted in Savannah (Ga.) *Tribune,* April 30, 1887.

41 Nixon, *Henry W. Grady: Spokesman of the New South,* 143–44; Williams Rutherford to Grady, May 9, 1877, in Grady Papers.

42 For these and other examples, see *Constitution,* July 10, 17, October 9, 1886; January 22, June 18, December 31, 1887; January 24, April 7, 28, June 8, November 24, 1888; August 24, November 30, 1889.

43 Ibid., April 1, 1888.

44 Ibid., May 2, 1888; Savannah (Ga.) *Tribune,* May 12, 1888.

45 Ayers, *Vengeance and Justice,* 238–55; Jacquelyn Dowd Hall, *Revolt Against Chivalry: Jessie Daniel Ames and the Women's Campaign Against Lynching* (New York, 1979), 147–48, 155–56.

46 *Constitution,* July 27, 28, 1887.

47 Ibid., July 10, 11, 31, 1887. All three of the mobs described above fit the classic description of a lynch mob. They took rumors at face value and asserted the total guilt of their victims. Arthur F. Raper, *The Tragedy of Lynching* (Chapel Hill, N.C., 1933), 8–9.

48 For these and other headlines, see the *Constitution,* September 17, December 4, 21, 1886; February 7, June 2, September 19, 1887; January 28, February 4, 29, April 21, June 4, July 16, August 20, 1888; July 11, September 27, 1889. Macon *Telegraph,* January 27, 1888. Also see Washington (D.C.) *Bee,* December 25, 1886.

49 Augusta (Ga.) *Weekly Sentinel,* quoted in the Huntsville (Ala.) *Gazette,* February 11, 1888.

50 Grady, "In Plain Black and White," 917; *Weekly Pelican* (New Orleans, La.), December 1, 1888.

51 Karl Schriftgiesser, *The Gentleman from Massachusetts: Henry Cabot Lodge* (Boston, Mass., 1945), 96–107; John A. Garraty, *Henry Cabot Lodge: A Biography* (New York, 1953), 117–20.

52 *Constitution,* February 19, 1889.

53 Ibid., May 22, July 27, August 21, 30, September 11, 1889. Grady did not

believe that the Negroes who followed the Liberty County Messiah were barbarians. He called them superstitious. Mills B. Lane, ed., *The New South: Writings and Speeches of Henry Grady* (Savannah, Ga., 1971), 146–47. See Thomas F. Armstrong, "The Christ Craze of 1889: A Millenial Response to Economic and Social Change," in Vernon Burton and Robert C. McMath, Jr., eds., *Toward a New South?* (Westport, Conn., 1982), 223–45.

54 *Constitution,* August 6, 7, 1889. Lyons is occasionally spelled Lyon.
55 Ibid., August 8, 1889.
56 Ibid., August 9, 1889.
57 Ibid., August 11, 1889.
58 Ibid., September 3, 4, 15, 25, 1889.
59 Ibid., September 6, 1889.
60 Ibid., September 7, 1889; Nixon, *Henry W. Grady: Spokesman of the New South,* 315.
61 *Constitution,* September 7, 1889.
62 Ibid., September 8, 18, 1889.
63 Ibid., September 19, 1889.
64 Ibid., September 20, 1889.
65 Ibid., September 23, 24, 1889.
66 *Weekly Pelican* (New Orleans, La.), September 28, 1889; New York *Age,* September 21, 1889.
67 What follows concerning the call for the meeting is from the *Constitution,* September 14, 1889.
68 Ibid., September 15, 1889.
69 Ibid., November 13, 1889.
70 Kousser, *The Shaping of Southern Politics,* 47.
71 Joel Chandler Harris, *Life of Henry W. Grady,* 186.
72 Ibid., 180–207.

6 *Development and Reconciliation*

1 Phillips, *A History Of Transportation,* 221–51; Jones and Dutcher, *Memorial History of Augusta, Georgia,* 481–501; Mary G. Cumming, *Georgia Railroad and Banking Company, 1833–1945* (Augusta, Ga., 1945), 9–77; W. K. Wood, "The Georgia Railroad and Banking Company," *Georgia Historical Quarterly,* LVII (Winter 1973), 544–61.
2 Russell, "Atlanta, Gate City of the South, 1847 to 1885," 32; Phillips, *A History of Transportation,* 252–302.
3 Russell, "Atlanta, Gate City of the South," 26; Phillips, *A History of Transportation,* 303–34; Garrett, *Atlanta and Environs,* I, 144–51; James Houstoun Johnston, comp., *Western and Atlantic Railroad of the State of Georgia* (Atlanta, Ga., 1931), 43–63.

4 Phillips, *A History of Transportation*, 364–66. Trains ran from the heart of Atlanta to East Point on the Atlanta-to-Macon line, then shunted off toward Alabama.
5 Stover, *The Railroads of the South*, 11.
6 Russell, "Atlanta, Gate City of the South," 39–42.
7 Ibid., 57–66; Wotton, "New City of the South," 153–63.
8 Augusta *Chronicle and Sentinel*, September 4, 19, 1875; *Constitution*, October 6, 1888.
9 Garrett, *Atlanta and Environs*, II, 21–23; Stover, *The Railroads of the South*, 196–99, 236, 240. The East Tennessee, Virginia, and Georgia combination gave Atlanta access not only to a second port but by 1890, access to 2,600 miles of additional track in four states.
10 *Constitution*, October 5, 1881. Atlanta acquired new feeder lines all through the decade. In 1887 the Atlanta and Florida Railroad was partially opened. It began service to Fayetteville just below Atlanta, with service extended to Fort Valley in short order. This useful road traveled through nine of the richest counties of Georgia. Garrett, *Atlanta and Environs*, II, 160. Also see Russell, *Atlanta: 1847–1890*, 237–39.
11 Woodward, "Bourbonism in Georgia," 29.
12 *Constitution*, October 5, 1881.
13 Harold Francis Williamson, *Edward Atkinson: The Biography of an American Liberal, 1827–1905* (Boston, Mass., 1934), 166–67.
14 *Constitution*, October 31, 1880.
15 Exposition stock sold for $100 a share. Atlantans bought 336 shares, or $36,600 worth. Augusta Wylie King, "International Cotton Exposition," *Atlanta Historical Bulletin*, XVIII (July 1939), 185.
16 Information concerning the exposition comes from the *Constitution*, September 1881–January 1882. Especially see the issues of October 5, 6, 28, December 15, 1881. Also see Garrett, *Atlanta and Environs*, II, 29–35; H. I. Kimball, *International Cotton Exposition: Report of the Director-General* (New York, 1882); Reed, *History of Atlanta, Georgia*, Pt. I, 472–76; E. Y. Clarke, *Atlanta Illustrated*, 3rd edition (Atlanta, Ga., 1881), 83–86, 202–204; Willie Mae Stowe Autry, "The International Cotton Exposition, Atlanta, Georgia, 1881" (M.A. thesis, University of Georgia, 1938); Alice E. Reagan, *H. I. Kimball: Entrepreneur* (Atlanta, Ga., 1983), 91–107; King, "International Cotton Exposition," 181–98. In 1957 Jack Blicksilver wrote two articles published with identical titles and pagination in the same magazine in succeeding months. They are Blicksilver, "The International Cotton Exposition of 1881 and Its Impact upon the Economic Development of Georgia," *Atlanta Economic Review*, VII (May and June 1957), 1–5, 11–12.
17 *Constitution*, November 5, 1881.
18 Blicksilver, "The International Cotton Exposition of 1881" (May 1957), 5, 11.

19 The largest attendance on any day was 10,293 on December 7. On October 27, the day that Colquitt and Bigelow got their suits, attendance was 6,594. Kimball, *International Cotton Exposition*, 124.

20 Blicksilver "The International Cotton Exposition of 1881" (June 1957), 1–5, 11–12.

21 Grady to Daniel S. Lamont, July 15, 1887, in Grover Cleveland Papers, Library of Congress, Washington, D.C., copy in Grady Papers, Box 1. Grady failed in his designs. Cleveland did not come to Atlanta alone.

22 Grady, *The New South*, 181–84. The theme of southern self-help was a recurring one. See the *Constitution*, June 17, 1887, and for a plea for local capital to develop Atlanta, May 12, 1889.

23 For an appraisal of Lee's role, see Buck, *The Road to Reunion, 1865–1900*, 250–52. Many of Grady's New South associates attempted reconciliation oratory. For a study of the efforts of John B. Gordon, see Huber W. Ellingsworth, "Southern Reconciliation Orators in the North" (Ph.D. dissertation, Florida State University, 1955).

24 For an overview of Grady's speech, see Nixon, *Henry W. Grady: Spokesman of the New South*, 237–53. For an analysis of Grady as a speaker, including the 1886 address, see Marvin G. Bauer, "Henry W. Grady," printed in William Norwood Brigance, ed., *A History and Criticism of American Public Address* (New York, 1960), I, 387–405. Also see Barton C. Shaw, "Henry W. Grady Heralds 'The New South,'" *Atlanta Historical Journal*, XXX (Summer 1986), with a reprint of the "New South" address, 55–66; David L. Metheny, "The New South: Grady's Use of Hegelian Dialectic," *Southern Speech Communication Journal*, XXXI (Fall 1965), 34–41; Charles F. Lindsay, "Henry Woodfin Grady, Orator," *Quarterly Journal of Speech Education*, VI (April 1920), 27–42. See Harold D. Mixon, "Henry Grady as a Persuasive Strategist," in Waldo W. Braden, ed., *Oratory in the New South* (Baton Rouge, La., and London, 1979), 74–116. Much of the description of the speech which follows comes from the *Constitution*, December 23, 24, 25, 27, 1886. George Christopher Wharton found a suggestion in the papers of Henry Watterson that the reconciliation editor of the Louisville *Courier-Journal* was asked to be the speaker before Grady was and declined. In light of the involvement of Inman, the prospect seems remote. See George Christopher Wharton, "Henry Watterson: A Study of Selected Speeches on Reconciliation in the Post-Bellum Period" (Ph.D. dissertation, Louisville State University, 1974), 125.

25 Nixon, *Henry W. Grady: Spokesman of the New South*, 241.

26 *Constitution*, December 25, 1886.

27 All quotations from this address are from Joel Chandler Harris, *Life of Henry W. Grady*, 83–93. The speech was transcribed by a stenographic reporter from the New York *Tribune*. Another text is Thomas D. Clark, "Henry W. Grady, *The New South*," in Daniel J. Boorstin, ed., *An American Primer* (Chicago, Ill., and London, 1966), I, 463–76.

28 Clark concludes that Grady's speech accomplished three ends. It fixed the term *New South* in the American mind; it assured capitalists that the South was a stable region; and in one evening, it raised Grady's rank among spokesmen for the Movement. Nothing about the speech is profound, and the part about the footsore Confederate soldier is melodrama. "Seldom again," however, "would the term 'New South' be used without invoking Grady's interpretation of it." Clark, "Henry W. Grady, *The New South*," 474–76.

29 Macon *Telegraph*, quoted in *Constitution*, December 27, 1886; New York *Times* and New York *Evening Post*, quoted in *Constitution*, December 25, 1886; Nixon, *Henry W. Grady: Spokesman of the New South*, 250–54.

30 Charleston (S.C.) *News and Courier*, December 29, 1886, quoted in E. Culpepper Clark, *Francis Warrington Dawson and the Politics of Restoration*, 141.

31 Buck, *Road to Reunion*, 107.

32 New York *Tribune*, April 30, 1886; Chicago *Inter-Ocean*, April 29, 1886, both quoted in Bauer, "Henry W. Grady, Spokesman of the New South," 62; *Constitution*, May 15, 1889. See editorials on March 26, June 17, 1887; March 11, 1888; September 7, 1886. On the anniversary of the battle of Gettysburg in 1887, to cite only one year, the paper had accounts on July 3, 4, and 5. On September 20, the blue and the gray were reported reunited at the Piedmont Exposition. The following month, on October 12, "Foes, Now Friends" were described on the field at Kennesaw Mountain, Ga.

33 *Constitution*, January 24, 1886.

34 Joel Chandler Harris, *Life of Henry W. Grady*, 204–205. Grady's colleague, Evan P. Howell, used a similar oratorical concept. A year before the version cited was recorded, Grady heard Howell make a talk using the same dramatic approach. *Constitution*, December 12, 1888.

35 *Constitution*, October 5, 1881.

36 Ibid., April 8, 1888. One scholar computes that Atlanta went backward in relation to the rest of the South in numbers of cotton spindles. In 1880 it had 2.7 percent of the spindles in the South; in 1890, 2.6. Chen-Han Chen, "The Location of the Cotton Manufacturing Industry in the United States, 1880–1910" (Ph.D. dissertation, Harvard University, 1939), 388. For an account of Elsas, May, and Company, see Garrett, *Atlanta and Environs*, I, 807–809.

37 *Constitution*, May 3, 6, 7, 1882; February 4, 8, 1883; February 6, 1884; November 21, 1886. For descriptions of business and manufacturing activity in Atlanta in 1881 and 1889, see Clarke, *Atlanta Illustrated*, 138–86, and Reed, *History of Atlanta, Georgia*, Pt. I, 455–56. Figures concerning the relative sizes of factories and shops in Atlanta and in Augusta are from United States census data. *Twelfth Census of the United States, Taken in the Year 1900, Manufactures*, Vol. VIII, Pt. II (Washington, D.C., 1902), 992.

38 *Constitution*, June 26, 1889.

39 Ibid., August 27, 28, 1886.

40 Grady Scrap Book No. 2, p. 102, in Grady Papers.
41 Cashin, *The Story of Augusta*, 152–56.
42 "A Stagnant Town" was published in the *Constitution* on January 27, 1885, and reprinted in the Augusta *Chronicle and Constitutionalist* the next day. Its author identified himself only by initials, which Walsh did not recognize. At other times, the *Constitution* commented generously upon the industry of Augusta. See a piece written by Grady on April 9, 1882.
43 See *Chronicle and Constitutionalist*, January 28, 1885; *Constitution*, January 29, 1885; Augusta *Chronicle*, May 5, 1886.
44 Augusta *Chronicle*, August 15, 1886. Also see August 19, 24, 25, 26, September 1, 1886.
45 *Constitution*, September 12, 1886.
46 Augusta *Chronicle*, September 15, 16, 17, 22, 1886.
47 Ibid., September 19, 1886. The labor difficulties were settled in mid-October 1886 by a compromise worked out between the mill owners and James A. Wright of the Knights of Labor. Wages stayed the same but working conditions improved. A board to hear future grievances was set up, and the workday was shortened by a half-hour. Cashin, *The Story of Augusta*, 157.
48 *Constitution*, April 5, 1882.
49 Ibid., October 17, 18, 1882; December 8, 1885; March 12, 1886.
50 Wright, *Old South, New South*, 172–73.
51 *Constitution*, July 23, 1881; April 29, 1885. Also see February 1, July 1, 1883; May 18, September 23, 1889.
52 The best overview of the creation of the Georgia Institute of Technology is in Robert C. McMath, Jr., et al., *Engineering the New South: Georgia Tech, 1885–1985* (Athens, Ga., 1985), 3–35. Except as indicated, the material used is from that source, written by James E. Brittain.
53 *Constitution*, October 2, 1886.
54 Ibid., October 9, 1886.
55 Ibid., October 24, December 20, 1886; January 1, October 6, 1888. Nathaniel E. Harris is well remembered today at the Georgia Institute of Technology. He is ranked among the foremost founders of the school.
56 *Twelfth Census of the United States, Taken in the Year 1900, Manufactures*, Vol. VIII, Pt. II, 131–35, 142–43. For an excellent study of the development of Atlanta during the 1880s, see Russell, *Atlanta, 1847–1890*, 241–58.

7 Epilogue

1 *Constitution*, November 16, 1890.
2 Ibid., June 30, July 6, 1887.
3 Evan P. Howell to Joseph E. Brown, May 10, 1888, in Joseph E. Brown Papers, Box 3, Folder 72.

4 *Constitution*, May 10, 29, 1888; Augusta *Chronicle*, quoted in ibid., May 17, 1888. When Grady's memorial services were held a year and a half later, Walsh was a principal orator.

5 Evan P. Howell to Joseph E. Brown, May 10, 1888, in Joseph E. Brown Papers, Box 3, Folder 72.

6 Alfred H. Colquitt to L. N. Trammell, May 23, 1888, in Trammell Papers.

7 Nixon, *Henry W. Grady: Spokesman of the New South*, 278–81; *Constitution*, March 28, May 25, July 29, August 29, 1888; Grady to Thomas Nelson Page, April 25, 1888, in Thomas Nelson Page Collection, Duke University, copy in Grady Papers, Box 1. Henry W. Grady to Joseph E. Brown, July 23, 1888, in Joseph E. Brown Papers, Box 3, Folder 72. Salt Springs, Georgia, today is known as Powder Springs.

8 Evan P. Howell to Joseph E. Brown, May 10, 1888, in Joseph E. Brown Papers, Box 3, Folder 72. It is interesting that as late as May 1888 Howell wanted Gordon to run against Colquitt if Grady did not. His view would shortly change. There were even reports that Howell might run against Colquitt. Macon *Telegraph*, November 12, 19, 1888; *Constitution*, November 16, 1890; November 18, 1888; John B. Gordon to Grady, July 5, 1889, in Letterbook F, 587–90, John B. Gordon Papers, Personal Letterbooks, Georgia Department of Archives and History, Atlanta.

9 Letter of James R. Holliday, in the *Constitution*, November 18, 1890.

10 John B. Gordon to Grady, July 5, 1889, in Gordon Papers, Personal Letterbook F, 587–90, Georgia Archives.

11 Brown's biographer says that Brown was in poor health as early as 1884 when Grady discouraged opposition for Brown and Henry D. McDaniel. Parks, *Joseph E. Brown of Georgia*, 564.

12 Five of the documents relating to the final rupture between Gordon and Grady are published in the Appendix, herein, including the ones containing the quotations cited.

13 Letter of James R. Holliday, in the *Constitution*, November 18, 1890; Letter of William M. Howard, Grady's brother-in-law, ibid.

14 *Constitution*, November 5, 6, 1890. In the Georgia Senate, Gordon got 25 votes to 18 against him; in the House, 97 to 72 against him. Brown vacated the Senate seat voluntarily because of bad health.

15 In that category, one does not include the defeat of the Lodge elections bill of 1890, the so-called Force bill. It failed to pass, a circumstance that would have pleased Grady, but he can be given little credit for that fact. It was derailed in Congress on a technicality. On the other hand, one is slow to blame Grady for the anti-Atlanta spirit in Georgia during so much of the twentieth century. That spirit was exacerbated in great part because political profit lay in stirring it up. The mechanics that made it profitable had to do with the county unit system, a method of vote counting in primary elections heavily weighted in favor of rural people. Politicians found they could get elected by attacking Atlanta. The system, however, was not created in re-

action to the prosperity and prominence of the city. Its structure was a part of the Georgia Constitution of 1868, written when Grady was eighteen years old. It was continued in slightly modified form in the Constitution of 1877. The county unit system was struck down by the federal courts in the 1960s.

16 *Constitution*, December 25, 1886.

Appendix

1 *Constitution*, June 9, 1889.
2 Julius L. Brown was a son of Senator Joseph E. Brown. He and Grady attended the University of Georgia together, and young Brown was sometimes a guest in Grady's boyhood home on Prince Avenue in Athens. They had been friends for twenty-three years when Grady died.
3 John B. Gordon to Grady, June 24, 1889, in Personal Letterbook F, 584–85, in John B. Gordon Papers, Georgia Department of Archives and History, Atlanta. Gordon wrote two versions of this letter, and they are similar. The other is found at pp. 582–83. They raise a question, for neither refers to Grady's "professed" friendship for Gordon, language that caused offense and which is a source of contention in two of the documents that follow. One concludes that Gordon either wrote and sent a third version of the letter containing that language, or that another entirely different letter passed between the men at a slightly later time. Never in his life did Grady like to deal in writing with disagreeable matters of a personal nature. At this point in his life, neither did Gordon. Both men customarily went to see adversaries to discuss points of disagreement in hopes of reconciliation. In June and July 1889 the offices of Grady and Gordon were within a casual stroll of each other, yet neither apparently tried to see the other under conditions where an understanding might have been sought.
4 *Constitution*, November 16, 1890. The letter from Grady to Gordon survived in the following way. In November 1890 Gordon ran for the seat in the United States Senate being vacated voluntarily by Brown because of bad health. The *Constitution* declined to support Gordon and said why in a long, unsigned editorial written by Clark Howell. Howell included a large part of Grady's response to Gordon in the editorial, and it is printed above.
5 Gordon was occupied with opening the new State Capitol in Atlanta on July 3–4, 1889. The building had been under construction since 1884.
6 Samuel Guyton McLendon was a well-known figure in Democratic politics. A former mayor of Thomasville and a representative of Thomas County in the Georgia House of Representatives, 1884–87, he knew both Gordon and Grady well. Like Grady, he had attended the University of Virginia, which formed a bond between them. After practicing law in Thomasville, he moved his practice to Atlanta and set up offices in the Kimball House. In

1919 he became secretary of state of Georgia and served until he died in 1928.

7 John B. Gordon to Grady, July 5, 1889, Personal Letterbook F, 587–90, in John B. Gordon Papers, Georgia Department of Archives and History, Atlanta. Gordon's letterpress copy of this letter, cited here, at first seems unreadable. His staff made the copy imperfectly. The original document was four pages long, typed with a blue ribbon. Copying involved dampening the surface of the original, placing a thin sheet of tissue paper on it, then pressing the two together in a machine. When done well, the tissue absorbed enough ink to make an acceptable copy. In the letter cited, the author discovered that by placing backgrounds of differing colors behind the tissue and using a bright light and a magnifying glass, virtually all of the letter can be read. The author thanks Edward Weldon, director of the Archives, for permission to undertake this process on these fragile documents.

8 Joel Chandler Harris, *Life of Henry W. Grady*, 382–84.

Bibliography

Manuscript Collections

Elijah Brown Papers. Atlanta Historical Society, Atlanta, Ga. This collection has important correspondence between Augustus O. Bacon and Joseph E. Brown bearing upon the gubernatorial campaign of 1882.

Joseph E. Brown Papers. University of Georgia Libraries, Athens, Ga. This indispensable collection contains a great many letters and telegrams bearing upon events in Georgia in the 1880s. Formerly, a part of this collection was known as the Felix Hargrett Papers, but all of it is now usually called the Joseph E. Brown Papers.

Grover Cleveland Papers. Library of Congress, Washington, D.C. These papers contain several letters and telegrams from Grady to Cleveland, as well as related correspondence.

Rebecca Latimer Felton Papers. University of Georgia Libraries, Athens, Ga. Mrs. Felton, an indefatigable enemy of the Bourbon leadership of Georgia and no admirer of Grady's, kept an invaluable set of scrapbooks to have a record on her enemies. Her papers also contain letters.

John B. Gordon Papers. Georgia Department of Archives and History, Atlanta, Ga. The John B. Gordon Personal Letterbook F has two letters from Gordon to Grady, dated July 24 and July 5, 1889, bearing upon the dissolution of friendship between the two men.

John B. Gordon Papers. Robert W. Woodruff Library, Emory University, Atlanta, Ga. This small collection contains a facsimile letter written by John B. Gordon in the gubernatorial campaign of 1886, as well as useful photographs.

Henry W. Grady Papers. Robert W. Woodruff Library, Emory University, Atlanta, Ga. The collection contains letters from all periods of Grady's life, numerous photographs and bits of memorabilia, two brief diaries, an account book, manuscripts of speeches, and twelve scrapbooks.

Joel Chandler Harris Papers. Robert W. Woodruff Library, Emory University, Atlanta, Ga. The collection contains items in which Grady is mentioned, but more important, it has scrapbooks with clippings from the Atlanta *Sunday Gazette.* This short-lived venture was published by Grady and Harris in 1878 and 1879.

William A. Hemphill Papers. Robert W. Woodruff Library, Emory University, Atlanta, Ga. Hemphill was business manager of the Atlanta *Constitution* and upon Grady's death helped to raise money to pay off the mortgage on Grady's home. An account of that effort is found in this collection.

Ralph E. McGill Papers. Robert W. Woodruff Library, Emory University, Atlanta, Ga. The McGill collection contains information concerning the early history and development of the Atlanta *Constitution.*

William J. Northen Papers. Georgia Department of Archives and History, Atlanta, Ga. Scrapbooks in the Northen collection contain manuscript letters from Grady to Northen bearing upon Northen's candidacy for governor in 1890, as well as other items.

L. N. Trammell Papers. Robert W. Woodruff Library, Emory University, Atlanta, Ga. The Trammell Papers have letters from various Georgia politicians commenting upon Grady and events in Georgia during the 1880s.

Newspapers

In the latter part of the nineteenth century, newspapers commonly printed speeches and letters that otherwise would be lost today. These documents are important original sources. The most useful newspaper published by Negroes in Georgia was the Savannah *Tribune.* The out-of-state newspapers below, beginning with the Huntsville (Ala.) *Gazette,* are black newspapers which had correspondents in Georgia, which commented upon Georgia affairs, or which reprinted material from black Georgia publications whose files no longer survive. Within the dates cited, most have gaps in their runs.

Atlanta *Constitution,* 1876–1892. Later editions of the newspaper have Grady materials. Especially see September 26, 1917; May 22, 1921; June 14, 1928; December 24, 1939; and September 1, 1942.
Atlanta *Evening Capitol,* 1885–86.
Atlanta *Evening Journal,* 1883–87.
Atlanta *Evening Star,* 1883.

Atlanta *Herald*, 1872–76.
Augusta (Ga.) *Chronicle*, 1872–90. The *Chronicle* at times was called the *Chronicle and Constitutionalist.*
Columbus (Ga.) *Enquirer-Sun*, 1880–90.
Hartwell (Ga.) *Sun*, 1886.
Macon (Ga.) *Telegraph*, 1880–90. The *Telegraph* at times was called the *Telegraph and Messenger.*
Milledgeville *Union and Recorder*, 1876–80.
Savannah *Morning News*, 1880–90.
Huntsville (Ala.) *Gazette*, 1879–90.
Indianapolis (Ind.) *Freeman*, 1886–90.
Leavenworth (Kans.) *Advocate*, 1888–91.
New Orleans (La.) *Pelican*, 1886–89.
New York *Age*, on microfilm reel with New York *Freeman* and New York *Globe*, 1880–90.
St. Paul (Minn.) *Western Appeal*, 1885–88.
Savannah (Ga.), *Tribune*, 1876–90.
Washington (D.C.) *Bee*, 1884–90.

Articles and Essays

Anderson, William. "The Resignation of John B. Gordon from the U.S. Senate, 1880." *Georgia Historical Quarterly*, LII (December 1968), 438–42.
Armstrong, Thomas F. "The Christ Craze of 1889: A Millenial Response to Economic and Social Change." In Vernon Burton and Robert C. McMath, Jr., eds. *Toward a New South?* Westport, Conn., 1982, 223–45.
Bartley, Numan V. "Another New South?" *Georgia Historical Quarterly*, LXV (Summer 1981), 119–37.
Bauer, Marvin G. "Henry W. Grady." In William Norwood Brigance, ed. *A History and Criticism of American Public Address.* New York, 1960, I, 387–405.
Blicksilver, Jack. "The International Cotton Exposition Of 1881: Its Impact upon the Economic Development Of Georgia." *Atlanta Economic Review*, VII (May and June 1957), 1–5, 11–12. These two pieces by Blicksilver were published with identical pagination in the same publication in succeeding issues.
Bonner, James C. "The Alliance Legislature of 1890." In James C. Bonner and Lucien E. Roberts, eds. *Studies in Georgia History and Government.* Athens, Ga., 1940, 155–71.
Brandon, William P. "Calling the Georgia Constitutional Convention of 1877." *Georgia Historical Quarterly*, XVII (September 1933), 189–203.
Cable, George Washington. "The Freedman's Case in Equity." *Century*, XXIX (January 1885), 409–18.

Campbell, J. Louis. "In Search of the New South." *Southern Speech Communication Journal*, XLVII (Summer 1982), 361–88.

Clark, E. Culpepper. "Henry Grady's New South: A Rebuttal from Charleston." *Southern Speech Communication Journal*, XLI (Summer 1976), 346–58.

Clark, Thomas D. "Henry W. Grady, *The New South*." In Daniel J. Boorstin, ed. *An American Primer*. Chicago, Ill., and London, 1966, I, 463–76.

Cobb, James C. "Beyond Planters and Industrialists: A New Perspective on the New South." *Journal of Southern History*, LIV (February 1988), 45–68.

Coleman, Kenneth. "The Georgia Gubernatorial Election of 1880." *Georgia Historical Quarterly*, XXV (June 1941), 89–119.

Crawford, T. R. "Early Home of Henry W. Grady." *New England Magazine*, II (June 1890), 425–36.

Davis, Harold E. "Henry W. Grady, Master of the Atlanta Ring, 1880–1886." *Georgia Historical Quarterly*, LXIX (Spring 1985), 1–38.

———. "Henry Grady, the Atlanta *Constitution*, and the Politics of Farming in the 1880s." *Georgia Historical Quarterly*, LXXI (Winter 1987), 571–600.

Eckert, Ralph L. "The Breath of Scandal: John B. Gordon, Henry W. Grady, and the Resignation-Appointment Controversy of May 1880." *Georgia Historical Quarterly*, LXIX (Fall 1985), 315–37.

Grady, Henry W. "Cotton and Its Kingdom." *Harper's New Monthly Magazine*, LXIII (October 1881), 719–34.

———. "In Plain Black and White." *Century*, XXIX (April 1885), 909–17. This piece, written in response to the George Washington Cable article cited above, gives an overview of Grady's views on race as expressed to a predominately northern audience.

Graves, John Temple. "Eulogy of Henry W. Grady." In Lucian L. Knight, *Georgia's Bi-Centennial Memoirs and Memories*. Atlanta, 1931, II, 352–57.

———. "Henry W. Grady." *Atlanta Historical Bulletin*, V (January 1940), 23–31.

Hadley, Dorothy Siedenburg. "Henry W. Grady as a Student Speaker." *Quarterly Journal of Speech*, XXV (April 1939), 205–11.

Hair, William I. "Review Essay—*Engineering the New South: Georgia Tech, 1885–1985*." *Georgia Historical Quarterly*, LXIX (Winter 1985), 509–17.

Holmes, William F. "Ellen Dortch and the Farmers' Alliance." *Georgia Historical Quarterly*, LXIX (Summer 1985), 149–72.

———. "The Georgia Alliance Legislature." *Georgia Historical Quarterly*, LXVIII (Winter 1984), 479–515.

———. "The Southern Farmers' Alliance: The Georgia Experience." *Georgia Historical Quarterly*, LXXII (Winter 1988), 627–52.

Hornsby, Alton, Jr. "Georgia." In Henry Lewis Suggs, ed. *The Black Press in the South, 1865–1979*. Westport, Conn., and London, 1983, 119–27.

Howell, Clark. "Henry W. Grady." *Chautauquan*, V (September 1895), 703–706.

King, Augusta Wylie. "International Cotton Exposition." *Atlanta Historical Bulletin*, XVIII (July 1939), 181–98.

Lindsay, Charles F. "Henry Woodfin Grady, Orator." *Quarterly Journal of Speech Education,* VI (April 1920), 27–42.

McDaniel, Ruth Currie. "Black Power in Georgia: William A. Pledger and the Takeover of the Republican Party." *Georgia Historical Quarterly,* LXII (Fall 1978), 225–39.

Metheny, David L. "The New South: Grady's Use of Hegelian Dialectic." *Southern Speech Communication Journal,* XXXI (Fall 1965), 34–41.

Mixon, Harold D. "Henry Grady as a Persuasive Strategist." In Waldo W. Braden, ed. *Oratory in the New South.* Baton Rouge, La., and London, 1979, 74–116.

Nixon, Raymond B. "Henry W. Grady, Reporter." *Journalism Quarterly,* XII (December 1935), 341–56.

Ransom, Roger L., and Richard Sutch. "The 'Lock-in' Mechanism and Overproduction of Cotton in the Postbellum South." *Agricultural History,* XLIX (April 1975), 405–25.

Reed, Thomas W. "Henry W. Grady: A Sketch Based upon Personal Recollections." *Bulletin No. 3a,* University of Georgia, Athens (February 1935), 5–15.

Roberts, Derrell C. "Joseph E. Brown and the Florida Election of 1876." *Florida Historical Quarterly,* XL (January 1962), 217–25.

———. "Joseph E. Brown and the Western and Atlantic Railroad." *Atlanta Historical Journal,* XXIX (Spring 1985), 5–40.

Russell, James Michael. "Politics, Municipal Services, and the Working Class in Atlanta, 1865 to 1890." *Georgia Historical Quarterly,* LXVI (Winter 1982), 467–91.

Shaw, Barton C. "Henry W. Grady Heralds 'The New South.' " *Atlanta Historical Journal,* XXX (Summer 1986), with a reprint of the "New South" address, 55–66.

Shingleton, Royce. "Atlanta Becomes the Capital: The Role of Richard Peters." *Atlanta Historical Journal,* XXVIII (Winter 1984–85), 39–50.

Spalding, Jack J. "Henry W. Grady." *Atlanta Historical Bulletin,* II (September 1937), 67.

Stephens, Lester D. "Farish Furman's Formula: Scientific Farming and the 'New South.' " *Agricultural History,* L (April 1976), 377–90.

Wade, John Donald. "Old Wine in a New Bottle." *Virginia Quarterly Review,* XI (April 1935), 239–52.

Wells, Della Wager. "King and Spalding: The Origins of the Partnership." *Atlanta Historical Journal,* XXVIII (Winter 1984–85), 5–17.

Wilson, Richard L. "Sam Jones: An Apostle of the New South." *Georgia Historical Quarterly,* LVII (Winter 1973), 459–74.

Wood, W. K. "The Georgia Railroad and Banking Company." *Georgia Historical Quarterly,* LVII (Winter 1973), 544–61.

Woodward, C. Vann. "Bourbonism in Georgia." *North Carolina Historical Review,* XVI (January 1939), 23–35.

Wynne, Lewis Nicholas. "New South Rivalry in the 1880s: Gordon versus Bacon." *Atlanta Historical Journal,* XXVII (Winter 1983–84), 41–55.

————. "The Bourbon Triumvirate: A Reconsideration." *Atlanta Historical Journal,* XXIV (Summer 1980), 39–55.

Theses and Dissertations

Autry, Willie Mae Stowe. "The International Cotton Exposition, Atlanta, Georgia, 1881." M.A. thesis, University of Georgia, 1938.

Bacote, Clarence A. "The Negro In Georgia Politics, 1880–1908." Ph.D. dissertation, University of Chicago, 1955.

Bauer, Marvin Grant. "Henry W. Grady: Spokesman of the New South." Ph.D. dissertation, University of Wisconsin, 1936.

Britt, Hiram Harvie. "The Georgia Delegation in Congress, 1880–1890." M.A. thesis, Emory University, 1930.

Bryan, Ferald Joseph. "Thomas E. Watson versus Henry W. Grady: The Rhetorical Struggle for the Mind of the South, 1880–1890." Ph.D. dissertation, University of Missouri at Columbia, 1985.

Chen-Han Chen. "The Location of the Cotton Manufacturing Industry in the United States, 1880–1910." Ph.D. dissertation, Harvard University, 1939.

Cherry, Jim David. "The Georgia Railroad Commission, 1879–1888." M.A. thesis, University of North Carolina, Chapel Hill, 1941.

Clark, E. Culpepper. "The Response to Urbanism in Henry W. Grady's New South." M.A. thesis, Emory University, 1968.

Coleman, Kenneth. "The Administration of Alfred H. Colquitt as Governor of Georgia." M.A. thesis, University of Georgia, 1940.

Cooper, Fleeta. "The Triumvirate of Colquitt, Gordon, and Brown." M.A. thesis, Emory University, 1931.

Ellingsworth, Huber W. "Southern Reconciliation Orators in the North." Ph.D. dissertation, Florida State University, 1955.

Fort, Randolph L. "History of The Atlanta Journal." M.A. thesis, Emory University, 1930.

Garrison, Ellen Barrier. "Old South or New? Georgia and the Constitution of 1877." Ph.D. dissertation, Stanford University, 1981.

Hahn, Steven. "The Roots of Southern Populism: Yeoman Farmers and the Transformation of Georgia's Upper Piedmont, 1850–1890." Ph.D. dissertation, Yale University, 1979.

Jones, George L. "William H. Felton and the Independent Democratic Movement in Georgia, 1870–1890." Ph.D. dissertation, University of Georgia, 1971.

Jones, Warren Lee. "Alexander Hamilton Stephens, Governor of Georgia, 1882–1883." M.A. thesis, Emory University, 1942.

Logan, Lena Crain. "Henry Watterson, Border Nationalist, 1840–1877." Ph.D. dissertation, Indiana University, 1942.

Nolen, Emmalu. "The History of the Atlanta Public Schools to 1907." M.A. thesis, Emory University, 1932.

Perdue, Robert. "The Negro as Reflected in the Atlanta Constitution, Atlanta Intelligencer, and Atlanta Daily New Era From 1868–1900." M.A. thesis, Atlanta University, 1963.

Pfennig, Dennis Joseph. "Evan and Clark Howell of the *Atlanta Constitution:* The Partnership, 1889–1897." Ph.D. dissertation, University of Georgia, 1975.

Racine, Philip N. "Atlanta's Schools: A History of the Public School System, 1869–1955." Ph.D. dissertation, Emory University, 1969.

Roberts, William Pittman. "The Public Career of Doctor William Harrell Felton." Ph.D. dissertation, University of North Carolina, Chapel Hill, 1952.

Russell, James Michael. "Atlanta, Gate City of the South, 1847 to 1885." Ph.D. dissertation, Princeton University, 1972.

Speers, Leona. "The Senatorial Career of Joseph E. Brown." M.A. thesis, University of Georgia, 1954.

Steelman, Lala Carr. "The Public Career of Augustus Octavius Bacon." Ph.D. dissertation, University of North Carolina, Chapel Hill, 1950.

Taylor, A. Elizabeth. "The Convict Lease System in Georgia, 1866–1908." M.A. thesis, University of North Carolina, Chapel Hill, 1940.

Thomas, Bettye Collier. "Race Relations in Atlanta from 1877 to 1890." M.A. thesis, Atlanta University, 1966.

Towery, James Gaston. "The Georgia Gubernatorial Campaign of 1886." M.A. thesis, Emory University, 1930.

Ward, Judson C. "Georgia Under The Bourbon Democrats, 1872–1890." Ph.D. dissertation, University of North Carolina, Chapel Hill, 1947.

Watts, Eugene John. "Characteristics of Candidates in City Politics: Atlanta, 1865–1903." Ph.D. dissertation, Emory University, 1969.

Werner, Randolph Dennis. "Hegemony and Conflict: The Political Economy of a Southern Region, Augusta, Georgia, 1865–1895." Ph.D. dissertation, University of Virginia, 1977.

Wharton, George Christopher. "Henry Watterson: A Study Of Selected Speeches on Reconciliation in the Post-Bellum Period." Ph.D. dissertation, Louisiana State University, 1974.

Wingo, Horace Calvin. "Race Relations in Georgia, 1872–1908." Ph.D. dissertation, University of Georgia, 1969.

Wotton, Grigsby Hart, Jr. "New City of the South: Atlanta, 1843–1873." Ph.D. dissertation, Johns Hopkins University, 1973.

Wynne, Lewis Nicholas. "The Alliance Legislature of 1890." M.A. thesis, University of Georgia, 1970.

———. "Planter Politics in Georgia: 1860–1890." Ph.D. dissertation, University of Georgia, 1980.

Books

Adams, Myron W. *A History of Atlanta University.* Atlanta, Ga., 1930.

Arnett, Alex Mathews. *The Populist Movement in Georgia: A View of the "Agrarian Crusade" in the Light of Solid-South Politics.* New York, 1967, originally published in 1922.

Avery, Isaac W. *The History of the State of Georgia from 1850 to 1881.* New York, 1881. Avery, a former editor of the Atlanta *Constitution*, was executive secretary to Governor Alfred H. Colquitt and two other governors and was a participant in many of the events he describes.

Ayers, Edward L. *Vengeance and Justice: Crime and Punishment in the 19th-Century American South.* New York, Oxford, 1984.

Baker, John William. *History of Hart County.* Atlanta, Ga., 1933.

Baker, Ray Stannard. *Woodrow Wilson: Life and Letters.* Garden City, N.Y., 1927, I.

Barnes, Donna A. *Farmers in Rebellion: The Rise and Fall of the Southern Farmers' Alliance and People's Party in Texas.* Austin, Tex., 1984.

Bartley, Numan V. *The Creation of Modern Georgia.* Athens, Ga., 1983.

Billings, Dwight B., Jr. *Planters and the Making of a "New South": Class, Politics, and Development in North Carolina, 1865–1900.* Chapel Hill, N.C., 1979.

Brooks, Robert Preston. *The Agrarian Revolution in Georgia, 1865–1912.* New York, 1971. Reprint of the 1914 edition.

———. *History of Georgia.* Spartanburg, S.C., 1972. Reprint of the 1913 edition.

Bruce, Philip Alexander. *The Rise of the New South.* Philadelphia, Pa., 1905.

Buck, Paul H. *The Road to Reunion, 1865–1900.* Boston, Mass., and Toronto, 1937.

Carlton, David L. *Mill and Town in South Carolina: 1880–1920.* Baton Rouge, La., and London, 1982.

Cash, W. J. *The Mind of the South.* New York, 1941.

Cashin, Edward J. *The Story of Augusta.* Augusta, Ga., 1980.

Clark, E. Culpepper. *Francis Warrington Dawson and the Politics of Restoration: South Carolina, 1874–1889.* University, Ala., 1980.

Clark, Thomas D. *Pills, Petticoats and Plows: The Southern Country Store.* Indianapolis, Ind., and New York, 1944.

Clarke, E. Y. *Atlanta Illustrated.* 3rd edition. Atlanta, Ga., 1881.

Cobb, James C. *Industrialization and Southern Society, 1877–1984.* Lexington, Ky., 1984.

Coleman, Kenneth, et al. *A History of Georgia.* Athens, Ga., 1977.

Coleman, Kenneth, and Charles Stephen Gurr, eds. *Dictionary of Georgia Biography.* Athens, Ga., 1983.

Cooper, Walter G. *The Story of Georgia.* New York, 1938.

Copeland, M. T. *Cotton Manufacturing Industry in the United States.* Cambridge, Mass., 1923.

Coulter, E. Merton. *James Monroe Smith: Georgia Planter Before Death and After.* Athens, Ga., 1961.

————. *The South During Reconstruction, 1865–1877.* Baton Rouge, La., 1947.

Cumming, Mary G. *Georgia Railroad and Banking Company, 1833–1945.* Augusta, Ga., 1945.

DeCanio, Stephen J. *Agriculture in the Postbellum South: The Economics of Production and Supply.* Cambridge, Mass., and London, 1974.

Degler, Carl N. *Place Over Time: The Continuity of Southern Distinctiveness.* Baton Rouge, La., and London, 1977.

Doster, James F. *Railroads in Alabama Politics, 1875–1914.* University, Ala., 1957.

Dunning, N. A., ed. *The Farmers' Alliance History and Agricultural Digest.* New York, 1975. Reprint of 1891 edition.

Felton, Mrs. William H. (Rebecca Latimer). *My Memoirs of Georgia Politics.* Atlanta, Ga., 1911.

Fields, Barbara J. *Slavery and Freedom on the Middle Ground: Maryland During the Nineteenth Century.* New Haven, Conn., and London, 1985.

Fite, Gilbert C. *Cotton Fields No More, Southern Agriculture, 1865–1980.* Lexington, Ky., 1984.

Flynn, Charles L., Jr. *White Land, Black Labor, Caste and Class in Late Nineteenth-Century Georgia.* Baton Rouge, La., and London, 1983.

Garraty, John A. *Henry Cabot Lodge: A Biography.* New York, 1953.

Garrett, Franklin M. *Atlanta and Environs: A Chronicle of Its People and Events.* Athens, Ga., 1969. Reprint of the 1954 edition, I and II.

Gaston, Paul M. *The New South Creed: A Study in Southern Mythmaking.* New York, 1970.

Gilman, Glenn. *Human Relations in the Industrial Southeast.* Chapel Hill, N.C., 1956.

Goldfield, David R. *Cotton Fields and Skyscrapers: Southern City and Region, 1607–1980.* Baton Rouge, La., and London, 1982.

Goodwyn, Lawrence. *Democratic Promise: The Populist Movement in America.* New York, 1976.

Grady, Henry W. *The New South: With A Character Sketch of Henry W. Grady by Oliver Dyer.* New York, 1890. In November and December 1889 Grady published six articles in the New York *Ledger.* They are reprinted in this volume with an appreciation of Grady written by a friend working for the New York *Sun.*

Griffith, Louis T., and John E. Talmadge. *Georgia Journalism, 1763–1950.* Athens, Ga., 1951.

Hahn, Steven. *The Roots of Southern Populism: Yeoman Farmers and the Transformation of the Georgia Upcountry, 1850–1890.* New York, 1983.

Hall, Jacquelyn Dowd. *Revolt Against Chivalry: Jessie Daniel Ames and the Women's Campaign Against Lynching.* New York, 1979.

Harris, Joel Chandler. *Life of Henry W. Grady, Including His Writings and Speeches.* New York, 1890. This memorial volume, published shortly after Grady's death to raise money for his family, contains most of Grady's major speeches as well as a valuable foreword by his intimate friend, Harris. It also contains other Grady materials. Quotations from most of Grady's speeches in the present work are from this source.

Harris, Julia Collier. *Joel Chandler Harris: Editor and Essayist.* Chapel Hill, N.C., 1931.

———. *The Life and Letters of Joel Chandler Harris.* Boston, Mass., and New York, 1918.

Harris, Nathaniel E. *Autobiography: The Story of an Old Man's Life with Reminiscences of Seventy-Five Years.* Macon, Ga., 1925.

Hawk, Emory Q. *Economic History of the South.* New York, 1934.

Haygood, Atticus G. *Pleas for Progress.* Nashville, Tenn., 1895.

Hicks, John D. *The Populist Revolt.* Lincoln, Nebr. Reprint.

Hillyard, M. B. *The New South.* Baltimore, Md., 1887.

Holland, L. M. *The Direct Primary in Georgia.* Urbana, Ill., 1949.

Howell, Clark. *History of Georgia,* Chicago, Ill., and Atlanta, Ga., 1926.

[Hudgins, H. C., and Company]. *Life and Labors of Henry W. Grady: His Speeches, Writings, Etc.* Atlanta, Ga., 1890. This work was produced to compete with the Joel Chandler Harris volume cited above. Generally inferior, it contains some material not in the Harris book, including one speech and useful recollections of Grady by important colleagues.

Johnston, James Houstoun, comp. *Western And Atlantic Railroad of the State of Georgia.* Atlanta, Ga., 1931.

Jones, Charles C., Jr., and Salem Dutcher. *Memorial History of Augusta, Georgia.* Syracuse, N.Y., 1890.

Kendrick, Benjamin Burks, and Alex Mathews Arnett. *The South Looks at Its Past.* Chapel Hill, N.C., 1935.

Kimball, H. I. *International Cotton Exposition: Report of the Director-General.* New York, 1882.

Klein, Maury. *History of the Louisville and Nashville Railroad.* New York and London, 1972.

Kousser, J. Morgan. *The Shaping of Southern Politics: Suffrage Restriction and the Establishment of the One-Party South, 1880–1910.* New Haven, Conn., and London, 1974.

[Lane, Mills B., ed.]. *The New South: Writings and Speeches of Henry Grady.* Savannah, Ga., 1971.

McClure, Alexander K. *Colonel Alexander K. McClure's Recollections of Half a Century.* New York, 1976. Reprint of 1902 edition.

McElreath, Walter. *A Treatise on the Constitution of Georgia.* Atlanta, Ga., 1912.

McMath, Robert C., Jr. *Populist Vanguard: A History of the Southern Farmers' Alliance.* Chapel Hill, N.C., 1975.

McMath, Robert C., Jr., et al. *Engineering the New South: Georgia Tech, 1885–1985.* Athens, Ga., 1985.

Martin, Thomas H. *Atlanta and Its Builders: A Comprehensive History of the Gate City of the South.* Atlanta, Ga., 1902.

Meier, August. *Negro Thought in America, 1880–1915: Racial Ideologies in the Age of Booker T. Washington.* Ann Arbor, Mich., 1963.

Mitchell, Broadus. *The Rise of Cotton Mills in the South.* Gloucester, Mass., 1966. Originally published in 1921.

Mitchell, Broadus, and George Sinclair Mitchell. *The Industrial Revolution in the South.* Baltimore, Md., and London, 1930.

Morgan, W. Scott. *History of the Wheel and Alliance, and the Impending Revolution.* New York, 1968. Originally published in 1891.

Nixon, Raymond B. *Henry W. Grady: Spokesman of the New South.* New York, 1943.

Northen, William J., ed. *Men of Mark in Georgia.* Atlanta, Ga., 1908.

Oliver, Robert T. *History of Public Speaking in America.* Boston, Mass., 1965.

Otken, Charles H. *The Ills of the South, or Related Causes Hostile to the General Prosperity of the Southern People.* New York and London, 1894.

Parks, Joseph H. *Joseph E. Brown of Georgia.* Baton Rouge, La., 1977.

Pearce, Haywood J., Jr. *Benjamin H. Hill: Secession and Reconstruction.* Chicago, Ill., 1928.

Phillips, Ulrich Bonnell. *A History of Transportation in the Eastern Cotton Belt to 1860.* New York, 1908.

Range, Willard. *A Century of Georgia Agriculture, 1850–1950.* Athens, Ga., 1954.

Ransom, Roger L., and Richard Sutch. *One Kind of Freedom: The Economic Consequences of Emancipation.* Cambridge, Mass., London, New York, and Melbourne, Australia, 1977.

Raper, Arthur F. *The Tragedy of Lynching.* Chapel Hill, N.C., 1933.

Reagan, Alice E. *H. I. Kimball, Entrepreneur.* Atlanta, Ga., 1983.

Reed, Wallace P. *History of Atlanta, Georgia.* Syracuse, N.Y., 1889.

Roberts, Derrell C. *Joseph E. Brown and the Politics of Reconstruction.* University, Ala., 1973.

Russell, James Michael. *Atlanta, 1847–1890: City Building in the Old South and the New.* Baton Rouge, La., and London, 1988.

Saloutos, Theodore. *Farmer Movements in the South, 1865–1933.* Berkeley and Los Angeles, Calif., 1960.

Saye, Albert Berry. *A Constitutional History of Georgia, 1732–1945.* Athens, Ga., 1948.

Schriftgiesser, Karl. *The Gentlemen from Massachusetts: Henry Cabot Lodge.* Boston, Mass., 1945.

Schwartz, Michael. *Radical Protest and Social Structure: The Southern Farmers' Alliance and Cotton Tenancy, 1880–1890.* New York, 1976.

Shadgett, Olive Hall. *The Republican Party in Georgia: From Reconstruction Through 1900.* Athens, Ga., 1964.

Shaw, Barton C. *The Wool-Hat Boys: Georgia's Populist Party.* Baton Rouge, La., and London, 1984.

Shingleton, Royce. *Richard Peters: Champion of the New South.* Macon, Ga., 1985.

Shurter, Edwin Dubois. *The Complete Orations and Speeches of Henry W. Grady*. Norwood, Mass., 1910. This book contains only some of the speeches.

Small, Samuel W. *A Stenographic Report of the Proceedings of the Constitutional Convention Held in Atlanta, Georgia, 1877*. Atlanta, Ga., 1877.

Spalding, Hughes. *The Spalding Family of Maryland, Kentucky and Georgia from 1658 to 1965*. Atlanta, Ga., 1963 and 1965.

Spalding, Jack J. *Sketch of the Life of Jack J. Spalding, His Family and His Spalding, Huston, and Johnson Ancestors*. Atlanta, Ga., 1926.

Steelman, Lala Carr. *The North Carolina Farmers' Alliance: A Political History, 1887–1893*. Greenville, N.C., 1985.

Stover, John F. *The Railroads of the South, 1865–1900: A Study in Finance and Control*. Chapel Hill, N.C., 1955.

Talmadge, John E. *Rebecca Latimer Felton: Nine Stormy Decades*. Athens, Ga., 1960.

Tankersley, Allen P. *John B. Gordon: A Study in Gallantry*. Atlanta, Ga., 1955.

Terrell, Russell Franklin. *A Study of the Early Journalistic Writings of Henry W. Grady*. Nashville, Tenn., 1927.

Thompson, C. Mildred. *Reconstruction in Georgia: Economic, Social, Political, 1865–1872*. Savannah, Ga., 1972. First published in 1915.

Thompson, Holland. *The New South: A Chronicle of Social and Industrial Evolution*. New Haven, Conn., Toronto, London, Oxford, 1919.

Tindall, George Brown. *South Carolina Negroes, 1877–1900*. Columbia, S.C., 1952.

U.S. Bureau of the Census. *Report on the Manufactures of the United States at the Tenth Census, 1880*. Washington, D.C., 1883.

———. *Report on Manufacturing Industries in the United States at the Eleventh Census: 1890*. Pt. I. Washington, D.C., 1895.

———. *Twelfth Census of the United States, Taken in the Year 1900. Manufactures*. Vol. VIII, Pt. II. Washington, D.C., 1902.

Wade, Richard C. *The Urban Frontier: The Rise of Western Cities, 1790–1830*. Cambridge, Mass., 1967.

Watts, Eugene John. *The Social Bases of City Politics: Atlanta, 1865–1903*. Westport, Conn., 1978.

Wayne, Michael. *The Reshaping of Plantation Society: The Natchez District, 1860–1880*. Baton Rouge, La., and London, 1983.

Webb, Walter Prescott. *Divided We Stand: The Crisis of a Frontierless Democracy*. New York, Toronto, 1937.

Wiener, Jonathan M. *Social Origins of the New South: Alabama, 1860–1885*. Baton Rouge, La., and London, 1978.

Williamson, Harold Francis. *Edward Atkinson: The Biography of an American Liberal, 1827–1905*. Boston, Mass., 1934.

Williamson, Joel. *The Crucible of Race: Black-White Relations in the American South Since Emancipation*. New York, Oxford, 1984.

Woodman, Harold D. *King Cotton and His Retainers: Financing and Marketing the Cotton Crop of the South, 1800–1925.* Lexington, Ky., 1968.

Woodward, C. Vann. *The Burden of Southern History.* Baton Rouge, La., 1960.

―――. *Origins of the New South, 1877–1913.* Baton Rouge, La., 1971. Originally published in 1951.

―――. *The Strange Career of Jim Crow.* 3rd revised edition. New York, 1974.

―――. *Thinking Back: The Perils of Writing History.* Baton Rouge, La., and London, 1986.

―――. *Tom Watson: Agrarian Rebel.* New York, 1938.

Wright, Gavin. *The Political Economy of the Cotton South: Households, Markets, and Wealth in the Nineteenth Century.* New York, 1978.

―――. *Old South, New South: Revolutions in the Southern Economy Since the Civil War.* New York, 1986.

Wynne, Lewis Nicholas. *The Continuity of Cotton: Planter Politics in Georgia, 1865–1892.* Macon, Ga., 1986.

Index

248 | *Index*

Education, (*continued*)
University of Georgia, 30, 52, 140,
188–89; Industrial College for Ne-
groes (Savannah, Ga.), 141; Georgia
Tech, 188–89; view of classical educa-
tion, 188; Grady's lack of interest in
education for blacks, 162
Edwards, Harry S., 188
Elberton, Ga.: Grady's address at, 126–
27
Elections Bill of 1890. *See* Force bill
Elsas, May, and Company. *See* Fulton
County Spinning Company
Emory College, 39–40
Estill, J. H., 70
Exposition Cotton Mill, 172, 181

Farm: Grady's imaginary, 130
Farm clubs, 118
"Farmer and the Cities, the" (speech at
Elberton, Ga., 1889), 2, 126–27
Farmer's Alliance exchange (store), 128,
187
Farmer's Alliance of Georgia: success at
recruitment, 120–21, 123; enemies de-
fined, 124; attacks jute trust, 124–25,
127; establishes exchange (store) in At-
lanta, 128; its friends win 1890 elec-
tion, 130–31, 187; its caucus, 195
Farmer's Alliance of Texas, 119
"Feeder" railroad lines, 168
Felton, William H., 68–69, 72, 145
Field, Cyrus W., 41, 66
Field, Stephen J., 41
Finch, N. P. T., 23, 26, 209 (n. 7)
Flagler, H. M., 176
Foodstuffs: decline in production of
(1880s), 116
"Footsore Confederate soldier," 177, 179,
227 (n. 28)
Force bill (Elections Bill of 1890), 159–
60, 229–30 (n. 15)
Fort McPherson, Ga., 158
Fulton County Spinning Company, 181
Furman, Farish, 213 (n. 17), 218 (n. 12)

Garfield, James A., 169
Gartrell, Lucius J, 73

Georgia Baptist (publication), 138
Georgia Baptist Sunday School Conven-
tion, 138
Georgia Democratic Convention of 1888,
192
Georgia Fruit Growers' Association, 118
Georgia Institute of Technology, 141;
fight over its location, 187–89; Atlanta
gets the school, 189; impetus to indus-
trial development, 190
Georgia Pacific Railroad, 167–68
Georgia Railroad, 164
Georgia (State) Agricultural Society, 118,
129
Georgia (State) Horticultural Society, 118
Georgia Stock and Agricultural Journal, 216
(n. 1)
Glenn, John T., 48
Glenn, W. C., 140–41
Goldsmith, George, 150
Gordon, John B., 7, 34, 38, 62; biographical data, 64–65; resigns from U.S. Senate (1880), 66–67, 70; runs for
governor (1886), 80–93; ability as a
campaigner—in Lee County, 84—at
Americus, 85—at Eatonton, 85—at
Augusta, 85–87—in Hart County, 89;
elected governor, 93–94; opens Intra-
State Farm Convention (1887), 119; informs Legislature Atlanta University is
integrated, 140; former lessee of convict labor, 146; investigates convict
lease system, 147–48; delays hanging
of Henry Pope, 149; alarmed at East
Point lynching and beatings, 156;
president of Georgia Pacific Railroad,
168; turns away from Grady, 191–94,
199–204; plans to run for U.S. Senate
(1890), 194; elected, 195, 229 (n. 14);
letter of protest to Grady, 200; Grady's
response, 200–01; answer to Grady,
202–03; memorial oration for Grady,
203–04, 210 (n. 35)
Governor's Day (1881), 171–72
Grady, Ann Gartrell (mother), 29
Grady, Annie King (sister), 29
Grady, Augusta King (daughter), 9–10,
36

250 | *Index*

Grady, William Sammons, Sr. (father), 29–30, 36
Grady County, Ga., 12
Grady family slaves, 29
Grady Memorial Hospital, 12
Grady statue (Marietta Street, Atlanta), 12
Grant, Ulysses S., 34
Greeley, Horace, 34
Griffith, Ross, 150
Guernsey, E., 3

Hall, George Daniel, 154, 157
Hamilton, Betsey, 52
Hancock, Winfield Scott, 169
Hangings: Grady's fascination with, 148
Hanson, John Fletcher, 114, 178, 188
Haralson, Frank L., 78
Harmony Baptist Church (Augusta, Ga.), 138
Harper, J. W., 89
Harris, Joel Chandler, 10; edits Grady memorial volume, 14–15, 25, 26, 37, 40, 128
Harris, Nathaniel E., 75, 188–89, 228 (n. 55)
Harrison, Benjamin, 152, 153, 159, 160, 161
Hart, Julia, 134
Hart County, Ga.: 1886 primary election in, 88–93
Hartwell (Ga.) *Sun*, 88–90, 215 (n. 67)
Hayes, Rutherford B., 37–38, 173
Haygood, Atticus G., 40, 133–34, 145, 162, 219–20 (n. 2)
Hemphill, Robert A., 23, 52–53, 209 (n. 7)
Hemphill, William A., 8, 21; biographical data, 22, 24, 28, 41, 43, 46; labor arbiter, 187; and Georgia Institute of Technology, 189; his *Constitution* stock, 209 (n. 7)
Henderson John T., 113–14, 118, 120, 216–17 (n. 5)
Hidell, W. H.: denounces Atlanta Ring, 82
Hill, Benjamin H., 34, 73, 175, 176
Hill, W. P., 157

Hill monument (statue): dedication in Atlanta, 80, 82–83
Hillyer, George, 46–47, 147
Hoar, George Frisbie, 151
Houghton Institute (Augusta, Ga.), 138
Howell, Clark: gets letter of advice from Grady, 9, 25, 26–27; covers Bacon-Gordon joint appearances (1886), 85–87; becomes assistant managing editor of *Constitution*, 209 (n. 9); becomes managing editor, 131; elected Speaker of Georgia House of Representatives, 131, 194–95; covers Augusta strike and lockout, 185–86, 230 (n. 3)
Howell, Evan P.: biographical data, 22–23; his office, 24, 28; employs Grady, 36–37, 39; notifies Grady he can buy one-fourth of *Constitution*, 41; leads wets in prohibition campaign, 46–47; manages Atlanta campaign to keep the statehouse, 60; a leader of the Atlanta Ring, 62–63; helps arrange abortive Tilden campaign (1884), 77–78; makes plans to bribe an editor for political purposes, 78; arranges Gordon's joint appearance schedule, 85; sides with Grady in disputes, 123; follows railroad developments, 168; director of International Cotton Exposition of 1881, 170; labor arbiter, 187; supports Atlanta as site of Georgia Institute of Technology, 189; rift with Colquitt, 191–92; his *Constitution* stock, 209 (n. 7); used "Pickens County Funeral" speech concept, 227 (n. 34); wanted Gordon to oppose Colquitt for U.S. Senate (1888) or he might oppose him himself, 229 (n. 8)
Hudgins, H. C., and Company: publishes Grady memorial volume (1890), 15
Hudson, Reuben, 150

Industrial College for Negroes (Savannah, Ga.), 141
Ingalls, John J., 151
Inman, John H., 175, 176
Inman, Samuel M., 46, 170, 175, 187, 189, 209 (n. 7)
Interest rates, 115, 217 (n. 7)